Mastering the
Globalization of Business

Palgrave Master Series

Accounting
Accounting Skills
Advanced English Language
Advanced English Literature
Advanced Pure Mathematics
Arabic
Basic Management
Biology
British Politics
Business Communication
Business Environment
C Programming
C++ Programming
Chemistry
COBOL Programming
Communication
Computing
Counselling Skills
Counselling Theory
Customer Relations
Database Design
Delphi Programming
Desktop Publishing
e-Business
Economic and Social History
Economics
Electrical Engineering
Electronics
Employee Development
English Grammar
English Language
English Literature
Fashion Buying and Merchandising
  Management
Fashion Styling
Financial Management
French
Geography
German

Global Information Systems
Globalization of Business
Human Resource Management
Information Technology
International Trade
Internet
Italian
Java
Language of Literature
Management Skills
Marketing Management
Mathematics
Microsoft Office
Microsoft Windows, Novell
  NetWare and UNIX
Modern British History
Modern European History
Modern United States History
Modern World History
Networks
Novels of Jane Austen
Organisational Behaviour
Pascal and Delphi Programming
Philosophy
Physics
Practical Criticism
Psychology
Public Relations
Shakespeare
Social Welfare
Sociology
Spanish
Statistics
Strategic Management
Systems Analysis and Design
Team Leadership
Theology
Twentieth-Century Russian History
Visual Basic
World Religions

www.palgravemasterseries.com

Palgrave Master Series
Series Standing Order ISBN 0–333–69343–4
(outside North America only)

You can receive future titles in this series as they are published by placing a standing order.
Please contact your bookseller or, in case of difficulty, write to us at the address below with
your name and address, the title of the series and the ISBN quoted above.

Customer Services Department, Macmillan Distribution Ltd.
Houndmills, Basingstoke, Hampshire RG21 6XS, England

Mastering the
Globalization of Business

Roger Cartwright, PhD

Business Series Editor
Richard Pettinger

First published 2004 by
PALGRAVE MACMILLAN
Houndmills, Basingstoke, Hampshire RG21 6XS and
175 Fifth Avenue, New York, N.Y.10010
Companies and representatives throughout the world

PALGRAVE MACMILLAN is the global academic imprint of the Palgrave Macmillan division of St. Martin's Press, LLC and of Palgrave Macmillan Ltd. Macmillan® is a registered trademark in the United States, United Kingdom and other countries. Palgrave is a registered trademark in the European Union and other countries.

ISBN 1–4039–2149–0 paperback

This book is printed on paper suitable for recycling and made from fully managed and sustained forest sources.

A catalogue record for this book is available from the British Library.

10 9 8 7 6 5 4 3 2 1
13 12 11 10 09 08 07 06 05 04

Printed and bound in Great Britain by
Creative Print & Design (Ebbw Vale), Wales

■ ⍙ Contents

Acknowledgements

Grateful thanks are due to my series editor, Richard Pettinger, and Suzannah Burywood, my editor at Palgrave for their assistance and patience in the writing of this text.

◪ Introduction

'The greatest challenge to our age is globalization'
Tony Blair – UK Prime Minister in a speech to the
Trades Union Congress, 10 September 2002

In June 2001 there were riots in the streets of Gothenburg, Sweden during a meeting of the European Union (EU) held in the city. In August/September 2002 there were demonstrations at the Earth Summit in the South African city of Johannesburg with Colin Powell the US Secretary of State being booed. These were just the latest in a series of protests that were becoming a feature of meetings of the World Trade Organization (WTO) and other such bodies. The protesters were expressing concerns about the dangers of **globalization**.

What is globalization?

Globalization has been defined by Ellwood (2001) as '... a new word that describes an old process: the integration of the global economy that began in earnest with the launch of the European colonial era five centuries ago. But (sic) the process has accelerated over the past quarter century with the explosion of computer technology, the dismantling of trade barriers and the expanding political and economic power of multinational corporation.'

Globalization as the term is used in this book is the process whereby organizations offer their products and services on a global rather than a local basis and in doing so become part of a global economy in addition to their role in local/regional economies. Globalization presents a series of opportunities and threats to organizations. It may well be that an organization or an individual does not perceive the global nature of its operations. However, once an organization sets up its own web site it has begun the move towards becoming global, as it has increased its access to a potentially huge customer base free of national boundaries.

While Ellwood (quoted earlier) states that it was Europeans who began the globalization process, today they have been joined by organizations from other parts of the world. US organizations, e.g. Microsoft, Ford, General Motors, Coca-Cola, IBM and Japanese corporations, e.g. Sony, Hyundai, Mitsubishi, Canon have joined ICI and P&O from the UK, Royal Dutch Shell from the Netherlands and Airbus Industrie, the pan-European commercial aircraft manufacturer as global players in their particular markets.

It is salutary to note that according to the 1999 *UN Human Development Report*, the total sales in 1997 of General Motors, Ford and Mitsui were each greater than the GDP (gross domestic product) of Saudi Arabia – an oil-rich country (sales in $US: General Motors – $163 billion, Ford – $147 billion, Matsui – $145 billion. GDP of Saudi Arabia – $140 billion). Many multinational companies are now richer than whole countries and it is the power that such financial resources provide that lies behind the concerns that are discussed in chapter 4. Many of the largest economies of the world are not in fact countries but large commercial organizations.

Trade and foreign direct investment (FDI)

To the average citizen of a country the main manifestation of globalization is the removal of trade barriers, i.e. it is easier to access products and services from other countries than was the case in the past. An unseen, but just as important manifestation of globalization, is the growth in foreign direct investment (see chapter 7). FDI is the process whereby foreign companies either set up operations abroad or buy local companies and integrate them into their operations. Partial or full ownership is transferred outside the country. According to Moore (2003) goods and services to the value of $8 trillion are traded across the world every 24 hours. In the same period the trading of stocks, shares and bonds is of the value of $188 trillion. It is this 'takeover' by foreign investors of local concerns that has become a major issue to the opponents of globalization – concerns that are considered in chapter 4.

Moore is an ex-prime minister of New Zealand and was, from 1999 until 2002, the Director General of the World Trade Organization (WTO) – see chapter 2. He argues that the free flow of capital and the ability to invest on a global rather than a purely national level is of benefit to all mankind and not just the investors and their organizations. He also takes issue with those who equate globalization with a form of Americanization. This is a common view among anti-globalization writers. It is a view, however, that does not take into account the massive FDI by organizations headquartered in other countries – Japan is a prime example. Of the top 10 companies as measured by total sales in 1997, three were from the US: General Motors (first place), Ford (second) and Exxon (ninth). Japanese companies dominated with Mitsui (third), Mitsubishi (fourth), Itochu (fifth), Marubeni (seventh), Sumitomo (eighth) and Toyota (tenth). The only European company in the top 10 was Shell (proper title: Royal Dutch Shell) in sixth place. All of these companies had annual sales in excess of the GDP of Malaysia. Many of the Japanese companies have expanded their global trade despite tariff barriers by the use of FDI. Toyota cars are not necessarily 'made in Japan' – they are also made in the UK and the US where Toyota (and other Japanese car manufacturers) have set up factories. Indeed some apparently Japanese companies have received massive European FDI making them more European than Japanese.

Not all authorities agree what globalization is or if it really exists. The distinguished UK academic Alan Rugman argues in *The End of Globalization* (2000) that what is described as globalization is either regionalization or trading between the three great trading blocs of the world – North America, Europe and the Far East. This view is discussed in chapter 6.

Globalization is far more than just an expansion of international trade. The latter has involved organizations expanding into an increasing number of geographically discrete markets. The ultimate objective (if a process can have an actual objective) is a single global market.

The aims of this book

This book sets out to provide an overview of the implications of globalization on management and business for those studying the subjects in college or university.

How to use this book

This book is laid out as shown below.

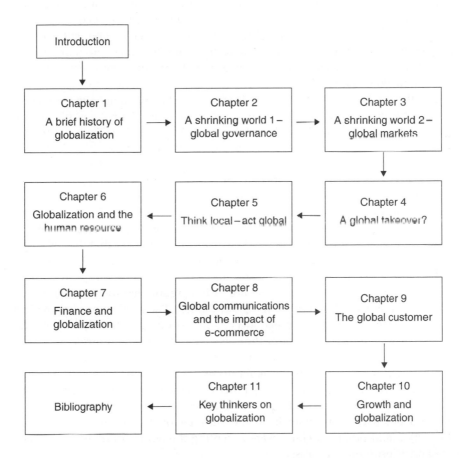

A list of resources and useful web sites is included at the end of the Bibliography. Chapter 11 contains details of some of the major thinkers on globalization.

Throughout the material there are **Think/Discussion points** that are useful for both readers and lecturers/facilitators to use in stimulating thought. At the end of each chapter there are some general questions and suggestions for further reading.

For additional support to this book, please see our web site at www.palgrave. com/masterseries/cartwright3.

The relevance of globalization to individuals and organizations

More and more organizations, for reasons that will be explored in this material, are reaching out to a wider, more global marketplace. As this process increases then an understanding of how globalization as a phenomenon may affect business and cause the requirements of senior management to become global rather than local leaders in the organization's particular field is becoming a prerequisite for an increasing number of organizations. For the same reasons courses and programmes on business and management can no longer confine their content to local conditions. International marketing has long been the main component considering global factors in business and management programmes, programmes that now also need to consider global finance, human relations and information in addition to global marketing.

Even the smallest local organization is affected by factors that have their causes beyond the local environs. Interest rates, exchange rates, the policies of supranational trading blocs such as the EU and the North American Free Trade Association (NAFTA) impact on large and small, local and global enterprises.

The riots and disturbances noted earlier had their roots in a belief that globalization was somehow replacing democracy with government by commercial organization or pan-regional governments. This belief is not confined to just one end of the political spectrum. While it is true that many of the rioters were from the extreme left as are many of the non-violent critics of globalization, there are also those from the far right such as the militias in the US who appear to believe that the UN wishes to take over firstly the US and then the world. In the UK it appears that a majority of the right of centre Conservative Party opposes a common European currency and the further political, social and economic integration that such adoption of the currency union would produce throughout the EU. Their objections are made in terms of protecting national (British) sovereignty – sovereignty that they believe will be in some way diluted by adopting the necessary economic conformity that a single currency involves. What is sometimes forgotten is that no country can ever be truly sovereign as the reaction of neighbours and trading partners needs to be considered as part of any decision-making process. As the largest trading partner of the UK are the other members of the EU, the UK government may decide not to adopt the euro but it cannot ignore it. In the summer of 2002, retailers in London, Edinburgh (and other UK cities) were accepting the euro – to refuse to accept it could have lost them business.

The relevance of this book to small businesses

Much of the literature on globalization concentrates on the activities of large, well-known organizations, e.g. Ford, General Motors, McDonald's, Canon, Shell. It can often be difficult to extrapolate from these giants of the global business world down to smaller organizations. At the end of each chapter therefore there is a short section that contextualizes the chapter content and ideas for the small business.

Chapter 4 examines the concerns raised by the critics of globalization, in particular the political and social implications. The chapter will attempt to explain why globalization appears such a danger to some sections of society as to bring people out onto the streets in violent protest.

The other chapters of the book will concentrate on how business organizations can expand into the global marketplace and how global factors are now impacting on even the most locally based enterprise.

Statistical information

A key characteristic of the late twentieth and early twenty-first centuries has been the currency of information. We live in a world where things change far more quickly than in the past. In the eighteenth century prices hardly changed from the beginning to the end of the century. In the wonderful situation comedy *Dad's Army* set in 1940, a bank manager refuses to cash a cheque for £5 because that is considered to be a large sum of money – what would £5 buy a mere 60 years later?

Fortunately for those studying business and management it is now possible via the Internet to have access to the most up-to-date information. Between the writing of the book and its publication (or at least soon after), a new tranche of countries will have joined the EU – its statistics will change dramatically. Rather than print tables of out-of-date material in the text, there is a list of web sites in the bibliography that will direct the reader to the most up-to-date information available.

Summary and key learning points

- Globalization as the term is used in this book is the process whereby organizations offer their products and services on a global rather than a local basis and in doing so become part of a global economy in addition to their role in local/regional economies.
- Not all authorities agree what globalization is or if it really exists.
- Transportation and communication technologies allow us to reach places far more quickly and with less effort than was the case in the past and to communicate across the globe very quickly indeed.
- More and more organizations are reaching out to a wider, more global marketplace.

- Organizations are affected by more than local factors.
- Courses and programmes on business and management can no longer confine their content to local conditions.
- Programmes now also need to consider global finance, human relations and information in addition to global marketing.

QUESTIONS

1   Why are business and management courses having to provide a global appreciation of topics such as finance, human resources etc?
2   Can any organization operate in such a way that it is only affected by its immediate local situation?

Recommended further reading

The Global City by Saskia Sassen (2001) and *The No-nonsense Guide to Globalization* by Wayne Ellwood (2001) provide useful background reading to the issues of globalization.

■ ᴍ 1 A brief history of globalization

Learning outcomes

By the end of this chapter you should understand:

• The way in which global trade has developed
• The means by which history has shaped organizations and trade
• The importance of government support to trading organizations

Definitions

Globalization, as the term is used in this book, is the process whereby organizations offer their products and services on a global rather than a local basis. As part of this process trade barriers are dismantled giving globalization a political as well as an economic impact. As stated in the Introduction Ellwood (2001) believes that globalization began with the launch of the European colonial era five centuries ago.

The view of Alan Rugman (2000) that what is described as globalization is actually either regionalization or trading between the three great trading blocs of the world – North America, Europe and the Far East – is also worthy of careful consideration. If what Rugman says is true then many of the perceived problems associated with globalization and put forward with considerable passion by, among others, Giddens (1999), Herz (2001), Klein (2000) and Korten (1996) may be illusionary. These perceived problems are discussed in chapter 4.

Think/Discussion point: Consider the everyday items that you use – foodstuffs, electrical equipment, motor vehicle etc. Examine them to see how many different countries they come from – does the answer surprise you?

The development of globalization

'Those who cannot remember the past are condemned to repeat it.'
George Santayana, 1905

In order to predict the future with any degree of accuracy it is necessary to understand the present. In order to understand the present requires knowledge of how the current situation came about, i.e. it is necessary to know about the past. There are those who believe that the history of a subject is unimportant and that texts on that subject need not devote any part to its history. The author is not of this view. To understand globalization and the opportunities and threats that it presents it is necessary to review its development. George Santayana's words as quoted above have a universal truth, as without a knowledge of history mistakes are likely to be repeated.

> **Think/Discussion point**: Consider a recent economic or political event such as the 2003 conflict in Iraq. How easy would it be to understand the event fully without a knowledge of the circumstances and actions leading up to it?

This chapter considers the development of firstly internationalization of trade and latterly globalization, i.e. the trend towards a single global market up to 1945. Post 1945 the institutions that govern world trade and relations – the United Nations, the International Monetary Fund, the World Bank and the World Trade Organization – were set up. Countries also began to come together as discrete trading blocs linked by treaty, the European Union being the prime example. Post-1945 developments form the substance of this book.

Globalization as described in this material began not as many believe towards the end of the twentieth century but with the voyages of discovery emanating in Europe from the fifteenth century onwards. Magellan, Drake, de Gama etc. are familiar figures in the pages of history books but they have also made a contribution to the commercial world as we see it today. While some of the explorers may have been concerned purely with extending knowledge about the world (a world many believed was both flat and at the centre of the universe as taught by the Church – heliocentricity, the idea that the earth revolved around the sun was a heresy for which death by burning could be ordered), most were concerned with commerce. They were seeking new markets for the products of their sponsors and new products to sell on their home market. The major developments in this process are considered in some detail below. It is not necessary to learn the names of people and dates but it is important that you understand the hazards that faced these explorers and the commercial and political imperatives that drove them. The ships of these explorers left with trading goods and the intention was that they would return with goods for the European markets.

It is worth noting at this point that much of the literature about globalization is 'Eurocentric', since the development of globalization is perceived to have begun with European exploration. There has been recent speculation that the Chinese were undertaking voyages of discovery across the globe to Africa, Australia, Europe and the Americas as early as 1421 (Menzies, 2002) and that they may have been the originators of globalization – a point discussed later in this chapter.

> **Think/Discussion point**: How easy is it to think outside one's culture? History is often supposed to be about dates and facts. As they are in the past, surely they can be verified? Try to find a history book from another culture that describes an event that is also covered in a history book from your culture – are the narrative

and the conclusions the same? Probably not. A Eurocentric view of Columbus sees him as a hero and discover. Many indigenous Central and South American peoples see him as a villain, conqueror and exploiter.

Trade is as old as civilization itself. The empires of the Persians, Carthaginians, Phoenicians, Greeks and Romans traded over large distances. The bulk of their trade, however, was regional. The Roman Empire was very large but even it was concentrated around the shores of the Mediterranean and up through Europe to the Rhine and Danube Rivers and, of course, the British Isles. Roman trade was essentially regional rather than global.

History has tended to concentrate on the military aspects of these early empires and their subjugation of conquered people. What is often forgotten is the reason for conquest. Whilst some military campaigns may have been for the personal aggrandizement of the ruler, the vast majority were concerned with seeking new resources and markets.

The first great European explorers were the Vikings who had by the eleventh century AD set up colonies in Greenland, the northeastern corner of North America, as far south as Kiev in what is now the Ukraine and were present in Constantinople, modern-day Istanbul. For the next 250 years there was little European exploration.

Marco Polo (1254–1324) was an Italian traveller and author, whose writings gave Europeans the first authoritative view of life in the Far East.

His father Nicolò and uncle Maffeo were Venetian merchants and business partners who had commercial interests in Constantinople and the Crimea. When Constantinople suddenly fell into the hands of rival Genoese merchants, Nicolò and Maffeo Polo set out in 1260 to search for new markets to the north of the Caspian Sea eventually reaching Bukhara (in present-day Uzbekistan). Bukhara was then one of the key cities on the caravan route that led from the Middle East to China. They remained there for three years, before joining Persian envoys on their way to visit the great Mongol Emperor Kublai Khan in his court at Shangdu (the 'Xanadu' of 'Coleridge's poem 'Kubla Khan') situated close to the site of present-day Beijing. The journey involved travelling along the famed Silk Road through Samarqand, the deserts of northern Tibet and the steppes of Mongolia. Kublai Khan commissioned them to return with 100 missionaries to convert his people to Christianity, as Islamic armies from the south were threatening him. The return to Venice, via Bukhara, Persia, Syria and Acre (near Jerusalem) took the Polo brothers three years.

Two years later in 1271 they took the 17-year-old Marco along with them on their return to China. They crossed Persia to Hormuz at the mouth of the Persian Gulf hoping to travel to India by sea, but unable to find a boat they considered safe, they travelled overland northeast through the deserts and mountains of Persia to Kashgar (present-day Kashi) on the Chinese border. Here Marco Polo was so ill that they were forced to rest for a year before continuing their journey up the River Oxus (now the Amu Darya) into the Hindu Kush and Pamir mountains where Marco observed the large horned sheep that would later bear his name (also known as the Argali), and commented on the effects of high-altitude sickness. They then skirted the Takla Makan Desert to the Lop Lake region of Sinkiang Province (present-day Xinjiang Uygur Autonomous Region), China; and finally across the Gobi Desert by camel caravan to the court of Kublai Khan at Shangdu, which they reached in 1275, three and a half years after leaving Europe. They were the first Europeans to visit most of the territory they traversed in this journey, particularly the Pamir and the Gobi Desert.

Marco Polo entered Kublai Khan's diplomatic service, acting as his agent on missions to many parts of the Mongolian Empire for the next 17 years. He travelled in Tibet and along the Yangzi, Yellow and upper Mekong Rivers, and was probably the first European to visit the interior of Burma. He visited the Mongol capital at Karakorum in modern-day Mongolia and may have reached Siberia in the north, as well as taking a sea voyage to the Indonesian archipelago. For three years from 1282 to 1285, he may also have been governor of the city of Yangzhou. His father and uncle served as military advisers to Kublai Khan. As Kublai Khan grew older, they became concerned about the stability of the Empire and in 1292 the three Polos left China, as escorts for a Mongol princess betrothed to the Persian Khan. War prevented the use of the overland route, and so they decided to travel to Persia by sea. They were provided with a fleet of 14 ships and a crew of 600. They sailed from Zaitun (present-day Quanzhou) on the Chinese coast by way of Sumatra and the Strait of Malacca to Sri Lanka, the Andaman and Nicobar islands, arriving in Hormuz in 1294. All but 18 of the original crew had died during the two-year journey. The ability of the Mongols and Chinese to undertake long ocean voyages was apparent and yet has rarely been commented on until 'Menzies' work, which will be considered later in this chapter. The Polos eventually arrived in their home city of Venice in 1295, 24 years after their adventures had begun, and extremely rich men mostly as a result of the jewels and precious stones they had sewn into their clothes for safe keeping.

When war broke out between Venice and Genoa, Marco Polo served as a captain in the Venetian fleet and was taken prisoner in 1298 along with 7000 others off the Dalmatian coast of Croatia. During his imprisonment by the Genoese, he dictated to a fellow prisoner and writer of romances, Rusticello of Pisa, the detailed account of his travels. He was released from prison in 1299 and returned to Venice where he married, had three daughters, and lived comfortably until he died at the age of 70, and was buried beside his father in the church of San Lorenzo.

The sea routes to the East

As word of Polo's journeys spread the Europeans began to search for a more advantageous route to facilitate trade between Europe and the Far East. The demand for silks and spices grew rapidly.

Henry the Navigator (1394–1460) the third son of John I, King of Portugal, is regarded as the patron of navigation and exploration – there is a huge statue of him looking out over the River Tagus in Lisbon. He established an observatory and the first school for navigators in Europe at Sagres, Portugal, near Cape St Vincent and he also made improvements in the art of shipbuilding. The caravel, a sailing ship, was designed at Sagres. There had been little progress in ship design from the Romans to the Vikings. Both used a large square sail that was at its most efficient with the wind in a position somewhere from the beam (side) of the ship around the stern. It might be thought that a square sail would be most effective with the wind directly behind the ship but this is not so. While a square sail is easy to rig and control it does not allow the ship to sail close to the wind in the way the triangular sails on a yacht do. Henry's caravel design used triangular (or lateen) sails and this allowed the sailors to make more advantageous use of the winds that blow from Europe down to Africa.

By the time Columbus sailed across the Atlantic larger ships carried both square and triangular sails thus allowing their crews to make fuller use of the wind.

Henry made no voyages himself, but under his direction important expeditions were undertaken along the west coast of Africa. The long-term aim of this effort was to find a sea route to India and the Far East, in order to establish trading links that were not controlled by Arab merchants, who were taking as much advantage as they could of their geographical situation to tax all goods passing through their territory. Religious tension in the Middle East was also rising at a time when the last outposts of Islamic civilization were being expelled from the Iberian Peninsula and replaced by indigenous Spanish rule, so a sea route was important for securing the safety and continuity of trade. Henry's navigators reached Madeira in 1420, and arrived off the mouth of the Gambia River in what is now the Gambia about 1446. The complete route to India was not pioneered until the expedition of Vasco da Gama in 1497–99.

Vasco da Gama was commissioned by Emanuel, King of Portugal, to reach India by sea. He sailed from Lisbon with four ships on 8 July 1497. In November he rounded the Cape of Good Hope (first rounded in 1488 by the Portuguese navigator Bartholomew Dias) having been out of sight of land for over 13 weeks. Natal was sighted and named at Christmas 1497. By the time he reached the port of Mozambique, he was running into Muslim opposition but at Malindi on the coast of what is now Kenya, he managed to secure a local pilot to guide him eastward. Da Gama reached Calicut on the Malabar Coast of India on 20 May 1498. He found that due to the hostility of Muslim merchants, and the poor quality of the goods he had brought with him, he was unable to sign a trade agreement with the ruler. With unfavourable winds the voyage back to Malindi took three months and many of his crew died of scurvy before they returned to Portugal in September 1499. He had navigated some 24,000 miles and demonstrated that the Indian Ocean was not the landlocked sea Europeans had thought it to be since the time of the ancient Greeks. Da Gama was rewarded with the title of Admiral of the Indian Ocean.

To follow up the discoveries of da Gama, Pedro Álvares Cabral was immediately dispatched to India, and he established a Portuguese trading post in Calicut. Sent back to India to deal with local hostility and a massacre of Portuguese traders da Gama collected a rich cargo of spice and sailed for Portugal establishing Portuguese colonies at Mozambique and present-day Beira on the coast of what is now Mozambique arriving back in 1524. He was named viceroy and sent to India to correct the mounting corruption among the Portuguese authorities there. Da Gama reached India in the autumn of 1524, but he died in Cochin only three months after his arrival.

By pioneering the Portuguese sea route to India, da Gama established Lisbon as the centre of the European spice trade, and laid the foundation for the Portuguese empire that controlled trade with the ports of eastern Africa, southwest India and Indonesia.

Columbus

Christopher Columbus (Italian, Cristoforo Colombo; Spanish, Cristóbal Colón) was born in 1451 in Genoa, Italy. In the mid-1470s he made his first trading voyage to the island of Khíos, in the Aegean Sea. In 1476 he is believed to have sailed with a convoy bound for England. It is further believed that the convoy was attacked by pirates off the coast of Portugal, where Columbus' ship was sunk, but he swam to shore and took refuge in Lisbon. Settling there, where his brother Bartholomew Columbus was already resident and working as a cartographer, he began to study charts and maps and concluded (wrongly) that the Earth was 25 per cent smaller than was previously believed and composed mostly of land. On the basis of these faulty beliefs, he decided that Asia could be reached quickly by sailing out towards the west. In 1484 he submitted his theories to John II, King of Portugal, petitioning him to finance a westward crossing of the Atlantic Ocean. His proposal was rejected by a royal maritime commission because of his miscalculations and because Portuguese ships were on the point of finding a sea route to Asia around Africa.

Soon after, Columbus moved to Spain, where his plans won the support of several influential people, and in 1486 he secured an introduction to Isabella I, Queen of Castile. In Spain, as in Portugal, a royal commission rejected his plan. However, Columbus continued to seek support, and in April 1492 his persistence was rewarded when Ferdinand V, King of Castile, and Queen Isabella agreed to sponsor the expedition. The signed contract stipulated that Columbus was to become viceroy of all territories he located; other rewards included a hereditary peerage and one-tenth of all precious metals found within his jurisdiction.

The modest expedition consisted of the *Santa María*, a decked ship about 35 m (115 ft) long under his command and the *Pinta* and the *Niña*, two small caravels, each about 15 m (50 ft) long, which were commanded by Martín Alonzo Pinzón and his brother Vicente Yáñez Pinzón.

By today's standards these were tiny ships for such a venture particularly when the *Santa Maria* is compared to the 25,000 GRT *Saga Rose*, a relatively small modern cruise ship.

The fleet sailed from Palos, Spain, on 3 August 1492, carrying perhaps 90 men. Three days out, the mast of the *Pinta* was damaged, forcing a brief stop at the Canary Islands. On 6 September the three vessels again weighed anchor and sailed due west. Columbus maintained this course until 7 October, when, at the suggestion of Martín Pinzón, it was altered to southwest. Meanwhile, the experienced crews grumbled about their foreign commander's failure to find his way, until signs appeared that they were approaching landfall.

Before dawn on 12 October land was sighted, and early in the morning the expedition landed on Guanahaní, an island in the Bahamas. Before an audience of uncomprehending natives, Columbus claimed that, by right of conquest, their island now belonged to Spain and renamed it San Salvador ('Holy Saviour', although recent research has suggested this island may have been Samana Cay). Additional landings made during the next few weeks included the islands of Cuba, which Columbus named Juana, in honour of a Spanish princess, and Española, later corrupted to Hispaniola (now comprising the Dominican Republic and Haiti), all believed by Columbus to be in Asian waters.

Columbus believed he had found 'India via the west', hence the name of Indians for the natives and West Indies for the area.

In December, the *Santa María* was wrecked off the coast of Española. A makeshift fort was built of materials salvaged from the vessel, and garrisoned with fewer than 40 men. The *Niña*, with Columbus in command, and the *Pinta* began the home-ward voyage in January 1493. After storms drove the ships first to the Azores and then to Lisbon, Columbus arrived at Palos, Spain, in March. He was enthusiastically received by the Spanish monarchs, who confirmed the honours guaranteed by his contract. Additional honours followed, including a noble title.

Columbus made three more voyages across the Atlantic taking with him the first 16 horses – the ancestors of all subsequent horses in North and South America, as horses had become extinct in the Americas after the last ice age. It was only on his fourth voyage that Columbus actually landed on the mainland of the Americas. Prior to that he had refused to acknowledge the existence of the landmass of North, Central and South America still believing that the Caribbean Islands were off the coast of China.

The Spanish conquest of the people of the Caribbean and Central America provided Spain with one of the factors that was to make her the first truly global economy – silver and gold. While there has been much made of the search for El Dorado and its streets of gold it was silver that provided the Spanish with their American treasure. Spain needed gold and silver to pay for purchases from the East – silks, spices etc. Silver was discovered in Mexico in 1534 and in Bolivia in 1545. The Spanish Conquistadors enslaved local people to provide a labour force for the mines.

By the Treaty of Tordesillas on 7 June 1494 Pope Alexander VI defined the spheres of Spanish and Portuguese possessions in the New World (North and South America). The line ran from north to south 370 leagues (1110 miles) west of the Cape Verde Islands. As a result of this change, Brazil became a Portuguese possession.

Neither England (it did not become Britain until after the Act of Union in 1707) nor France who were also actively engaged upon exploration in North America were consulted about the demarcation.

The English in particular were none too pleased and by the 1560s the vessels of Drake, Hawkins and Raleigh were challenging the Portuguese and Spanish domina-tion using well-built ships that were capable of long voyages. It was not just national pride that fuelled the numerous conflicts that followed the Pope's decision but the wish for fair trading rights and a share in the wealth of the newly discovered lands.

North America and the Caribbean became the battleground for European strug-gles in later years.

Ferdinand Magellan's (a Portuguese in the service of Spain) fleet was the first to find a route between the Atlantic and the Pacific. On 21 October 1520, Magellan sailed into the passage to the Pacific Ocean that is now named after him, the Strait of Magellan. It took 38 days to navigate the treacherous strait, and the crew of the *San Antonio* deserted and returned to Spain. Fires were seen along the shores to the south, causing Magellan to name this land Tierra del Fuego (land of fire). After a journey of 530 km (330 miles), on 28 November 1520, his three ships sailed into the ocean, which Magellan named 'Pacific' (meaning 'peaceful') because of its calmness.

Magellan reached the Philippines in March 1521 during his attempted circum-navigation of the Earth in the service of Spain. He claimed the islands in the name of Spain. The following month Magellan was killed on the island of Mactan when he tried to impose Christianity and Spanish sovereignty on the local chief. The rout of Magellan's men ended the authority Magellan had sought to establish.

The Spanish claim to the islands was disputed by Portugal, which was already in possession of the nearby Moluccas and could invoke the Treaty of Tordesillas of 1494 (see above), whereby the eastern hemisphere was reserved to Portuguese colonization. In addition, although in the service of Spain, Magellan was Portuguese. In 1542, however, a Spanish expedition reasserted the claims of Spain and named the archipelago the Islas Filipinas, or Philippine Islands, in honour of the royal heir, later King Philip II.

Spain now had a base in the Far East from which to trade. Before long there was regular trade across the Pacific to the west coast of Central America, then by land over the narrow Isthmus of Panama (first crossed in 1515 by Vasco Nuñez de Balbo) using the Camino Real (Royal Road) built at the cost of thousands of native lives and thence to the Spanish mainland. The silver from Central America facilitated the purchase of goods from the Far East.

Much of the Americas remained Spanish until the middle of the nineteenth century and many of the countries in the region still speak Spanish. The exception is Brazil where the language remains Portuguese – a link right back to the Treaty of Tordesillas.

The voyages of Columbus and Magellan led to the foundation of an economy that was much more global than regional.

The Chinese

Up to the beginning of the twenty-first century it has always been assumed by Europeans and their descendents in the Americas that it was Columbus who made the discovery of the New World. However, in 2002, Gavin Menzies, an ex Royal Navy submariner, put forward the theory that Columbus actually used maps dating from the early years of the fifteenth century. By studying manuscripts and artefacts Menzies believes that the Chinese were the first outsiders to land in not only the Americas but also in Australia. He contends that in 1421 the Emperor Zhu Di sent out four huge fleets to return ambassadors and tributes from Africa, the Middle East and the Far East. He believes that the Chinese already had major trading links with these areas and may have had the first global economy. The fleets were then sent on voyages of exploration returning in 1423.

The ships, 500-foot long junks made from the finest teak and mahogany, were led by Emperor Zhu Di's loyal eunuch admirals. Their mission was 'to proceed all the way to the end of the earth to collect tribute from the barbarians beyond the seas and unite the whole world in Confucian harmony' (Menzies, 2002). The journey lasted over two years and encircled the entire globe. When they returned Zhu Di had fallen from power and China was beginning its long, self-imposed isolation from the world it had so recently embraced. It has been suggested that a series of natural catastrophes struck China around 1423 and the Emperor may have believed that the gods were displeased with the idea of encircling the globe and thus he ordered the records destroyed. Menzies' reconstruction of the possible routes show the Chinese sailing across the top of Russia (the Northeast Passage). While this has only been possible with modern ships fairly recently discussions with authorities in navigation have led the writer to conclude that the hull form of a junk may (and it is a big may) have been suitable for sailing through such inhospitable and icy conditions. Doubtless more will be heard of this theory in years to come.

European venture capital and exploration

The European voyages of exploration (Columbus, Magellan, Cabot, Verrazano, Vespucci, Drake etc.) were also responsible for the development of modern financing. They were a partnership between the explorer and those who risked not only their lives but also their capital on a successful venture. While the original ventures tended to be single projects with cargo and ship being sold off upon return to harbour it was not long before organizations as they exist today began to develop – organizations with an existence that lasted longer than a single venture.

Think/Discussion point: Modern explorers undertake risks for personal achievement. Why is it that in earlier times exploration was linked to commercial enterprise? (Clue – think about risk and likelihood of coming back in one piece.)

Most businesses in the world at the time were local, forced to be so by the logistics of perilous overland and ocean travel. Sea journeys took months and even years and there were few roads except between major trading centres. European explorers soon came to find that they were not unique in the way they organized their economies and society as they discovered thriving civilizations in China, India and South America. Initially only in the case of the latter did the Europeans, driven by thoughts of gold and conversion of the natives to Christianity, seek to overthrow the rulers and take over. In respect of China and India the Europeans were content initially to set up trading stations in the coastal areas and to work with local rulers.

As sea travel was the easiest means of moving goods it is paradoxical that ports such as Bristol in England and the Hanseatic ports on the Baltic were international before they were national. The only national organizations until well into the sixteenth/seventeeth centuries were the ruler and the Church – the logistics of setting up national commercial organizations either in terms of transport or financing did not exist.

The 'India' companies

There were a number of commercial enterprises formed in Western Europe during the seventeenth and eighteenth centuries to further trade with both India itself and the East Indies. The companies, which had varying degrees of governmental support, grew out of the associations of merchant adventurers who voyaged to the East Indies following the discovery in 1498 of the Cape of Good Hope route by the

Portuguese navigator Vasco da Gama (described earlier). The most important of the companies were given charters by their respective governments, authorizing them to acquire territory wherever they could and to exercise in the acquired territory various functions of government, including legislation, the issuing of currency, the negotiation of treaties, the administration of justice, and even the waging of war. Governments needed to work through such companies as at the time there was no means that a European government could make its will felt thousands of miles away without a large navy, an army that could function in the heat and humidity of the tropics and a great deal of expense. However, if private individuals were prepared to set up trading posts in these areas and finance the infrastructure, all the government had to do was provide a governor, a small number of 'official' troops and an occasional visit by a naval frigate. The Danes, the Dutch (who held the Cape of Good Hope in modern South Africa at the time) with the extension of their interests throughout present-day Indonesia, being a major power and influence in the area until well after 1945, the Portuguese in Goa (until removed by India in 1961), and the French all set up East India companies, but the most important was the company that received its charter from Elizabeth I of England.

English later British Honourable East India Company

The most important of the various East India companies, this company was a major force in the history of India for more than 200 years. Queen Elizabeth I granted the original charter on 31 December 1600, under the title of 'The Governor and Company of Merchants of London Trading into the East Indies'. At this time England and Scotland were two separate countries, joined by a joint monarch (James I of England and VI of Scotland) after the death of Elizabeth. The company was initially granted a monopoly of trade in Asia, Africa and America but in practice kept its activities confined to India and the East Indies.

The company was managed by a governor and 24 directors chosen from its stock-holders. Early voyages by the company's ships penetrated as far as Japan, and in 1610 and 1611 its first factories, or trading posts, were established in India in the provinces of Madras and Bombay. Under a perpetual charter granted in 1609 by King James I, the company began to compete with the Dutch trading monopoly in the Malay Archipelago, but after a military defeat conceded the area that became known as the Netherlands East Indies and later Indonesia to the Dutch. The company's armed merchant ships, however, continued sea warfare with Dutch, French and Portuguese competitors. In 1650 and 1655 the company absorbed rival companies that had been incorporated under the Commonwealth and Protectorate by Lord Protector Oliver Cromwell after the English Civil War. In 1657 Cromwell ordered it reorganized as the sole joint-stock company with rights to the Indian trade – a very lucrative monopoly. During the reign of Charles II, after the restoration of the monarchy, the company acquired sovereign rights in addition to its trading privileges; in effect it became the representative of the British Crown in India. In 1689, with the establishment of administrative districts called presidencies in the Indian provinces of Bengal, Madras and Bombay, the company began its long rule in India.

The victories of Robert Clive, a company official, over the French at Arcot in 1751 and at Plassey in 1757 made the company the dominant power in India. With the

French defeat at Pondicherry in 1761, the British and the Company were effectively the rulers of all of India although native Princes were allowed to keep their courts and rule as long as they followed British policies. It is interesting to see how, just as in North America the rivalry between Britain and France was fought out in India – a long way from the European battlefields. The East India Company was the first instance of a modern global organization and its taking over of French possessions in India the first example of warfare on a global scale as Royal Navy vessels also took part in actions in addition to the Company's ships. Later in this book the concerns and views of David Korten, author of *When Corporations Rule the World* (1996), are considered. The history of the East India Company shows that the idea of a commercial organization 'ruling' over a large population is not a recent phenomenon but has its roots in the seventeenth and eighteenth centuries.

In 1773 the British government established a Governor-Generalship in India, thereby greatly decreasing administrative control by the company. Nevertheless the Company's Governor of Bengal, Warren Hastings, became the first Governor-General of India. In 1784 the India Act created a department of the British government to exercise political, military and financial control over the Indian affairs of the Company, and during the next half-century British control was extended over most of the subcontinent. In 1813 the Company's monopoly of the Indian trade was abolished, and in 1833 it lost its China trade monopoly. Its annual dividends of 10.5 per cent were made as a fixed charge on Indian revenues. The company continued its administrative functions until the Indian Mutiny of 1857–58. The catalyst for the mutiny was a concern that animal fats had been used to grease rifle cartridges. The cartridges of the time had to be bitten off before loading and such fats were considered unclean for religious reasons by many of the sepoys as the native soldiers were called. However, the real cause was bitterness about the Company's handling of taxation and justice. Much savagery occurred on both sides before the mutiny was put down. By the Act for the Better Government of India (1858), the British Crown assumed all governmental responsibilities held by the Company, and its 24,000-man military force was incorporated into the British army. The company was dissolved on 1 January 1874, when the East India Stock Dividend Redemption Act came into effect.

Think/Discussion point: Why might a government want to curtail the global operation of one of its companies?

The East India Company (John's Company as it was nicknamed) was the first example of an organization that was moving towards the more modern definition of global. Despite being confined in its trading activities to India its influence as a commercial player was felt much more widely, to the East where it purchased goods and along the sea route back to the UK where its ships had to provision etc. By its involvement in the political and social life of India and its domination of the economy it was much more than just a business. In the modern world a large commercial organization can also dominate an area by virtue of its buying power and as will be demonstrated later in this book, can influence political decisions by its decisions to stay or relocate as a result of taxation etc.

The East India Company in its heyday controlled a staggering 50 per cent of world trade and 25 per cent of the world's population.

The industrial revolution

The industrial revolution that began in the UK at the beginning of the nineteenth century was a time when local organizations and companies had the opportunity to become national. The building of a rail network, first in the UK and the eastern seaboard of the US and then throughout Europe, ensured that goods and people could be transported swiftly and safely in a fraction of the time previously possible. From a twenty-first century viewpoint with aircraft travelling at anything up to twice the speed of sound it is perhaps difficult to comprehend the difference that rail travel brought, especially in Europe where distances between major population and manufacturing centres are less than in the US. By 1888 the average speed on the UK's Great Western Railway was 46 mph. By 1890 the UK rail network was complete and there were few if any towns or even villages more than 5 miles from the nearest station, except in more remote areas. In 1865 at the end of the Civil War there were 35,000 miles of track in use in the US; by 1888 this number had increased by a factor of over four to 156,000. The national expansion of large organizations was now possible. The railroads themselves together with the shipping companies that were moving increasing numbers of emigrants across the Atlantic were amongst the largest of these new industrial giants, as were the iron and steel works, mining, engineering and chemical plants that were being developed at an increasing rate.

Originally national in nature it was not long before growth outside national boundaries was contemplated. Imperial powers, of which the UK was by clear the largest, could expand into their colonies. The introduction of cotton weaving into India by UK entrepreneurs eventually led to the downfall of the home industries in the north of England after 1945 because they could no longer compete on price.

Imperial preference

From about 1870 until 1945 a school atlas showed much of the world in red – a sign that the territory in question was part of the British Empire. In many ways Britain did not seek an empire as such but resources and then markets for its goods. The Empire formed a strong trading bloc. Raw materials from colonies and dominions were transported in British ships to the UK, where there was a strong manufacturing industry that was able to manufacture goods that could then be sent back to the colonies for sale. Many of the smaller colonies were the result of the need for coaling stations for the merchant ships and the warships of the Royal Navy that protected the sea-lanes so vital to British interests. Countries outside the Empire could face tough tariff barriers if they wished to sell to areas controlled by Britain. As these areas flexed their muscles and demanded greater autonomy they began to agitate for the removal of tariffs and be allowed to trade freely with whosoever they wished.

In the early years of the twentieth century there was a fierce debate in Britain as to whether it was better to keep the concept of Imperial preference or to lower tariff barriers and move to a regime of free trade. The revolution of the American colonies was not just a revolution against Stamp Duty and the tax on tea. There was also the discontent brought about by the Navigation Acts (the first was in 1651) that forbade goods entering Britain unless they were carried in a British ship or one from the country of origin (this was before the days of flags of convenience). As far as colonial goods were concerned the ship would have to be British whether or not the British shipowner was the cheapest. In a free trade system not only are tariff barriers lowered but the means of transporting goods are also liberalized. Echoes of the Navigation Acts can still be found in those countries that have not deregulated their air services. For many years only British and French airlines could carry passengers between London and Paris. Deregulation means that provided that there are available landing and take-off slots, an airline from another country could offer such a service. In the US shipping industry cabotage is only being liberalized slowly. Cabotage is the reservation to a country of transportation within its territories. A cruise from Los Angeles to Hawaii and back in a non-US flagged cruise liner is required to make a stop in Mexico so as to avoid the cabotage regulations, because the trip from Los Angeles to Hawaii, although thousands of miles, is classified as an internal US journey. Cabotage allows a country to protect its transport infrastructure and while it is a major impediment to free trade it does have strategic military advantages in that some control of transportation systems is retained by the government. In the 1982 Falkland Islands conflict between Britain and Argentina the UK government used its STUFT (Ships Taken Up From Trade) powers to acquire the necessary transport ships from UK shipping companies. They could not have requisitioned foreign flag vessels in this way.

> **Think/Discussion point**: Why might a country wish to keep its cabotage laws?

J P Morgan

The first of the twentieth-century global operations was masterminded from the US by the financier J P Morgan using the financial power of the Morgan Guarantee Trust. By 1900 the banker and venture capitalist Morgan controlled a number of the most important US railroads and was later to help form the mighty US Steel Corporation. The industrial revolution was fuelled by iron (and later steel) and railways and thus Morgan had at his command the major economic levers of his day. A philanthropist and collector of important works of art, Morgan was also a ruthless businessman, a facet of his nature shown quite clearly in the operations of the IMM (International Mercantile Marine) Company. Ostensibly IMM was a UK operation run by the chairman of the White Star Line, J Bruce Ismay. In reality IMM was controlled and financed by Morgan from the US with the objective of gaining a monopoly of the lucrative transatlantic passenger traffic. That traffic included the transportation of emigrants from Europe to the US and the trade used the largest liners yet seen in the world. Morgan had attempted to acquire two German companies but had failed and he then turned his attentions to the UK giants of Cunard and White Star.

Shipping was the most important factor in world trade (in many ways it still is). France and later the UK had sponsored and supported the building of the Suez Canal in the latter years of the nineteenth century and the US considered the Panama Canal opened in 1914 as part of its strategic interest even to the extent of purchasing the Danish Virgin Islands in the Caribbean (St Thomas etc.) to guard its Atlantic end.

Morgan acquired interests in White Star and a number of other UK and European shipping lines and then tried to buy Cunard but was thwarted by the UK government. He was helped in his acquisition by the chairman of the Harland and Wolff shipbuilders in Belfast. Harland and Wolff built all of White Star's ships on a failsafe cost plus arrangement. As a company Harland and Wolff could expand by accessing Morgan's money for ships that they would then build on a building cost plus commission basis (Harland and Wolff could not lose on such an arrangement as their costs would always be met in full). Under Morgan's invisible control they built the *Titanic* and her two sisters, the *Olympic*, which had a long and successful career and the *Britannic*, sunk in the First World War while serving as a hospital ship.

It is therefore a little known fact that the infamous *Titanic*, well known for sinking on her maiden voyage after colliding with an iceberg in April 1912, was actually ultimately owned by a US company. She might have flown the blue ensign (her Captain was an officer in the Royal Naval Reserve and thus entitled to fly the blue and not the red ensign), be officered and crewed almost entirely with UK citizens, be registered in Liverpool and owned by the apparently British White Star Line but she was in fact the property of J P Morgan and the Morgan Guarantee Trust. Morgan was due to sail on her maiden voyage and cancelled at the very last minute – history might have been very different had he been on board. More care might have been taken and the ship would now be just a footnote in history books.

The loss of the *Titanic* and subsequent losses in the First World War denied Morgan his ambition on the global stage but it is interesting to note that few on either side of the Atlantic were aware that a US financier had acquired no fewer than five UK and one Belgian shipping companies including White Star and its large fleet of passenger liners. When the UK government realized that as a maritime nation part of its strategic reserve was under the control of a foreigner, it acted immediately to subsidize Cunard to build the record-breaking *Mauretania* and her ill-fated sister the *Lusitania* torpedoed and sunk in the First World War with a terrible loss of life. Part of the subsidy was a requirement that Cunard must remain British, a condition not changed until Carnival (started by the US entrepreneur Ted Arison in 1972 with one ship and now the largest cruise company in the world) acquired the Cunard brand and its ships in 1998 – see the case study at the end of chapter 5.

Had the First World War not broken out there is a considerable likelihood that Morgan's global ambitions would have increased and that might well have started the process of globalization as it is known today decades earlier that it actually began.

Between the wars

The First World War put the expansion plans of many companies on hold, those of companies located in the Triple Alliance (Germany, Austro-Hungary and Turkey)

Krupp, I C Farben, Skoda etc. to be shelved for decades. However, the war had a dramatic effect in shifting the nature of the basic world economy. Prior to 1918 the world was a coal-based economy, thereafter and through to the present day it has been oil-based. The leaders in the new global economy depended on securing sources of oil of which the US and the then neglected Middle East had an abundance. Many of the conflicts of the early twenty-first century have their roots on the need for large supplies of oil and thus a need to control the world's oilfields.

The US government that had been so suspicious of trusts and cartels before the war now began to secure the nation's supplies by encouraging such syndicates of oil companies. Collier and Horowitz (1976) have commented that the US government was actually orchestrating the formation of a powerful syndicate of US oil companies abroad. Whereas in the past such syndicates would have been illegal, the government refused to assist Standard Oil in expanding into Mesopotamia insisting that it be part of a consortium of US companies.

The UK was also encouraging its oil companies to explore foreign fields and ensure that they controlled not only the oil but also the policies of the governments beneath whose land it lay. Many of the German, Italian and Japanese strategic problems in the Second World War lay in their lack of a friendly supply of oil and their need to try to take oil by force thus removing military forces from other objectives. Germany's only friendly source of oil was in Romania and those were not very large reserves and vulnerable to air attack. Germany's attempts to produce synthetic oil products were largely unsuccessful in that they could not be employed on a large enough scale.

The world was hit by the great depression between the wars and many smaller companies were taken over; the foundations for the future giant multinationals were being laid. The Wall Street Crash of 1929 and the subsequent depression had a knock-on effect all over the world, not just in the US. National economies were shown to be susceptible to factors outside their immediate control – the world was experiencing the birth pangs of a global economy.

Post 1945

The US emerged out of the Second World War as the major economic force in the world. Europe and Japan had been devastated by bombing with many vital industries destroyed. The UK had escaped invasion but had been heavily bombed and was near to bankruptcy despite the use of lend-lease from the US to equip its fighting forces. The US had not been bombed and its industry had prospered. Only the US had the industrial capacity to provide the goods needed to rebuild the post-war world. The capacity required in wartime was not run down to peacetime levels but was tasked to the process of rebuilding through initiatives such as the Marshall Plan and the Cold War meant that the military manufacturers did not have to completely scale down as had happened in 1918.

In 1944 the Bretton Woods conference in New England brought together 44 nations (associated with the Allies) to discuss the economic shape of the post-war world. The conference was cantered on the concept of free movement of goods backed by the US dollar as an international currency. The results of Bretton Woods have been far reaching leading to the setting up of a series of international institutions as detailed in the next chapter.

As will be shown in the remaining chapters of this material, the growth of global trade and organizations operating on a global basis has been massive since 1945. The same clothes, foodstuffs, soft drinks, alcoholic drinks, automobiles and aircraft are seen in every corner of the globe. News organizations such as CNN reach more and more homes and the Internet makes a mockery of the barbed wire and watchtowers of some national borders.

Implications for small businesses

At either end of the operations of companies such as the Honourable British India Company (HIC) was a web of smaller businesses. Small businesses in India collected or manufactured goods that were then sold to the HIC who in turn sold them to other smaller businesses in the UK. This pattern is repeated today. There are still many small retailers and service companies that buy their stock from large wholesale operations that in turn may deal directly with the product or service source. The small business needs to keep open good and effective relationships with its suppliers, as they may be its main link to global products and services. One of the implications of the Internet has been the ability of information and communication technology (ICT) to bring the original product/service provider and the end user closer together thus eliminating many of the other organizations in the supply chain.

Microsoft

Among those organizations that are truly global (Ford, Coca-Cola, Shell, McDonald's etc.), the Microsoft Corporation is possibly the one that impacts on more lives and in more situations than any other. Just as Polo, Columbus and their colleagues opened up the world for trade so has Microsoft (and its entrepreneurial co-founder Bill Gates) opened up a new world of electronic information transfer, communication and commerce.

The success of Microsoft and its domination of the personal computer software market through the WINDOWS® operating system stem from the entrepreneurial nature of the company's founders, William Henry (Bill) Gates and Paul Allen.

Gates formed his first company while still in high school. He had shown an aptitude for computer technology and devised a system for carrying out traffic counts. The 1970s saw the beginnings of a hobby market in self-build primitive computers. The introduction of kits for the Altair 880 computer system in 1975 provided Gates and Allen with the opportunity to build software to use on the machine. Interestingly software was the neglected area of development. At that time the 'intellectual' stimulation of building a machine that would work seemed to be the main focus of hobbyists rather than using the machine to run applications that would be of commercial or domestic use.

It was very astute of Gates and Allen to realize that their futures lay not in designing and supplying computer hardware but in providing the software for the machines built by others. The software supplier has become a vital link between the computer manufacturer and the user just as the HIC provided the link between suppliers and users in the eighteenth and early nineteenth centuries for much of the early British Empire.

Gates' great contribution may well be remembered not so much in the names of his products but in his realization that the developing IT (information technology) sector would eventually require standardization. In the beginning each machine used its own, sometimes unique operating system. Gates foresaw that compatibility would be the route to success.

Many of the early computer enterprises were concerned with the development of small machines suitable for desktop use, what has become known as the PC (personal computer) – a term originally applied to the products of IBM (International Business Machines), a company that entered the market quite late having previously concentrated on mainframe hardware. From the earliest days of the PC users required word processing and spreadsheets. There was also a growing games market, primitive as the early offerings were, as users realized the 'fun' and entertainment potential of computers.

While there might have been a temptation to go into hardware manufacture, Gates took the view that the future of Microsoft lay in providing applications etc. for a range of hardware and that Microsoft should enter into partnership agreements with OEMs (original equipment manufacturers). Microsoft would provide DOS (disc operating system – developed by Microsoft as the operating system originally used by IBM for its PCs before that company introduced OS/2 as its own operating system) and applications for a manufacturer's machines, and while each version might be slightly different due to the design of the hardware, the user would not notice this. The concept of a 'one-size fits-all' approach to software is what has made Microsoft the force in the world that it is today. No matter who made the hardware, by forming an early partnership with that OEM, by the time the equipment reached the market, Microsoft would have software available.

Packages

It was but a short step from having applications available for a new computer system at its launch to having it already pre-installed, making the whole package ready to run from the box – a considerable boon to the growing number of users who had no interest in computers as technology but who needed the applications for work and pleasure. They did not want to go through a process of installing software; they wanted the whole package ready to run.

The development of WINDOWS® as an operating environment originally by Apple but later becoming a name synonymous with Microsoft allowed for multi-functionality and multitasking to be offered to even the most inexperienced user. Packages such as Microsoft Office containing as they do a word processor (WORD) and a spreadsheet (EXCEL) etc. provide for a complete set of applications using similar commands and icons all in a mouse-driven, WINDOWS environment.

Microsoft's grew because of the development of MS (Microsoft) DOS, as this standardized operating system became the platform upon which WINDOWS® (up to WINDOWS XP®) was to be placed and the myriad of Microsoft and other WINDOWS compatible applications run.

DOS has had competitors notably OS/2 but the world appears to have accepted DOS and WINDOWS® as the standard. The development of computer networks and the importance of communication between machines made the adoption of a common standard a necessity. It is a feature of the growth of globalization that individual companies and even countries can no longer afford to be out of step with each other. Compatibility between products and common standards are all-important.

Microsoft has made compatibility its stock in trade, compatibility that is actually on Microsoft's terms as the company has been setting the compatibility standards, in effect writing the rules and nothing is as fundamental in the computer business as the operating system.

Windows

Apple were the first to offer an operating environment that used a mouse and icons to point and click rather than keyboard inputs. Indeed one idea was to remove the keyboard completely as some of the small hand-held organizers and computers have done.

Microsoft developed what is now known as Microsoft WINDOWS® and this product has gone through a series of developments, e.g. WINDOWS® 3.0 in 1990, 3.1 in 1992, 95 (7 million copies sold in 2 months), 98, ME, and has become the major system used world-wide. Indeed it was the complete domination of WINDOWS® and the fact that more and more computers were being sold not only with Microsoft applications pre-loaded but also with Internet access through a Microsoft application that the world began to ask, 'was Microsoft controlling access to the Internet for an increasing percentage of the global population?' This was a question that the US government put before the courts with the result that Microsoft was ordered to split itself into two separate organizations to avoid any conflict of interest.

It is hardly surprising that so many of the world's computers come pre-loaded with Microsoft products and not in the least sinister. Microsoft took an entrepreneurial decision to work with OEMs and provide applications for different computers. That was clearly a sensible commercial decision. Unfortunately the world has become so dependent on ICT that any monopoly looks dangerous hence the action by the US government.

CASE STUDY QUESTIONS

1   To what extent can the desire for maximum compatibility be said to have contributed to the adoption of WINDOWS and the global growth of Microsoft?

2 What are the dangers of such global dominance of the global ICT market?

3 Could Microsoft have succeeded without the decision to work so closely with OEMs?

Summary and key learning points

- The development of global organizations is not a new phenomenon.
- The British in India, J P Morgan and the US oil companies were pursuing global strategies long before globalization became an issue.
- Countries can be very concerned when their strategic assets are threatened by foreign ownership.
- Governments will act so as to protect strategic assets from foreign ownership.
- Governments will assist companies in acquiring control of strategic resources such as oil.
- Once a company becomes involved in another country in a major role it also becomes involved in the politics etc. of that country.
- Since 1945 the move has been towards free trade with the easing of barriers to world trade a major goal.

QUESTIONS

1 Globalization is not a recent phenomenon – discuss this statement with reference to Spain and the various 'India' companies.

2 Why might governments wish to regulate the global operations of their companies?

3 J P Morgan invented modern globalization – discuss.

Recommended further reading

Wild (2000), *The East India Company*, provides details of the Company's history and Strouse (2000), *Morgan: an American Financier*, gives an insight into the financier J P Morgan. Gavin Menzies' (2002) theory of the Chinese discovery of the Americas is expounded in his book, *1421 – the Year China Discovered the World*.

Further information about Microsoft and Bill Gates can be found in Manes and Andrews (*Sales*, 1994) and Dearlove (*Doing Business the Bill Gates' Way*, 2001).

▣ ⊠ 2 A shrinking world I – global governance

Learning outcomes

By the end of this chapter you should understand:

- What is meant by the world becoming smaller
- The need for international organizations
- The role of the United Nations (UN)
- The role of the International Monetary Fund (IMF)
- The role of the World Bank
- The role of the World Trade Organization (WTO)/General Agreement on Tariffs and Trade (GATT)
- The role of the International Labor Organization (ILO)
- The growth in non-governmental organizations (NGOs)

It is often said that the world is becoming smaller. While this is not true in a literal sense most people know what is meant – that transportation and communication technologies allow us to reach places far more quickly and with less effort than was the case in the past and to communicate across the globe very quickly indeed.

To illustrate the second point: on 24 December 1814 (less than 200 years ago) Britain and the United States signed the Treaty of Ghent bringing what has become known as the War of 1812 to a close. The conflict had been precipitated by the British insistence that US vessels could be searched for British seamen who could then be impressed into the Royal Navy. The war's deeper roots concerned the trade relations between the US, Britain and the ambitions of the US to acquire Canada. The war was to all intents and purposes a draw. This treaty was ratified by Britain on 28 December and by the US Senate on 16 February 1815. Between these dates a final battle was fought on 8 January, when a British army, not knowing of the treaty, landed at the mouth of the Mississippi River and was defeated near New Orleans by forces under Andrew Jackson. Word of the treaty had not reached the opposing generals.

The first powered flight – the Wright Brothers in 1903 – was less than the length of a modern Boeing 747 'Jumbo Jet'. By 1969 mankind had not only mastered flight but had also walked on the moon – such has been the progress in making the world smaller over the past 100 years.

On 6 April 2003 UK forces acting as part of the US-led coalition to remove both weapons of mass destruction and the regime of Sadaam Hussein from Iraq

(Operation Iraqi Freedom) entered the City of Basra – Iraq's second city. With the troops were 'embedded' journalists who accompanied them into battle. UK television viewers were, in their own homes, able to see live coverage via videophone from the streets of Basra – a clear demonstration of how communication speeds have increased.

Think/Discussion point: In what ways has 'the world become smaller' in your lifetime? How has this made your life different from that of your parents or grandparents?

There was still one facet of the world that for many years had proved difficult to make 'smaller' and that was the issue of time zones. Despite the speed of communication it will always be the case that at noon in London it is only 07:00 a.m. in New York. For many years this caused problems of communications for companies operating on a global basis. As will be shown in chapter 8, however, recent developments in information and communication technology (ICT) have nullified many of the disadvantages caused by time zones and imaginative thinking has led some organizations to break free of national boundaries and locate 'real-time' call centres in a variety of places across the globe.

Think/Discussion point: What kinds of problems can time zones cause to a global organization?

Assuming that regular office hours are (for the sake of argument) 09:00–17:00, an organization with offices in London, New York, Tokyo and Moscow may find that there are few occasions in the day when they are all fully staffed. The overlap between them is shown in Figure 2.1 with the base times at GMT, i.e. the time at the London office. Tokyo closes one hour before London 1ns.

Think/Discussion point: Britain and Eire are one or two hours behind their EU partners. Is there a case for a standard EU time based on the Paris meridian?

By the end of the nineteenth century the increase in the ease of communication across much of the world had already led to multilateral agreements on postal services, telegraphs and railways.

The huge growth in global trade and the speed of communications since 1945 has led to a need for more formal governance in the relationships between countries. In addition to military treaty organizations such as NATO (North Atlantic Treaty Organization) there has been considerable expansion of global governance since the ending of the Second World War in 1945.

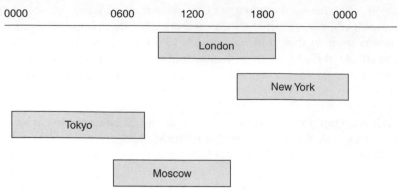

| 0000 | 0600 | 1200 | 1800 | 0000 |

Figure 2.1 **The time zone problem.**

The first real attempt at some form of world order occurred at the end of the First World War. Woodrow Wilson, the US President had suggested that a 'League of Nations' be set up as a forum in which nations could discuss their differences without recourse to war – a laudable aim in 1919. The Paris Peace Conference of 1919 adopted this concept and the League of Nations was set up by the victorious allies. Ironically the US Senate voted to stop the US joining – Wilson's dream was in tatters as without the US the League was unlikely to be successful. Indeed it did nothing to halt the spread of fascism that led to the Second World War. The only surviving institution of the League of Nations is the International Labor Organization (ILO) – see later in this chapter. Further information about the Paris Peace Conference can be found in Margaret Macmillan's (2001) *Peacemakers – Six Months that Changed the World.*

In 1945 a more serious attempt at a form of world governance was put in place with the institution of the United Nations – a move again sponsored by the victorious allies.

The United Nations (UN)

The UN is an international organization of nation-states, based on equality between its members. Under its charter, the UN was established 'to maintain international peace and security'; 'to develop friendly relations among nations'; and 'to achieve international cooperation in solving ... economic, social, cultural, or humanitarian problems' and in 'encouraging respect for human rights and for fundamental freedoms'. Members are pledged to fulfil the obligations they have assumed, to settle international disputes by peaceful means, to refrain from the threat or use of force, to assist the UN in actions ordered under the charter and to refrain from assisting any country against which such UN action is being taken, and to act according to the charter's principles. The UN won the Nobel Prize for Peace in 2001. There has been much comment that the UN has failed to keep the peace and that its resolutions are marred by the individual agendas of its large members especially as the permanent members of the Security Council – the US, Russia, the UK, France and China have a veto. The US has vetoed resolutions demanding action against Israel while the Soviet Union (as Russia was for much of the past

50 years) has vetoed resolutions against its allies. In 2003 France announced that it would veto any additional resolution against Iraq if that resolution was designed to permit the use of force to disarm and change the regime of Sadaam Hussein. Both the UK and the US believed that an earlier resolution (1441) allowed the use of force and they used 1441 as legitimization for the invasion of Iraq in March 2003. Nevertheless the UN provides a forum for conflict resolution and through its many agencies (UNESCO, UNICEF etc.) assistance is provided to developing countries.

The first commitment to establish a new international organization was made in the Atlantic Charter, signed by President Franklin D Roosevelt of the US and Prime Minister Winston Churchill of Great Britain on 14 August 1941, at a conference held on a warship off the coast of Newfoundland. They pledged to establish a wider and permanent system of general security and expressed their desire to bring about the fullest collaboration between all nations in the economic field. The principles of the Atlantic Charter were more widely accepted in the Declaration by the United Nations, signed on 1 January 1942 by representatives of the 26 allied nations that were fighting against the Axis powers of Germany, Italy and Japan during the Second World War. In this document the term United Nations, suggested by Roosevelt, was first used formally.

Direct action to form the new organization was taken at a 1943 conference in Moscow. On 30 October, representatives of the Union of Soviet Socialist Republics (USSR), Great Britain, China and the US signed a declaration in which they recognized the need to establish 'at the earliest practicable date a general international organization'. Meeting in Tehran a month later, Roosevelt, Churchill and Soviet Premier Joseph Stalin reaffirmed 'the supreme responsibility resting upon us and all the United Nations to make a peace which will ... banish the scourge and terror of war'.

Following up on the Moscow declaration, representatives of the four powers met at the Dumbarton Oaks estate in Washington, DC in the autumn of 1944 to work out a series of proposals for an international organization. They agreed on a draft charter that specified its purposes, structure and methods of operation, but they could not agree on a method of voting in the proposed Security Council, which was to have the major responsibility for peace and security.

The voting issue was settled at the Yalta conference in February 1945, when Roosevelt, Churchill and Stalin met for the last of their wartime negotiating summits. Essentially, the Soviet leader accepted the Anglo–American position that limited great-power prerogatives on procedural matters, but retained the right of veto on substantive issues. It is this veto that is coming under increasing criticism as the other members of the UN cannot see the rationale behind such power being invested in just a handful of members. At the same time, the allied leaders called for a conference of United Nations to prepare the charter of the new organization.

Delegates from 50 nations met in San Francisco on 25 April 1945, for what was officially known as the United Nations Conference on International Organization. During a two-month period, they completed a charter consisting of 111 articles, based on the draft developed at Dumbarton Oaks. The charter was approved on 25 June and signed the next day; it became effective on 24 October 1945, after ratification by a majority of the signatories. The bonds of the wartime alliance against common enemies undoubtedly hastened agreement on establishing the new organization.

On 10 December 1945, the US Congress invited the UN to establish its headquarters in the US. The organization accepted and in August 1946 moved to a temporary location in Lake Success, New York. Later that year a site was purchased bordering the East River in Manhattan, and plans for a permanent headquarters were drawn up. The site was granted a measure of extraterritoriality under an agreement between the US and the UN. The complex was completed in mid-1952.

Under the charter, UN membership is open to all peace-loving states that accept the obligations of the organization – whether a country would admit to being 'non-peace loving' is a mute point. The 50 nations that attended the San Francisco conference, with the addition of Poland, became founding members of the UN. Until 1971 China was represented by a delegation from the Nationalist government of Taiwan; in October of that year, however, the General Assembly voted to include a delegation from the People's Republic of China in its stead.

New members are admitted by a two-thirds' vote of the General Assembly on the recommendation of the Security Council. Since 1945, membership has increased more than threefold, mainly with the admission of many new African and Asian countries that had been European colonies. As of late 2002, the UN had 191 members.

The charter established six principal UN organs: the General Assembly, the Security Council, the Economic and Social Council, the Trusteeship Council (no longer in operation), the International Court of Justice and the Secretariat.

All member states are represented in the General Assembly, which is the main deliberative body of the UN. The General Assembly meets annually in regular sessions and in special sessions at the request of a majority of its members or of the Security Council. The Assembly has no enforcement authority: its resolutions are recommendations to member states that carry the political and moral force of majority approval but lack power of direct implementation. The charter, however, permits the Assembly to establish agencies and programmes to carry out its recommendations; among the most important of these are the following: the United Nations Development Programme (UNDP), the United Nations Conference on Trade and Development (UNCTAD) and the United Nations Children's Fund (UNICEF).

The Security Council, which is in continuous session, is the UN's central organ for maintaining peace. The Council has 15 members, of which five – China, France, Great Britain, Russia and the US – have been accorded permanent seats. Periodically proposals have been made for new permanent members to be added (e.g. Germany, Japan), and old ones removed (e.g. France, Britain) to reflect the changing balance of world power, but to date no substantive revision has been made. Non-permanent members serve for two years, with five new members elected by the General Assembly every year. Decisions of the Council require nine votes, including the concurring votes of the permanent members on substantive issues.

The Economic and Social Council (ECOSOC), which meets annually, has 54 members: 18 members are elected each year by the General Assembly for three-year terms. ECOSOC coordinates the economic and social activities of the UN and its specialized agencies such as the World Health Organization (WHO); the United Nations Educational, Scientific and Cultural Organization (UNESCO); the Food and Agriculture Organization (FAO); and the International Labor Organization (ILO). In practice, ECOSOC's functions are limited because each specialized agency is organized separately and is governed by its own constitution and elected bodies: the agencies submit annual reports to ECOSOC. The UN and the specialized agencies together are called the UN System.

The International Court of Justice, situated in The Hague, the Netherlands, is the judicial body of the UN. The Court hears cases referred to it by UN members, who retain the right to decide whether they will accept the Court's ruling as binding. When asked to do so by the UN, its principal organs, or the specialized agencies, the International Court of Justice may also render advisory opinions. Fifteen judges sit as members of the court; they are elected for nine-year terms by the General Assembly and the Security Council.

The Secretariat serves the other UN organs and carries out the programmes and policies of the organization. The body is headed by the secretary-general, who is appointed by the General Assembly on the recommendation of the Security Council.

The UN's operating costs are met by contributions from member states in accordance with a schedule of assessments approved by the General Assembly. Only the regular budget, constituting ongoing activities under the charter, is covered by fixed assessments: special programmes such as UNICEF and the UNDP are usually financed through voluntary contributions. The largest contributors are the US (25 per cent) and the former USSR (10 percent). Of the other members, only Japan, Germany, France, Great Britain, Italy and Canada contributed more than 2 per cent. In the mid-1980s the UN underwent a serious financial crisis. Many member states, including the US and the USSR, withheld part of their contributions due to national fiscal problems and dissatisfaction with certain aspects of the UN system.

Under the charter, the Security Council is primarily responsible for matters of peace and security. Articles 33–38 of the charter authorize the Security Council to encourage disputing nations to settle their differences through peaceful means, including negotiations, enquiry, mediation, conciliation, arbitration and judicial settlement.

When the Council determines that a dispute threatens peace, it may, under Articles 39–51, enforce its recommendations, either by non-military means, such as economic or diplomatic sanctions, or by the use of military forces. This is the only place where the charter authorizes enforcement action. Such action is subject to the concurring votes of the five permanent council members, however, and thus emphasizes the significance of the great-power veto on important issues. Military action is also subject to the availability of armed forces from the UN members. UN peace-keeping forces are formed from the forces of member countries but wear UN insignia (the blue beret) and not national insignia. The UN has undertaken peace-keeping roles across the globe. These are always difficult operations as both warring sides may see the UN forces as an 'enemy'. The only UN military action under its own flag was the 'police action' in Korea in the early 1950s. Better known as the Korean War the UN intervened after the invasion of South Korea by communist North Korea. The peace negations are still under way!

Impact of the UN

While it is claimed that the UN has been nowhere near as effective as it could have been – critics citing its failures in Rwanda, the Congo, Bosnia and Kosovo in particular, there are those who believe that the impact of international organizations has been quite profound. Akira Iriye, a prominent historian, has suggested that the central influence on the international scene in the period since 1945 was not the Cold War, but rather a deepening web of international interactions. In *Global*

Community: the Role of International Organizations in the Making of the Contemporary World (2002) Iriye goes beyond the usual framework for studying international relations – politics, war, diplomacy and other interstate affairs – and traces the crucial role played by international organizations in determining the shape of the world today. Iriye's discussion of international organizations around the world examines multinational corporations, religious organizations, regional communities, transnational private associations, environmental organizations and other groups to illuminate the evolution and meaning of the global community and global consciousness. Iriye points out that while states have been preoccupied with their own national interests such as security and prestige, international organizations, both intra-government and non-governmental organizations (see below), have been actively engaged in promoting cultural exchange, offering humanitarian assistance, extending developmental aid, protecting the environment and championing human rights. Iriye contends that they have made important contributions to making the world a more interdependent and peaceful place.

> **Think/Discussion point**: How effective can an organization comprising nearly 200 members each with their own agendas actually be in promoting peace and harmony?

The governance of international trade and finance

In 1944 the Bretton Woods conference in New England brought together 44 nations (associated with the allies) to discuss the economic shape of the post-war world. The conference was cantered on the concept of free movement of goods backed by the US dollar as an international currency. The results of Bretton Woods have been far reaching leading to the setting up of a series of international institutions as detailed below.

The International Monetary Fund (IMF)

The IMF is an international organization comprising 184 member countries, i.e. most of the countries of the world. It was established to fulfil three main functions. The first was the promotion of international monetary cooperation, exchange stability and orderly exchange arrangements. Secondly the fund was tasked with fostering economic growth and high levels of employment. Thirdly it was given the role of providing temporary financial assistance to countries to help ease balance of payments adjustment.

At the UN conference held at Bretton Woods, representatives from the western allies then fighting the Second World War agreed on a framework for economic cooperation designed to avoid a repetition of the policies that had contributed to the Great Depression of the 1930s and the subsequent rise of fascism.

The organization of the IMF

The IMF is accountable to the governments of the member countries. The creators of the fund believed that this accountability would be essential to its effectiveness. In recent years, the IMF has become increasingly open, making a large proportion of its documents available to the public on its web site (www.imf.org). The move to a degree of public accountability has been driven in part by worries that the IMF was too secretive given its huge power in making loans to countries conditional on the country accepting IMF conditions. Many of these conditions impose cuts in public expenditure and the privatization of state enterprises.

The IMF is headed by the Board of Governors, which is composed of ministers of finance or heads of central banks (or other officials of comparable rank) from each of the IMF's 184 member countries. Apart from those Governors that are represented on the IMF Committee (see below), the Governors gather only on the occasion of the IMF–World Bank Annual Meetings to deal formally with IMF matters. During the rest of the year, they communicate the wishes of their governments for the IMF's day-to-day work through their representatives on the Executive Board (see below). It would be cumbersome and ineffective if the Board of Governors were involved in the day-to-day running of the fund. A large board is necessary to ensure that all of the IMF members are represented. Without such inclusive representation the IMF would be open to charges that it only acted on behalf of some of its members. Despite all members being represented the charge is often levelled that the IMF is in fact an offshoot of US policy making.

The IMF Committee consists of 24 Governors representing constituencies or groups of countries, corresponding to those of the Executive Board (see below). It meets twice a year, on the occasion of the IMF–World Bank Annual and Spring Meetings, to advise the IMF on the functioning of the international monetary system.

The Executive Board

The Executive Board consists of 24 Executive Directors representing the IMF's 184 member countries. The Board, which is based at IMF headquarters in Washington, DC, is responsible for conducting the day-to-day business of the IMF and meets at least three times a week in formal session. In 2003 eight Executive Directors represented individual countries: China, France, Germany, Japan, Russia, Saudi Arabia, the UK and the US. The 16 other Executive Directors each represent groupings of the remaining countries. The Executive Board rarely makes its decisions on the basis of formal voting, but relies instead on the formation of consensus among its members. The managing director, appointed by the Executive Board, is head of IMF staff and chair of the Executive Board.

How the IMF works

There are three main areas of IMF activity:

- Surveillance
- Credits and loans
- Technical assistance.

Surveillance

The IMF maintains a policy dialogue with each of its members through a process known as surveillance. It appraises members' exchange rate policies within the overall framework of their economic policies in what is known as an Article IV consultation. This is usually undertaken on an annual basis. Surveillance is carried out based on the conviction that strong and consistent domestic economic policies will lead to stable exchange rates and a growing and prosperous world economy. The IMF also carries out multilateral surveillance, the results of which are summarized in the *World Economic Outlook* (twice a year), and in the *Global Financial Stability Report* (quarterly).

Credits and loans

The IMF provides credits and loans to member countries with balance of payments problems to support policies of adjustment and reform. A main function of the IMF is to provide loans to countries experiencing balance-of-payments problems so that they can restore conditions for sustainable economic growth. The financial assistance provided by the IMF enables countries to rebuild their international reserves, stabilize their currencies and continue paying for imports without having to impose trade restrictions or capital controls. Unlike development banks, the IMF does not lend for specific projects. As of 31 January 2003, it had credits and loans outstanding to 89 countries for an amount of about $96 billion. The IMF makes its financial resources available to its members through a variety of financial facilities (loan programmes). In addition to its regular facilities (Stand-By Arrangements; the Extended Fund Facility; the Supplemental Reserve Facility; Contingent Credit Lines; and the Compensatory Financing Facility), the IMF also provides concessional assistance under its Poverty Reduction and Growth Facility (PRGF) and debt relief under the Heavily Indebted Poor Countries (HIPC) Initiative. The IMF and the World Bank (see later) have designed a framework to provide special assistance for heavily indebted poor countries that pursue IMF- and World Bank-supported adjustment and reform programmes, but for whom traditional debt relief mechanisms are deemed as insufficient. The HIPC Initiative entails coordinated action by the international financial community, including multilateral institutions, to reduce to sustainable levels the external debt burden of these countries. The IMF is not the only possible lender of funds to countries.

Both the World Bank (see later in this chapter) and commercial banks also lend to countries. The IMF is, however, often the lender of last resort. Much of the criticism of the IMF stems from the conditions that it makes in order for a country to lend money from it. Countries that need loans so badly have no choice but to accept IMF conditions, however severe, as the UK found out in the 1960s.

Technical assistance

The IMF offers technical assistance and training to help countries strengthen their human and institutional capacity, and design and implement effective macroeconomic and structural policies. Technical assistance is offered in the areas of:

- Fiscal policy
- Monetary policy
- Statistics.

Emergencies

The IMF provides emergency assistance to help member countries with urgent balance of payments financing needs in the wake of natural disasters or armed conflicts. Given that such disasters often strike at the poorest countries such assistance is of critical value.

The World Bank

From its inception during the Second World War at the Bretton Woods Conference, the World Bank initially helped rebuild Europe after the war. Its first loan of $250 million was to France in 1947 for post-war reconstruction. Reconstruction has remained an important focus of the Bank's work, given the natural disasters, humanitarian emergencies and post-conflict rehabilitation needs that affect developing and transition economies.

The World Bank is one of the world's largest sources of development assistance. The primary focus of the Bank is on helping the poorest people and the poorest countries.

In 2002 the World Bank provided $19.5 billion to developing countries and worked in more than 100 developing economies, bringing finance and/or technical expertise towards helping them reduce poverty. It is worth noting that according to the Bank's figures, more than half the people in developing countries live on less than £440 ($700) a year. Of these, 1.2 billion earn less than 60 p ($1) per day.

While the title may seem akin to that of just a huge high street bank, the World Bank is not a commercial bank, as the term is used and understood. It is one of the UN's specialized agencies, and is made up of 184 member countries, i.e. most of the countries of the world. It is the member countries that are jointly responsible for how the Bank is financed and how its money is spent. The World Bank is a combination of the International Bank for Reconstruction and Development (IBRD) and the International Development Association (IDA), a trust fund managed by the IBRD to provide grants and interest-free credits to the world's poorest countries. Together these organizations provide low-interest loans, interest-free credit and grants to developing countries.

It can be very difficult for poor countries to raise large sums on the international money markets and yet they need money in order to fund the developments that, it is hoped, will lead them out of poverty. Even if money can be borrowed the interest rate may be prohibitive – the greater the risk, the higher the interest charged. In addition to direct contributions and loans from developed countries, poorer countries can receive grants, interest-free loans and technical assistance from the World Bank to enable them to provide basic services. In the case of the loans, countries have 35–40 years to repay, with a 10-year grace period.

Some 40 countries provide the money for this funding by the IDA by making contributions every four years. The fund was replenished most recently in 2002, with nearly £5.5 billion ($9 billion) from donors and another £4 billion ($6.6 billion) from the Bank's resources. At that time, donors agreed on increased use of IDA grants – up to 21 per cent of resources – to help address the special difficulties, such as the HIV/AIDS epidemic, faced by the poorest and most vulnerable countries.

IDA credits make up about one-quarter of the Bank's financial assistance. With the exception of IDA funds, very little of the Bank's income is provided by its member countries.

In 2002 the IDA provided £5 billion ($8.1 billion) in financing for 133 projects in 62 low-income countries.

Those developing countries with higher national incomes can also receive loans from the IBRD at rates of interest that are lower than in the commercial market. Countries that borrow from the IBRD have more time to repay than if they borrowed from a commercial bank – 15 to 20 years with a three-to-five-year grace period before the repayment of principal begins. Developing country governments borrow money for specific programmes, including poverty reduction efforts, delivery of social services, protection of the environment and promotion of economic growth that will improve living standards. In 2002 the IBRD provided loans totalling £7 billion ($11.5 billion) for 96 projects in 40 countries.

The IBRD raises almost all its money in the world's commercial financial markets. With a Triple A (AAA) credit rating it can issue bonds to raise money and then pass on the low interest rates to its borrowers.

The World Trade Organization (WTO)/General Agreement of Tariffs and Trade (GATT)

The WTO is the only global international organization dealing with the rules of trade between nations. At its heart are the WTO agreements, negotiated and signed by the majority of the world's trading nations and ratified in their parliaments. The aim of the WTO is to help producers of goods and services, exporters and importers conduct their business.

The GATT was established after the Second World War to set up rules for the governance of world trade and to promote the free movement of goods and services without tariff barriers. The years since GATT's creation have seen a huge growth in world trade in both products and services. Merchandise exports grew on average by 6 per cent annually. Total trade in 2000 was 22 times the level of 1950.

The governance system was developed through a series of trade negotiations, or rounds, held under GATT. The first rounds dealt mainly with tariff reductions but later negotiations included other areas such as anti-dumping and non-tariff measures. The last round under GATT auspices was the 1986–94 Uruguay Round and led to the creation of the WTO.

The WTO was established in 1994 as an international organization to pursue the concept of free trade. The WTO settles trade disputes by allowing the aggrieved member to place restrictions on goods of an offender. For example, in 2000 the WTO ruled in favour of the US over preferential imports bananas from ex Caribbean colonies into the EU – see chapter 4. Through the Lomé Convention drawn up in 1975 the EU protects the banana industries in former colonies of EU countries (the ex-colonies being mainly those of Britain and France in the Caribbean) by allowing them preferential entry into EU markets. The US threatened to place tariffs on certain goods, e.g. Scottish cashmere imported from the EU into the US. This would have devastated the economy of the Scottish borders region and manufacturers there rightly complained that their futures were being jeopardized over Caribbean bananas (Ellwood, 2001 and Ransom, 2001). As in the majority of such cases, a compromise was agreed ending the 'banana war' in June 2001. The EU argued that such WTO restrictions on agreements like the Lomé Convention deny sovereign governments the ability to take decisions based on national interest.

In July 2003 the WTO ruled against the US and in favour of the EU. The issue was that US tariff barriers on steel designed to protect the US steel industry broke WTO rules. Not surprisingly the EU announced that it would be planning to raise tariffs to price some US products out of Europe – so much for free trade!

Of current concern is the WTO rules that try to force countries to take foodstuffs that they believe may be hazardous due to the addition of hormones or genetic modification. When the EU protested that hormone-fed beef was illegal in Europe, the US took the EU to the WTO and received a favourable ruling with the result that the US applied 100 per cent tariffs to certain EU food products. The WTO can only force a country to accept products and services from another for offer in its markets – it cannot force consumers to buy. Anecdotal evidence suggests that compulsion may be counter-productive as consumers in a country forced to accept a WTO ruling on behalf of another country may begin to boycott the goods of that country.

The WTO sees its role as providing assurance. Consumers and producers know that they can enjoy secure supplies and greater choice of the finished products, components, raw materials and services that they use. Producers and exporters know that foreign markets will remain open to them.

The WTO fulfils its role by:

- Administering trade agreements
- Acting as a forum for trade negotiations
- Settling trade disputes
- Reviewing national trade policies
- Assisting developing countries in trade policy issues, through technical assistance and training programmes
- Cooperating with other international organizations.

This, the WTO believes leads to a more prosperous, peaceful and accountable economic world. Virtually all decisions in the WTO are taken by consensus among all member countries and they are ratified by members' parliaments. Trade friction is channelled into the WTO's dispute settlement process where the focus is on interpreting agreements and commitments, and how to ensure that countries' trade policies conform to them. That way, the risk of disputes spilling over into political or military conflict is reduced.

By lowering trade barriers, the WTO's system also breaks down other barriers between peoples and nations.

At the heart of the WTO system – known as the multilateral trading system – are the WTO's agreements, negotiated and signed by a large majority of the world's trading nations, and ratified in their parliaments. These agreements are the legal ground-rules for international commerce. Essentially, they are contracts, guaranteeing member countries important trade rights. They also bind governments to keep their trade policies within agreed limits to everybody's benefit.

The agreements were negotiated and signed by governments, although their purpose is to help producers of goods and services, exporters and importers conduct their business. As will be discussed in chapter 4, there are those who believe that the WTO system works best for richer countries whose suppliers gain access to larger markets. Poorer counties are not able to protect vulnerable local businesses and it is large multi-nationals that benefit from WTO activities. Mike Moore, Director General of the WTO from 1999 until 2002 refutes such suggestions strongly in his book, *A World Without Walls* (2003), a book that is recommended as further reading.

In February 1997 agreement was reached on telecommunications services, with 69 governments agreeing to wide-ranging liberalization measures that went beyond those agreed in the Uruguay Round.

Also in 1997 40 governments successfully concluded negotiations for tariff-free trade in information technology products, and 70 members concluded a financial services deal covering more than 95 per cent of trade in banking, insurance, securities and financial information.

In 2000, new talks started on agriculture and services. These have now been incorporated into a broader agenda launched at the fourth WTO Ministerial Conference in Doha, Qatar, in November 2001.

The agenda adds negotiations and other work on non-agricultural tariffs, trade and environment, WTO rules such as anti-dumping and subsidies, investment, competition policy, trade facilitation, transparency in government procurement, intellectual property and a range of issues raised by developing countries as difficulties they face in implementing the present WTO agreements. The deadline for the negotiations is 1 January 2005.

The WTO has more than 140 members, accounting for over 97 per cent of world trade. Around 30 others are negotiating membership.

Decisions are made by the entire membership. This is typically by consensus. A majority vote is also possible but it has never been used in the WTO, and was extremely rare under the WTO's predecessor, GATT. The WTO's agreements have been ratified in all members' parliaments.

The top-level decision-making body of the WTO is the Ministerial Conference that meets at least once every two years.

Below this is the General Council (normally ambassadors and heads of delegation in Geneva, but sometimes officials sent from members' capitals), which meets several times a year in the Geneva headquarters. The General Council also meets as the Trade Policy Review Body and the Dispute Settlement Body.

At the next level, the Goods Council, Services Council and Intellectual Property (TRIPS) Council report to the General Council.

Numerous specialized committees, working groups and working parties deal with the individual agreements and other areas such as the environment, development, membership applications and regional trade agreements.

The WTO Secretariat, based in Geneva, has around 550 staff and is headed by a director-general. Its annual budget is roughly 143 million Swiss francs. It does not have branch offices outside Geneva.

The International Labor Organization (ILO)

The ILO is the UN's agency that seeks the promotion of social justice and internationally recognized human and labour rights. It was founded in 1919 and is the only surviving major creation of the Treaty of Versailles that brought the League of Nations into being (see earlier in this chapter). The ILO became the first specialized agency of the UN in 1946.

The ILO formulates international labour standards in the form of Conventions and Recommendations that set minimum standards of basic labour rights: freedom of association, the right to organize, collective bargaining, abolition of forced labour, equality of opportunity and treatment, and other standards regulating conditions across the entire spectrum of work-related issues. It provides technical assistance primarily in the fields of:

- vocational training and vocational rehabilitation
- employment policy
- labour administration
- labour law and industrial relations
- working conditions
- management development
- cooperatives
- social security
- labour statistics and occupational safety and health.

The ILO promotes the development of independent employers' and workers' organizations and provides training and advisory services to those organizations. Within the UN system, the ILO has a unique tripartite structure with workers and employers participating as equal partners with governments in the work of its governing organs.

The ILO was created in 1919, at the end of the First World War, at the time of the Peace Conference that convened first in Paris, then at Versailles. The need for such an organization had been advocated in the nineteenth century by two industrialists, Robert Owen (1771–1853) of Wales and Daniel Legrand (1783–1859) of France.

Their ideas were first tested within the International Association for Labour Legislation, founded in Basel in 1901 and they were then incorporated into the Constitution of the ILO, adopted by the Peace Conference in 1919.

The initial motivation was humanitarian. The condition of workers, more and more numerous and exploited with no consideration for their health, their family lives and their advancement, was less and less acceptable. This preoccupation appears clearly in the Preamble of the Constitution of the ILO, where it is stated, 'conditions of labor exist involving ... injustice, hardship and privation to large numbers of people'.

There was a second political motive. Politicians began to realize that without an improvement in their condition, the workers, whose numbers were ever increasing as a result of industrialization, would create social unrest, even revolution as had happened in Russia in 1917. The Preamble notes that injustice produces 'unrest so great that the peace and harmony of the world are imperilled'.

The third motive was economic. Because of its inevitable effect on the cost of production, any industry or country adopting social reform would find itself at a disadvantage vis-à-vis its competitors. By setting standards it was hoped that nations would refrain from using their people as a cheap labour force to attract foreign capital and increase their competitive advantage. This is an issue examined in chapter 4 where such practices seem all too prevalent at the start of the twenty-first century.

A final reason for the creation of the ILO was added by the participants of the Peace Conference, linked to the end of the war to which workers had contributed significantly both on the battlefield and in industry. This idea appears at the very beginning of the Constitution: 'universal and lasting peace can be established only if it is based upon social justice'.

The ILO Constitution was written between January and April 1919, by the Labor Commission set up by the Peace Conference. The Commission was composed of representatives from nine countries, Belgium, Cuba, Czechoslovakia, France, Italy, Japan, Poland, the UK and the US. The Constitution set up a tripartite organization, the only one of its kind bringing together representatives of governments, employers and workers in its executive bodies. The ILO Constitution became Part XIII of the Treaty of Versailles.

The first annual International Labor Conference, composed of two representatives from the government, and one each from employers' and workers' organizations from each member state, met in Washington on 29 October 1919. It adopted the first six International Labor Conventions, which dealt with hours of work in industry, unemployment, maternity protection, night work for women, minimum age and night work for young persons in industry. It is many of these rights that opponents of globalization believe are ignored in low wage economies.

In 1926, an important innovation was introduced when the International Labor Conference set up a supervisory system on the application of its standards, which still exists today. It created the Committee of Experts composed of independent jurists responsible for examining government reports and presenting its own report each year to the Conference.

In 1934, under the presidency of Franklin D Roosevelt, the US, which did not belong to the League of Nations (see earlier), became a Member of the ILO.

In 1969, the ILO was awarded the Nobel Peace Prize as it commemorated its fiftieth anniversary.

Non-governmental organizations (NGOs)

The last few years of the twentieth century saw a huge rise in the number of what have become known as non-governmental organizations (NGOs). Composed of both charities and pressure groups NGOs have become a part of global governance and discussion demanding a voice at such events as the Earth Summits in Rio in 1997 and Johannesburg in 2003. Many NGOs have been critical of globalization claiming that its main beneficiaries are not the poor but multinational corporations and the US.

Think/Discussion point: Why do you believe the US comes in for such global criticism?

Greenpeace, Friends of the Earth, Oxfam and Action Aid are now globally recognized NGOs, the first two being effective pressure groups and the last two have gone far beyond the simple distribution of charity. The programmes of Oxfam and Action Aid are developmental as they seek to improve the long-term condition of people through education and infrastructure projects rather than alleviating short-term problems with the provision of food aid etc.

In 1980 there was only one independent organization working to protect the environment in Indonesia, by 2003 there were more than 2000. Similar organizations have been emerging across much of the world. In the Philippines, registered non-profit organizations grew from 18,000 to 58,000 between 1989 and 1996 whilst in the US, aside from religious groups and private foundations, 70 per cent of non-profit organizations filing tax returns are less than 30 years old; a third are less than 15.

There is no little doubt that the growth of citizen-led organizations is reshaping politics and economics both at the domestic and global levels. Ordinary people are becoming more and more involved in environmental, developmental and human rights issues. At the same time the numbers of those exercising their right to vote in democracies is dropping. In the 2003 Scottish parliamentary elections, only the second since devolution in 1999 the turnout was less than 50 per cent. The figures suggest that the apathy is with politics and politicians and not with causes and issues.

The ending of apartheid in South Africa and the movement of that country to majority rule and the overthrow of communist regimes in Central Europe were citizen led.

There is nothing new in the concept of organizations founded by private individuals playing a role in democracies – it is the growth in such activities in recent years that has been astonishing. Before the US Civil War in 1861 Europeans were expressing admiration for the number of citizen-based associations that could be found in the US.

Today such associations are not only a feature of societies on a global basis but they are now a distinct sector of civil society, a sector that, like government, serves essential social functions, but that has many of the entrepreneurial qualities of business. The profit, in this case, is welfare and social progress. NGOs need to compete for charitable funds just as business needs to compete for the customer's pound, dollar, euro etc. William Drayton, the president of Ashoka, an organization named for an altruistic emperor of India, that supports people working to bring about social changes in Asia, Africa, Latin America and Central Europe, has referred to the founders of many NGOs as social entrepreneurs – people who have vision, practical ability and drive that they direct not towards profit but harness for social problems not just locally, but system-wide.

The NGO sector is rapidly moving away from charity functions towards a desire to find more systemic and sustained solutions to social problems. In doing so they are showing an increased readiness to experiment with mainstream business methods and market-based approaches. Many of the charity shops on UK high streets have run up against opposition from commercial retailers as they have adopted a more commercially minded approach by selling new goods in addition to second-hand ones. Paid managers for such shops are becoming more and more common.

NGOs have grown as people have begun to question the ability of the state to carry out a whole host of functions. They represent another way of organizing the common business of society by involving grass-roots participation.

An example of how NGOs are now combining to challenge governmental actions is shown by group of more than 50 NGOs (including Oxfam from the UK) and social society movements from developed and developing countries that called for the rejection of the launch of negotiations on an investment agreement at the WTO Ministerial meeting in Cancun in September 2003.

The NGOs and social movements contend that instead of promoting sustainable development, the WTO negotiations on investment, promoted by the EU, the US and Japan, will create a global bill of rights for transnational corporations (TNCs) and infringe upon the right of individual governments to regulate the entry, operation and exit of foreign investors for development purposes. They argue that whilst foreign direct investment (FDI) – see chapter 4 – can make a positive contribution to sustainable development, it can also lead to foreign exploitation with TNCs enjoying many rights and making huge profits at the expense of workers' salaries and local firms' capacity.

Governments are not always happy at the prospect of dissention from NGOs. Members of the Global Unions group accused the government planners of the Second Meeting of the Preparatory Committee for the World Summit on the Information Society (WSIS) of stifling voices of dissent after excluding many NGOs from the debate over the draft conclusions.

Governments voted to keep non-governmental groups and civil society activities out of discussions on a draft declaration and plan of action for the summit in Geneva in December 2003.

The summit, organized by a range of UN agencies led by the International Telecommunications Union, concerns world-wide policy and regulation issues arising from the introduction of new communications technologies, use of the Internet and the expansion of the global information market. A follow-up conference is to be held in Tunis in 2005.

The position of NGOs within society received a boost in 2002 with the results of a survey in the US that showed that Americans' faith in their government increased from 27 per cent to 48 per cent over the past year. But the confidence extended to NGOs grew as well by up to five percentage points over the 2001 survey to 41 per cent. Both sectors now enjoy credibility roughly on a par with that of business, which earned a score of 44 per cent – the same mark it received in the 2001 report. NGOs can operate outside vested interest and it is this that makes them attractive

Think/Discussion point: Why do you think NGOs have grown as rapidly as they have and what is their attraction for ordinary citizens?

to many of those who are disillusioned by perceptions of too close a relationship between governments and large commercial corporations and interests.

Quite clearly NGOs will form a permanent part of future national and global governance, something that both politicians and business will need to consider, especially as many NGOs have been highly critical of globalization as will be shown in chapter 4.

Implications for small businesses

In agreeing to assist countries, organizations such as the IMF often make stringent demands on public spending, lowering tariff barriers and interest rates. These can have a dramatic effect on local businesses. It beholds the operators of small businesses to look at the international situation to see if there are any likely threats or indeed opportunities. While the WTO and the IMF may seem remote, their actions can affect the smallest operation.

Oxfam

The Oxford Committee for Famine Relief met for the first time on 5 October 1942 amidst concerns about the famine among people in the countries occupied by Germany as a result of the Allied sea blockade of the Axis Powers. Among its founding members were Canon T R Milford of the University Church and Professor Gilbert Murray, a member of the national committee and former Regius Professor of Greek at Oxford.

After the ending of hostilities in 1945 the Oxford Committee saw a continuing need and enlarged its objectives to include the relief of suffering in consequence of the war (i.e. the Second World War). Activity centred on the provision of food parcels and clothing to Europe, much of which was then in the grip of famine conditions. From 1948 grants were made to projects in Europe and elsewhere and in 1949 the Committee's objectives were again broadened to the relief of suffering arising as a result of wars or of other causes in any part of the world. The Committee gradually became known by its abbreviated telegraph address, Oxfam, this name was adopted formally in 1965 (this was before the days of email addresses when the quickest way to send messages was either the telephone or the telegram system).

The 1960s brought great changes to the work of Oxfam and greater public awareness not least through the growth of television. Concern for the world's poor grew among the general public and the charity's income trebled over the course of the decade. The organization worked to present a different picture of poor people: one in which they were portrayed as human beings with dignity, not as passive victims. It was also a time when a less patronizing view of people in what was then called the 'Third World' was being encouraged. Oxfam produced education and information materials for schools, churches and individuals that explained the root causes of poverty and suffering, the connections between the rich North and the poorer South of the globe, and the role of people in the North in creating, and potentially solving, poverty in the developing world.

The major focus of work, managed by a growing network of Oxfam field directors overseas, became support for self-help schemes whereby communities improved their own water supplies, farming practices and health provision. The idea that by teaching a person to fish can make them self-sufficient for a lifetime was gaining public acceptance.

As Oxfam continued to expand its work through the 1970s, many new ideas and theories were put forward about development and poverty, including the decision to employ local people to run and work on projects rather than imposing outsiders from developed nations. The principles of community involvement and control are still behind Oxfam's work today.

In the 1970s it became clear that many of the problems associated with poverty required government and international action. Oxfam started – within the bounds set by charity law – to campaign on behalf of the people it worked with overseas and to talk to decision-makers who shaped policy on relevant issues. Oxfam moved from being a charity to being an NGO.

Oxfam's Public Affairs Unit (PAU) was set up to provide research into and analysis of the causes of poverty. By the mid-1980s the unit was lobbying on a range of issues including pesticides, food aid and Third World debt – all of which are still issues today.

In addition to charitable donations Oxfam was one of the first UK charities/NGOs to run its own shops. Operated by volunteer groups around the country they became one of the main sources of income in the late 1960s, selling donated items and handcrafts from overseas. They are now a familiar sight on most high streets. Approximately 22,000 volunteers work in more than 830 Oxfam shops in the UK.

Oxfam Trading rapidly expanded its Bridge programme and sales of fairly traded products during the 1970s and 1980s. Fair trade is considered in the next chapter of this book.

Introducing a mail-order catalogue boosted annual sales above £1 million by the early 1980s. The programme took the name Fair Trade in 1996 (trading under the name Oxfam Fair Trade Company) to bring it in line with the wider Fair Trade movement, which included campaigning for improvements in the terms of trade and conditions of workers.

Emergency relief and rehabilitation in the Horn of Africa dominated Oxfam's work in the 1980s as it did with other NGOs. With other aid agencies, Oxfam had been warning of the impending crisis and had sought to galvanize the international community into action. Nearly half of the £51 million that Oxfam raised in 1984/85 was spent on relief and rehabilitation in the Horn of Africa, where Oxfam confirmed its pre-eminence as a provider of water and sanitation in emergencies. This was the time of the massive 'Feed the World' relief effort promoted by rock musicians to aid the famine relief in the Horn of Africa.

The growth in income enabled Oxfam to expand its support for development projects worldwide. In parallel, increased resources were dedicated to policy, research and campaigning work to address the structural causes of poverty, such as crippling debt burdens, unfair terms of trade and inappropriate agriculture policies.

With the escalating number of conflicts following the collapse of the Soviet Union and the Eastern bloc, Oxfam began emergency and rehabilitation work in this region. During the 1990s, Oxfam supplied humanitarian aid to affected civilians on all sides of the wars in the former Yugoslavia.

Oxfam's largest ever response to a humanitarian disaster was in the Great Lakes region of Central Africa in the mid-1990s. Oxfam realized that aid alone could not provide solutions to the political, economic and social problems of the region. The relief work on the ground was matched by international lobbying and campaigning aimed at the UN, the Organization of African Unity and powerful governments, in an effort to build a lasting peace that would provide the opportunity for individual and economic development.

During 1997/98, Oxfam undertook a major review of the way it works, its aims and how it fits into the world around it. Thorough research, both within and outside Oxfam, helped the organization to focus on its core beliefs, and to develop a strategy so that, no matter how the world changes, it can respond and make a major impact on poverty and suffering.

From its start in the university city of Oxford, Oxfam is now one of the best-known NGOs in the world. The aims of the organization are that every individual should have the right to a living wage, good quality education, affordable health care, protection from disasters and violence, the right to have a say in his or her own future and equality of opportunity. These aims form the basis of all Oxfam's work and are translated into its work on the ground.

CASE STUDY QUESTIONS

1 Why do you believe there has been a trend for NGOs to move from the charitable to the political sphere?
2 To what extent do NGOs provide a representative outlet for ordinary people?
3 Should organizations such as Oxfam adopt a commercial approach to fundraising through competing on the high street?

Summary and key learning points

- In 1945 a serious attempt at a form of world governance was put in place with the institution of the United Nations (UN).
- The huge growth in global trade and the speed of communications since 1945 has led to a need for more formal governance in the relationships between countries.
- International governance is seen as a means of reducing conflict.
- Increasing world trade needs international governance.
- Finance for development needs to be provided at an international level.
- The International Monetary Fund (IMF) is an international organization comprising 184 member countries. It was established to fulfil three main functions.

The first was the promotion of international monetary cooperation, exchange stability and orderly exchange arrangements. Secondly, the fund was tasked with fostering economic growth and high levels of employment. Thirdly, it was given the role of providing temporary financial assistance to countries to help ease balance of payments adjustment.

- The World Bank is one of the world's largest sources of development assistance. The primary focus of the Bank is on helping the poorest people and the poorest countries.
- The easing of barriers to world trade has been a major goal since 1944.
- The World Trade Organization (WTO) is the international organization dealing with the rules of trade between nations.
- The General Agreement of Tariffs and Trade (GATT) was established after the Second World War to set up rules for the governance of world trade and to promote the free movement of goods and services without tariff barriers.
- The International Labor Organization (ILO) is the UN's agency that seeks the promotion of social justice and internationally recognized human and labour rights.
- Non-governmental organizations (NGOs) are citizen-led organizations involved in charity, development and lobbying work at both the domestic and global levels.
- NGOs are often better at encouraging individual participation in international matters than formal government programmes.
- There has been a dramatic rise in the number of NGOs in the past 20 years.

QUESTIONS

1   Can international organizations such as the UN really change the behaviour of nation states?
2   NGOs are more popular than governments – discuss.
3   Why is an organization such as the WTO necessary in today's world of high-speed global trade?

Recommended further reading

Joseph Stiglitz, ex chief economist at the World Bank, sets out his views on the WTO and IMF in *Globalization and its Discontents* (2002). Mike Moore, Director General of the WTO from 1999 until 2002 provides an insight into the WTO in *A World Without Walls* (2003), while a *Global Community* by Akira Iriye (2002) and Fowler's (2000) *The Virtuous Spiral* provide useful information on the role of NGOs. Kapur Lewis and Webb (1997) provide information about the World Bank.

☑ 3 A shrinking world 2 – global markets

Learning outcomes

By the end of this chapter you should understand:

- What markets are
- The nature of a customs union
- Regionalization v. globalization
- The European Union (EU)
- Currency union
- The European Free Trade Association (EFTA)
- The North American Free Trade Association (NAFTA)
- Association of South East Asian Nations (ASEAN)

The previous chapter was concerned with global institutions and governance. This chapter examines markets, regional trade blocs and customs unions. The European Union (EU) and the North American Free Trade Association (NAFTA) are the two best known but there are a number of others. The EU differs from other free trade associations in that it is concerned not only with trade but also with ever closer political ties between its members. It is the political integration within the EU that has caused much heart searching within the UK over the past decade, heart searching that has increased with the introduction of a common currency, the euro by a number of EU members.

Markets

A market can be something as local as a set of stalls laid out in a public space as still seen in a number of market towns throughout the world to this day through to the international transactions required to purchase oil, weapons, financial services or aeroplanes.

A market is purely the forum for an exchange between parties. As discussed in a companion volume to this book, *Mastering Marketing Management* (Cartwright, 2002) from which this next section is adapted, while twenty-first century shopping malls throughout the world may seem to have little in common with the medieval markets depicted in films and books or the thriving markets of many African,

Caribbean or Asian countries, they are in fact just a modern version of the same mechanism for exchange.

Think/Discussion point: What if any are the differences, other than in scale and facilities, between a street market in Tobago and the Trafford Centre shopping mall just outside Manchester in the UK?

A market facilitates the exchange process by bringing a seller and a buyer together. While in the vast majority of cases the exchange is one of good and or services for money although it may involve barter, i.e. the seller exchanges his goods/services as required by the buyer for goods/services that the buyer holds and that the seller requires. Such barter is not unusual in trade between governments especially where oil or weapons are concerned.

In the days when travelling was difficult, it made sense for people to carry out as many transactions as possible at the same time and in the same place. Medieval towns vied with each other for the right to hold a market and as such a right was often within the patronage of the local ruler, considerable political machinations could occur.

For any one product or service there may well be a number of quite disparate markets and customer bases.

Geographically markets types can be expressed as the following types:

- Local
- National regions
- National
- Supra-national regions
- International/global
- Virtual.

However, this is somewhat simplistic, as it is necessary to distinguish between the product and the means of getting that product to the customer. For instance, a chocolate bar may be national or international in its appeal but because of the means by which it is sold, the actual point of sale may serve a purely local market. Coca-Cola (see chapter 5) is a global product manufactured, bottled and served on a local basis. Indeed one would be unlikely to order a coke from America if one were thirsty in Thailand. Conversely Scottish whisky is a local product widely available in a global market as by legal definition it must be manufactured in Scotland.

Local

Organizations operating locally are perhaps among the most familiar. They include the vast majority of small owner-managed organizations. Their operations are designed to serve a local market. Being part of the locality they can often react and adapt to changing local conditions more rapidly than organizations operating in a wider region. However, because of their smaller size, they are often unable to compete with larger organizations on price and range of products/services. The average corner shop in the UK has found it very difficult to compete with the large national supermarket chains. Initially they were able to compete by opening earlier and shutting later but some supermarkets now operate on a 24-hour basis. In more rural areas they have the advantage of being closer to their customers but they are still unable to match the economies of scale offered by the supermarkets with their ability to buy in huge bulk quantities. A number of corner shops have banded together in confederations enabling them to buy in bulk and gain the advantages of economies of scale.

There is no doubt that as shopping malls and out-of-town supermarkets etc. grew in the developed world throughout the latter years of the twentieth century, it was the smaller retailers who felt the pinch and the increasing number of closures of such retailers in UK towns was evidence of this.

Other organizations, e.g. local builders, plumbers, electricians etc. have managed to hold onto their business, as it is easier for them to provide an immediate service (if you need a plumber, you need one now) than larger national organizations, which may find it harder to respond in a flexible and immediate manner.

One other method for the local organization to gain the benefits of size that accrue to regional/national/international organizations is to become part of a franchise. Perhaps the best known of these is the McDonald's® chain of fast-food restaurants, which offers almost identical menus and service standards over much of the world, the vast majority of the operations being franchises. This aspect of globalization is covered in chapter 10.

> **Think/Discussion point**: To what extent has there been a move in your local area to national/global organizations acting locally?

National regions

In geopolitical terms a region can be described as an area with clearly defined boundaries. Such boundaries do not have to be political or geographic, they can be cultural, e.g. the Basque region that straddles parts of the Franco–Spanish border.

The UK is often divided up into a series of regions: London and the Home Counties, South East, South West (and the West Country), Midlands, North West, North East, Northern Ireland, Wales and Scotland. Scotland, Wales, Northern Ireland together with the Isle of Man, the Scilly Islands and the Channel Islands also have their own devolved government (that of the Isle of Man being one of the world's oldest parliaments) together with (Wales excepted) their own versions of the standard sterling currency.

The US is often divided up into regions for marketing purposes, e.g. the North East Corridor, the Pacific Northwest, the West Coast, the Deep South etc.

Regions can often exhibit quite different cultural norms, as anybody who has lived in both London and, say, the North West of the UK or has moved from California to New York will appreciate.

National

A trend of the late twentieth century carried on into the twenty-first has been for the development of products and services that have a more than purely national appeal. Motor car manufacturers such as Ford, Chrysler, BMW etc. have been developing models that appeal to more than one nationality. Indeed the Japanese may be considered to have started this trend when as part of the rebirth of the Japanese economy after the Second World War they developed motor vehicle products for the European market rather than for specific countries. In Western Europe, where there are countries with very similar road networks and infrastructure, it is not difficult to design a model that can appeal to different nationalities with only superficial details being changed, often just the brand or model name (see chapter 7). The UK and Ireland market is somewhat more problematic given that both countries drive on the left rather than the right, but modern manufacturing techniques make light of that problem. Interestingly it is not a problem for the Japanese who also drive on the left.

The vast majority of organizations operate within their own national borders; hence brand names that are familiar to the people from one country may be unknown to those from others. There are, however, some products and names that have become truly international.

The advantages to remaining within a single national segment are those of language, currency and law: factors that tend to be consistent within national entities albeit with some deviation. For example laws differ between US states and between Scotland and England (especially in respect of property and contract law) and certain regions may speak a different language, although there is nearly always a common tongue. In Europe the advent of the euro is making currency transactions easier, although at the time of writing not all EU members had joined the eurozone, the UK appearing very reticent.

Products such as literature, many TV programmes, some motion pictures and comedy often do not work when placed in another culture and these may well remain national in character.

Supra-national regions

The EU is an example of a supra-national regional market. It is a free market open to organizations from all members. While this may increase competition it also provides opportunities. The functioning of the EU and similar groupings form the main core of this chapter.

International/global

Ford, Sony, McDonald's, Shell etc. are household names across much of the globe. These organizations do have a national home, the US for Ford and McDonald's, Japan for Sony, the Netherlands for Shell (the company is actually Royal Dutch Shell) but in fact operate on a global basis with headquarters, manufacturing, distribution etc. in either individual countries or pan-national regions. Products and services may be developed for particular national groups or the same product may be sold everywhere with only slight changes to reflect particular usage etc. For instance North America works almost universally on 110 volts for the electric supply compared to 220/240 volts in Europe. If you are manufacturing electrical goods, certain different components will be needed depending on the voltage in the area of sale. It is noticeable that consumer electrics designed for travel such as electric razors and laptop computers are nearly always supplied with 110–240 adaptors as they themselves operate on low voltages. Even within the EU, however, there is not a standard electrical outlet socket.

Somebody from the UK studying the goods on sale in a New York department store might conclude that the market is becoming more and more global and they would be right, not withstanding the fact that some goods and services do not travel as well as others. Just because something has been successful in one market does not guarantee similar success in others, however similar. While some US convenience foods and drinks (two soft drinks ending in the word Cola spring to mind) have been highly successful globally, other such items have failed to penetrate other markets, especially the lucrative European markets.

Virtual

The latter years of the twentieth century saw a dramatic growth of the so-called dot.com organizations linked to the Internet. While it was initially thought that there might be vast sums of money to be made trading internationally over the net, reality produced some outstanding financial failures but some successes especially in book retailing and home banking. Christopher Price (2000) has looked at a group of Internet pioneers and concluded that although the losses up to 2000 were considerable, the eventual long-term gains make the virtual market an inevitability especially for those such as Davis at Lycos, Yang at Yahoo! and Schrock at AltaVista, who are supplying search engines etc. to facilitate Internet use. On a smaller scale many purely local retailers and manufacturers were able to reach a much larger market by taking online orders and providing product/service information through their web pages. The chairman of IBM was certainly wrong (spectacularly so) when he said in 1943 that there would be a world market for only five computers (quoted in Aldrich, 1999).

It is to be expected that there will be a growth in this type of marketing especially as customers become more confident in the security of credit card transactions and delivery mechanisms. The virtual global marketplace is covered in chapter 8, which looks at the impact of the Internet on globalization.

Working online frees organizations from any local/regional/national constraints and allows them to be truly international but perhaps at the loss of the personal touch.

Customs unions

Countries often act to protect their business by imposing tariffs on imports. Restricting imports not only protects indigenous suppliers but also eases the country's balance of trade, as it does not have to use up its currency buying from another country. However, if country A places tariffs on the products of country B the likelihood is that country B will place tariffs on the products of country A in retaliation. The rationale behind the WTO as described in the previous chapter is the removal of tariffs in order to allow a free flow of goods and services. What occurs in a customs union is that the members reduce tariffs on trade between themselves and negotiate tariff deals with other customs unions or individual customers.

Being in a country that is a member of a customs union provides a local business with a potentially vastly increased marketplace. While this presents opportunities there is also the threat of increased competition from other businesses within the customs union that will also have access to the local area.

Regional trade groupings

Alan Rugman (2000) has described the major trading blocs of the world in terms of a 'triad'. There are three such blocks: North America, Europe and Japan. One of the war aims of Japan in 1941 was to create the greater South East Asia Co-Prosperity Sphere, a Japanese equivalent of the then declining British Empire. The difference between the North American Free Trade Association and the European Union and the British Empire or its Japanese equivalent is that the former are not based on a singe hub nation that is the main beneficiary.

Organizations in and/or trading with much of Europe and North America need to be aware of the European Union (EU) and the North American Free Trade Agreement (NAFTA).

The European Union (EU)

In April 1951, a treaty forming the European Coal and Steel Community (ECSC) was signed by Belgium, Luxembourg, the Netherlands, Italy, France and Germany. The driving force behind the formation of the ECSC was Robert Schuman, foreign minister of France between 1949 and 1953. The concept was that there would be a free market in the vital commodities of coal and steel between the partners. This economic aim was also overlaid by a political one, the first post-war West German Chancellor, Konrad Adenauer, making the point in 1950 that there were important political considerations as a degree of sovereignty in national policy making would need to be abnegated as a result of ECSC's formation. By agreeing to coordinate the production of coal and steel and their associated products, the partners would be operating in a supra-national manner. Coal and steel are strategic materials and the cooperation of the partners would, it was believed, make another war between France and Germany much less likely. The ESCS needed supra-national institutions to manage the partnership and these have evolved into the institutions of firstly the EEC (European Economic Community) often referred to as the Common Market and latterly the EU (European Union). It was recognized early on that there would be a need for a higher authority, indeed it was called just that, a court of justice to settle disputes between the partners, an assembly to provide a democratic input (members were not actually elected by the citizens of the partner countries but chosen by national parliaments) and a council of ministers representing the needs and aspirations of the partners.

The EEC was instrumental not only in removing trade barriers in strategic materials between the partners but also in encouraging officials and politicians to work together.

The success of the ECSC was such that the partners agreed to extend its operation beyond that of the coal and steel industries and in 1957 they signed the two treaties of Rome. The first treaty established the European Economic Community (EEC) and the second, Euratom was designed to expand ESCS operations into nuclear energy. While the UK was initially interested in the proposal, initial membership was restricted to the six original members of ECSC. Austria (forbidden by the settlements arrangements following the Second World War to become involved with any form of political and economic union with West Germany), Denmark, Norway, Portugal, Sweden and Switzerland formed the European Free Trade Association (EFTA) in 1960 to act as a free trading bloc outside the EEC. EFTA was configured to give a greater emphasis on being a free-trading association without the political institutions being developed within the EEC. Nevertheless in 1961, the UK, Eire and Denmark applied to join the EEC. President Charles de Gaulle of France vetoed the entry of the UK and all three applications fell. The UK then joined EFTA.

As the EEC grew in stature and its institutions gained more supra-national authority and influence, a debate began that is still ongoing. Should the Community become wider and accept more members or deeper and develop further towards political and economic union.

In respect of expansion, the 1961 application by the UK, Denmark and Eire has already been mentioned; there was an associate agreement between the EEC and Greece in 1961, the UK, Denmark and Eire re-applied for membership in 1967 together with Norway although France still opposed UK membership. The EEC was renamed the European Community (EC) in 1967 (and the European Union (EU) in 1993). Special agreements were made with Spain in 1970 and in 1972 the UK, Denmark and Eire were finally admitted to the EEC. Norway's membership was agreed but the Norwegian population voted in a referendum not to become EC members. Membership meant that all UK businesses were now part of a supranational market in addition to their market within the UK. A referendum on continuing membership was held in the UK in 1975 with a large majority voting in favour of remaining within the UK.

There was further expansion in 1981 when Greece became a member and again in 1985 when Spain and Portugal joined. By 2000, Austria (relieved of an obligation not to enter any form of union with Germany), Finland and Sweden had also joined the Community (1995) and there were a large number of countries mainly from the old communist Eastern bloc but also Turkey having made applications. While Turkey's application has been rejected on human rights grounds, the applications of the Czech Republic, Hungary, Latvia, Malta, Poland, the Slovak Republic and Slovenia to join the EU from 2004 were accepted. The accession of Cyprus to EU membership in 2004 depends on an agreement between the Cypriot authorities and the authorities of the Turkish North Cyprus. Many of the existing EU countries adopted the euro as a common currency in January 2002 although the UK elected not to join the eurozone at that time.

The North American Free Trade Association (NAFTA) – see later – was made between the US, Canada and Mexico on 1 January 1984. The aim of NAFTA is to remove virtually all tariffs between the three members by 2008. NAFTA is far less of a political agreement than the EU as its main focus is purely on the removal of trade barriers rather than setting up supra-national institutions.

EU law

Community law, adopted by the Council or by the Parliament may take the following forms:

- **Regulations:** these are directly applied without the need for national measures to implement them.
- **Directives:** bind member states as to the objectives to be achieved while leaving the national authorities the power to choose the form and the means to be used.
- **Decisions:** these are binding in all their aspects upon those to whom they are addressed. A decision may be addressed to any or all member states, to undertakings or to individuals.
- **Recommendations and opinions:** these are not binding.

EU directives and decisions normally require national legislation to be enacted according to the procedures of the member states before becoming law. That legislation must ensure that the directive/decision is followed to the letter although the wording etc. may differ between states according to national procedures.

Think/Discussion point: Why is it necessary to have EU law superior to national laws and for all national laws to be in compliance with EU law?

Community legislation, as well as the Council's common positions transmitted to the European Parliament, is published in the *Official Journal* in all the official languages as listed on the EU web site.

The EU economy

Table 3.3 (see later) shows that the EU is largest customs union and trading bloc in the world. Statistics change month by month and an up-to-date view of the EU economy can be gained from the Eurostat pages on the EU web site (see Bibliography).

In 2003 the EU was showing a healthy trading balance with the rest of the world as the surplus figures in Table 3.1 show.

Outside its own members or candidate members the major trading partners of the EU are shown in Table 3.2 together with the rounded up/down value of exports and imports to the nearest € billion and the growth rate in both during the first half of 2003, i.e. January–June 2003.

The importance of the Chinese market to the EU is clearly demonstrated and this may be a battlefield with the North Americans. The importance of Switzerland, Norway and Turkey is hardly surprising. The first is surrounded by EU states, the

Table 3.1   EU external trade surplus,
second quarter 2003.

Month (2003)	Surplus (€ billion)
May	3.7
June	5.4
July	12.2

Source: EU web site.

Table 3.2   EU major trading partners.

Country	Exports from EU (€ billion)	Growth rate %	Imports to EU (€ billion)	Growth rate %
USA	121	−10	93	−15
Switzerland	36	−3	30	−4
Japan	21	−6	34	0
China	16	+20	38	17
Russia	14	+24	24	−11
Norway	13	+1	23	+11
Turkey	12	+10	11	+11

Source: EU web site.

second applied to become a member but its people voted against and Turkey appears desperate to join.

A positive balance of trade gives the EU considerable muscle in trading negotiations. The position with the US is more problematic. At present the EU sells more to the US than it buys and this gives the power to the US as a customer. However, the differences are small and the EU may soon become a net customer of the US in which case it will have a greater proportion of what Michael Porter (1996) has described as the bargaining power of the customer. These issues are reflected in the case study at the end of this chapter, a case that deals with EU/US commercial conflict.

Social Charter

For an organization such as the EU to both function and to be accepted by all its citizens, it must ensure that there are no major disparities between those living in one part of the EU from those in others. As Pettinger (1998) has pointed out, the harmonization of social policy had been a long-term aim of the original six founders of what was the EEC. A format for such harmonization was agreed in 1989 with the Social Charter (as it became known) being a separate part of the Maastricht Treaty, which changed the name of the EEC into the EU. The reason for the separation was the refusal of the then Conservative government in the UK to adopt any form of social charter, thus the UK was provided with an opt-out clause. The Labour government elected in 1997 signed up for the Social Charter in November of that year. Despite the opt out, the UK government put into law the Trade Union Reform and Employment Rights Acts in 1993 at the behest of the EU in addition to minimum statutory maternity rights, secret ballots for trade union activities, protection for employees who were transferred between organizations and absolute rights regarding health and safety at work. As UK citizens would have been entitled to take any issues relating to these to the European Court (see chapter 10), the government had to mirror EU legislation hence the Social Charter entered the UK political scene via a back door.

The Social Charter deals with provisions in the following areas, many of which provide for a statutory obligation upon employers and are thus also covered in chapter 10:

- Freedom of movement for workers within the EU
- Protection for employment and pay
- Improvements in living and working conditions
- Adequate social protection and social security
- Freedom to join trade unions etc. (and of course the right not to join)
- Adequate and continual vocational training
- Equality of treatment regardless of gender
- Information to all workers on workplace issues
- Health and safety at work protection
- Access to labour markets for the elderly
- Access to labour markets for the disabled
- Protection for children and young persons at work.

The last provision was the cause of much concern in the UK media as it was feared that youngsters might be forbidden to undertake paper rounds – this has not proved to be the case but illustrates the 'Europhobia' that occasionally sweeps the UK!

A full explanation of the Social Charter and the implications for organizations can be found in *The European Social Charter* by Richard Pettinger (1998).

Banks and the euro

The European Investment Bank (EIB)

The European Investment Bank (EIB), the financing institution of the EU, was created by the Treaty of Rome. The members of the EIB are the member states of the EU, which have all subscribed to the Bank's capital.

The EIB has its own legal personality and financial autonomy within the Community system. The EIB's mission is to further the objectives of the EU by providing long-term finance for specific capital projects in keeping with strict banking practice.

The EIB grants loans mainly from the proceeds of its borrowings, which, together with 'own funds' (paid-in capital and reserves), constitute its 'own resources'. Outside the EU, EIB financing operations are conducted principally from the Bank's own resources but also, under mandate, from Union or member states' budgetary resources.

The European Central Bank (ECB)

It was in June 1988 that the Council of Ministers confirmed the objective of the progressive realization of economic union and mandated a Committee, chaired by the then President of the European Commission (Jacques Delors), to study and propose concrete stages leading to this union. The Committee was composed of the governors of the EC national central banks and specialist experts.

On the basis of the *Delors Report*, the European Council decided in June 1989 that the first stage of the realization of economic and monetary union should begin on 1 July 1990 – the date on which, in principle, all restrictions on the movement of capital between member states were abolished.

In view of the relatively short time available and the complexity of the tasks involved, the preparatory work for the final stage of Economic and Monetary Union (EMU) was also initiated. The first step was to identify all the issues which should be examined at an early stage, establish a work programme until the end of 1993 and define accordingly the mandates of the existing sub-committees and working groups established for that purpose.

The euro

The European Currency Unit (ECU) became the common unit of exchange of the EU (as part of the European Monetary System (EMS) in 1979. It took the place of the European Unit of Account (EUA), which had been used as an accounting tool for calculating the relative value of payments into and out of the accounts of the European Community (EC) as it then was. The ECU is a composite of the EC members' currencies, weighted according to those countries' share of output and their share of EU commerce. It is supported by a reserve fund, the European Monetary Cooperation Fund (EMCF). The ECU plays a fundamental part in the exchange rate mechanism (ERM), under which member countries have to keep the value of their national currencies within a percentage band (divergence factor) of a central parity. The divergence factor varies from country to country. However, the ECU is not only concerned with the ERM. The currencies of members of the EU, which are not members of the ERM, such as the UK and Italy (both left the ERM in 1992 as a result of financial problems, the issue in the UK resulting in the later resignation of the Chancellor of the Exchequer, Norman Lamont), are still component parts of the ECU. The composition of the ECU has been changed from time to time, but was frozen on 1 November 1993, when the Treaty on European Union (the Treaty of Maastricht) came into effect.

The ECU was not a hard currency, and so could not be used for everyday transactions. ECU coins were minted, but only for ceremonial use and as collector's items. However, the ECU was used for syndicated loans and for money market business.

Under the Maastricht Treaty signed in 1991 it was agreed that a common currency should be in place by 1999 but with an opt-out clause for those countries such as the UK and Denmark that did not wish to join the first members of the 'eurozone'. At the EU Madrid summit in December 1995, it was decided that the common currency would be called the euro. However, at the summit the following decisions were also made: on 1 January 1999, the currency rates for those that qualify for EMU would be fixed, the euro replacing the ECU. On 1 January 2002, the euro became hard currency and the national currencies of participating EMU member states (the mark, franc, peseta, lira, guilder etc.) were abolished. The ECU was duly replaced by the euro when this came into being in January 1999.

> **Think/Discussion point**: How could a common currency lead to a loss of sovereignty?

On 2 May 1998 the Council of the European Union – in the composition of heads of state or government – unanimously decided that 11 member states (Belgium, Germany, Spain, France, Ireland, Italy, Luxembourg, the Netherlands, Austria, Portugal and Finland) fulfilled the necessary conditions for the adoption of the single currency on 1 January 1999. They formed the first tranche of countries adopting the euro.

The heads of state or government also reached a political understanding on the persons to be recommended for appointment as members of the Executive Board of the ECB.

On 1 January 1999 the final stage of EMU commenced (in respect of participating members) with the irrevocable locking of the exchange rates of the currencies of the 11 member states participating in the euro area and with the conduct of a single monetary policy under the responsibility of the ECB.

The UK and the euro

The Conservative Party (the main UK opposition party at the time of writing) has become increasingly hostile to the idea of EMU.

One of the main reasons expressed for this hostility relates to national sovereignty. There are those who believe that monetary union is but a step on the road to full political union which will set up a United States of Europe, something many UK politicians are against. The argument is that as monetary union negates the influence a national government has on fiscal policy, the natural step is political union.

However, while remaining outside the euro zone, the UK's fiscal policy cannot help but be influenced by the relationship of sterling to the euro. The high pound of the early months of 2000 and the UK's reluctance to embrace EMU is one of the reasons given by the board of BMW when it divested itself of its only recently acquired UK subsidiary, Rover, in March 2000. The UK government refuted these comments but nevertheless a number of global organizations have expressed a wish to see the UK within the euro zone and trading in the currency. Supporters of EMU argue that Britain will be marginalized by its major trading partners (other EU members) unless the country joins France, Germany etc. in adopting the euro.

The UK Chancellor of the Exchequer, Gordon Brown, set five economic tests that must be met before the UK would consider adopting the euro. There would then be a referendum of the British people. At the time of writing (2003) there is still deep division over whether the UK should adopt the euro. Many to the political right believe that losing control of the national currency will lead to a loss of sovereignty.

Even if the UK does not adopt the euro for some time to come, organizations will often be dealing with suppliers and customers who are in member states that have adopted the common currency and thus they will need to be cognizant of the exchange rates etc. It may well be that the UK experiences 'creeping euroization' as more and more organizations begin to quote using the euro.

Economic groupings such as the EU and NAFTA are breaking down previous political, economic and trade barriers. However, despite this opening of the world to trade and global organizations, famine and war are still all too common in many areas. That is perhaps the next big challenge for globalization.

The European Free Trade Association (EFTA)

The EU is not the only trade association in Europe; there is also the lesser known EFTA of which the UK was once a member.

The European Free Trade Association (EFTA) was founded to promote free trade as a means of achieving growth, prosperity and economic cooperation among its member countries. The seven founding members of EFTA – Austria, Denmark, Norway, Portugal, Sweden, Switzerland and the UK – were members of the Organization for European Economic Cooperation (OEEC), which was established in 1947 to implement the Marshall Plan that had been devised in the US to aid the economic recovery of war-torn Europe and to promote economic cooperation between member countries. The OEEC was successful in freeing trade and payments in Western Europe and improving the economic relationships between Western European countries.

By the 1950s there were many politicians in Western Europe who wished to move in the direction of a more rapid and more complete economic integration of its nation states. Some European governments were making plans to go beyond 'cooperation' as exemplified in such intergovernmental organizations as the OEEC. They proposed to begin the process of close integration of their national economies and to create strong central institutions under a common authority to help bring this about.

The first successful move on this path had been the conclusion in April 1951 of the Treaty establishing the European Coal and Steel Community (ECSC), which created a common market for coal and steel within the territories of its six member states: Belgium, France, the German Federal Republic, Italy, Luxembourg and the Netherlands. The next move was even more important. It came in 1955 and took the form of proposals for the formation of a European Economic Community (EEC). Its objective in the field of trade was to operate a customs union applying to all types of goods. The EEC and its successor the EU were covered in earlier in this chapter.

In 1956, while discussions concerning the establishment of the EEC were taking place, some other members of the OEEC presented the idea of a broad free trade area, covering the whole of Western Europe. This initiative led to the establishment of an intergovernmental Committee of Ministers to negotiate a free trade area agreement. A special committee examined the complex issues involved and considerable progress was made in finding solutions to the numerous problems, solutions that were later to be applied in the negotiations of the EFTA Convention. Nevertheless, these negotiations were suspended at the end of 1958 mainly due to differences between France, which was devoted to the EEC, and Britain, which sought to form a looser alliance based on free trade.

The governments of other OEEC countries outside the EEC then began to explore the idea of a free trade arrangement between themselves with the aim of counter-balancing the EEC and finding a joint agreement with the six EEC member states. In June 1959 officials from seven governments (the UK, Denmark, Norway, Sweden, Austria, Switzerland and Portugal) met in Sweden, to draw up a draft plan for a European Free Trade Association (EFTA). On the basis of this draft, government ministers agreed to the creation of such an association among the seven countries. Officials assembled again at the beginning of September and completed the final text of the Convention establishing EFTA in the short period of eight weeks. The Convention was signed on 4 January 1960 and entered into force after parliamentary approvals (a national referendum in the case of Switzerland) on 3 May 1960.

The Stockholm Convention

The Convention established a framework within which the necessary minimum set of rules was spelt out together with a statement of certain guiding principles and the indication of procedures that could be applied in actual situations. In one area, however, the Convention went into specific detail. This was for provisions for tariff.

As originally provided for in the Stockholm Convention, the abolition of tariffs was to take 10 years. This timetable was drawn up with the hope of achieving parallelism with the similar process then taking place in the EEC. When the latter decided to accelerate the process, EFTA followed suit. As a result, tariffs on industrial goods traded between the EFTA countries were, with few exceptions, abolished three years ahead of schedule, on 31 December 1966. The timetable for the abolition of quantitative restrictions on trade was also accelerated and was brought to completion by the middle of 1965.

The Association Agreement with Finland and the accession of Iceland

From the beginning of EFTA, Finland expressed interest in a relationship with the Association because of the importance of its trade with the seven members. The result was an Agreement, signed in Helsinki on 27 March 1961, creating an association between the member states of EFTA and the Republic of Finland.

The Finland–EFTA Agreement established a new free trade area on the basis that Finland was to have the same rights and obligations towards the EFTA member states as these had among themselves. In practice, this was achieved by the simple expedient of making all the provisions of the EFTA Convention that concerned trade and economic aspects also applicable to the commercial relations between Finland and the seven EFTA countries. Finland became a full member of EFTA on 1 January 1986.

Although the other countries participating in the Nordic Council, Denmark, Finland, Norway and Sweden, took part in EFTA from the beginning of the 1960s, Iceland did not join them in the Association until the end of the 1960s. Of some importance in this connection was the fact that the economy of Iceland depended almost exclusively on its fisheries exports, which could not benefit fully from the industrial free trade provisions of the EFTA Convention.

The accession of the UK and Denmark to the EEC

The preamble to the Stockholm Convention reiterated the desire for a wider European solution to the question of economic integration. Accordingly, throughout the 1960s the EFTA countries continued their efforts, which had begun in the OEEC in 1956–8, to find an acceptable solution to the problem created by the division of Western Europe into two regional economic groups: the EEC and EFTA. A number of proposals were put forward to bridge the gap.

At a meeting of EFTA ministers in London in June 1961 it was agreed to try the bilateral approach. On this basis, the EFTA member countries made applications for membership of, or association with, the EEC. In the following years, various unsuccessful attempts were made to arrive at some arrangement between EFTA and the EEC, including renewed efforts by the British government in 1966 and 1967 for membership (see earlier in this chapter). In December 1969, a meeting of the heads of government of the six EEC countries was held at The Hague. One decision made at this meeting was to open negotiations on Community membership for the four countries that had applied for it: Denmark, Ireland, Norway and the UK. It was also decided to begin talks with the six other EFTA countries that were not applicants for EEC membership but that wished to arrive at suitable trading arrangements with the Community.

The UK and Denmark, along with Ireland, became members of the Community on 1 January 1973. However, Norway did not join, as at a referendum held in Norway in September 1972, the majority of voters opted against Community membership. As a result, Norway negotiated the same type of free trade agreement with the Community as had in the meantime been concluded by those EFTA countries not seeking EEC membership.

The EEC members had decided at The Hague Summit in December 1969 that negotiations should also take place with the EFTA countries, on the understanding that the enlargement of the EEC should not involve the re-erection of tariff barriers in Europe and that the agreements with the non-candidate EFTA countries should, if possible, enter into force at the same time as the candidate countries took up membership of the EEC.

In general, the free trade agreements between the EFTA members and the EEC provided for a gradual reduction of import duties, arriving at zero duties for almost all industrial products by July 1977. This timetable was respected by all concerned, with the result that by that date virtually all trade in industrial products between the 16 countries was free of duty.

The EFTA/EEC agreements also applied to trade with any new members of the EEC. This was the case when Greece and Spain, which had negotiated a free trade arrangement with EFTA in 1979, joined the EEC in 1981 and 1986, respectively.

When Portugal – an EFTA member since its foundation – joined the EC, the trade liberalization achieved between Portugal and other EFTA countries remained intact, while transitional arrangements with Portugal as an EC member were negotiated.

The conclusion of the free trade agreements between EFTA and the EEC was seen as progress towards the original goal of building bridges between the two main areas of economic integration in Western Europe by providing the basis for closer and more substantial cooperation between EFTA and the EC.

The European Economic Area (EEA)

On the 17 January 1989, in a speech before the European Parliament, Jacques Delors, the then President of the EC Commission, proposed 'a new, more structured partnership, with common decision-making and administrative institutions' with the EFTA countries. The rationale behind Delors' ideas was to increase the efficiency of the cooperation between the EC and EFTA. He therefore raised the question whether the EFTA countries were prepared to strengthen their internal structures and to accept the same discipline as the Community member states in the numerous fields of cooperation.

North American Free Trade Agreement (NAFTA)

NAFTA is an economic pact for the gradual removal of tariffs and other barriers to free trade on most goods produced and sold in North America, the elimination of barriers to international investment and the protection of intellectual property rights. NAFTA was signed by Canada, Mexico and the US on 17 December 1992, and went into effect on 1 January 1994. Unlike the EU, NAFTA is concerned only with the free movement of goods and services and not people. There is no NAFTA equivalent of EU citizenship.

NAFTA was preceded by bilateral customs agreements between the US and Mexico established in 1987 and the Canadian–US Free Trade Agreement implemented in 1989, in which many tariffs between the two countries were eliminated or reduced. After several years of debate, NAFTA was approved in 1993 by the legislatures of Canada, Mexico and the US. In the same year, the absence of comprehensive provisions on environmental degradation, labour rights and import surges led to negotiations on supplemental agreements in these three areas. NAFTA called for the immediate elimination of duties on half of all US goods shipped to Mexico. Other tariffs are to be phased out gradually. Tariff barriers are divided into six separate categories, with each category having a different timetable for tariff reduction. Each member can choose to reduce tariffs ahead of schedule, subject to the consent of the other NAFTA signatories. NAFTA contains provisions for suspending the timetables in order to protect industries adversely affected by an influx of imported goods.

Canada was the first signatory to ratify the agreement: the Canadian parliament passed the appropriate measure on 23 June 1993. The debate over NAFTA in the US divided members of both the Democratic and Republican Parties and led to fierce opposition from environmental and labour groups. Many feared that jobs would be lost as a result of US production plants moving to Mexico where they could take advantage of a cheaper labour force and lax enforcement of environmental and workers' rights laws. Environmental groups opposed NAFTA because of concerns that pollution and food safety controls would be more difficult to enforce. In response to these concerns, three side agreements covering environmental and labour issues were established in 1993. After a long battle NAFTA was only passed by a narrow margin in the US Congress. Mexican opposition ranged from objections to loss of economic sovereignty to fears that the accord reinforced the position of the ruling Institutional Revolutionary party. Nonetheless, the agreement was finally ratified in November.

Even after its passage, NAFTA continues to be debated among its supporters and opponents. The administration of US President Bill Clinton claimed the pact created 100,000 US jobs within its first year, but opponents say that the higher number of imports to the US under NAFTA caused a loss of jobs. Further flaws in the agreement were highlighted by the collapse in the Mexican stock market following a government devaluation of the peso (the Mexican currency) in December 1994, which exposed structural weaknesses and incomplete modernization in Mexico's economic and political systems. In addition to the lack of consensus over the number of jobs lost or gained under NAFTA, economists find it difficult to distinguish economic changes caused by NAFTA from other factors.

NAFTA forms the world's second-largest free trade zone after the EU/EFTA (see earlier) by uniting Canada, Mexico and the US in an open market, the grouping brings together 365 million consumers. The world's largest free trade zone is the European Economic Area, which came into effect at the same time as NAFTA. Talks on including all Latin American nations in NAFTA – with the exception of Cuba – began in late 1994. Negotiations to include Chile in NAFTA formally began in 1995. These talks include plans for the creation of a free trade zone throughout the Americas sometime in the early 2000s. However, the inclusion of more countries in NAFTA is expected to be a difficult procedure, as some countries are far from being able to agree to, and implement, the stringent economic requirements of a free trade accord, which includes mandates for minimum wages, working conditions and environmental protection.

Think/Discussion point: Why do you think that NAFTA has not followed the common currency, citizenship, freedom of movement of people etc. model that the EU has?

EU and NAFTA

In 1992, Lester Thurow suggested that the 1990s and early twenty-first century would see a major trade conflict between the US (which now includes NAFTA), Japan and the EU. He concluded that the EU had the greater long-term economic power and would win.

Using the 2000 population statistics for NAFTA and the EU Table 3.3 shows how the EU will compare with NAFTA, compare in respect of size of potential home market after the accession of new members in 2004. Europe is the bigger market.

Other customs unions

Throughout the world, especially in South America and Asia similar customs unions and pacts have been signed. An example is the Association of South East Asian Nations (ASEAN).

ASEAN is a regional alliance of 10 independent countries of South East Asia founded in Bangkok in 1967 by Indonesia, Malaysia, the Philippines, Singapore and Thailand; Brunei became a member after attaining independence in 1984; Vietnam – the Association's first communist partner – joined in 1995; Laos and Myanmar were admitted in 1997 and Cambodia in 1999. The permanent secretariat is in Jakarta, Indonesia.

ASEAN was established during the Vietnam War initially to develop a new relationship between Malaysia and Singapore. Principal objectives of the organization, outlined in the Bangkok Declaration (1967), were to accelerate economic growth and promote regional peace and stability, as well as to collaborate on economic, social and cultural issues of mutual concern. A joint forum with Japan was established in 1977, and a cooperation agreement with the European Community was signed in 1980.

Table 3.3 Population of custom's unions in 2004.

EU country	Population (millions)	NAFTA country	Population (millions)
Germany	83.25	USA	278
France	59.8	Mexico	102
UK	59.65	Canada	31
Italy	57.67		
Spain	40		
Poland	38.63		
Netherlands	16		
Greece	10.6		
Belgium	10.26		
Czech Republic	10.25		
Hungary	10.1		
Portugal	10		
Sweden	8.88		
Austria	8.15		
Slovak Republic	5.4		
Denmark	5.35		
Finland	5.18		
Ireland	3.84		
Latvia	2.39		
Slovenia	1.93		
Luxembourg	0.44		
Malta	0.39		
TOTAL	448.16		411

The organization's activities and policies are coordinated by the Secretariat, established at the 1976 summit in Bali, Indonesia, and by its secretary-general. ASEAN maintains national secretariats in member countries, and has also established committees in the capital cities of countries with which it cooperates: Berlin, Brussels, Canberra, London, Moscow, New Delhi, Ottawa, Paris, Riyadh, Seoul, Tokyo, Washington and Wellington. There is also an ASEAN committee in Geneva. Heads of governments of member countries meet annually, there are also annual ministerial meetings (AMM) and meetings of economic ministers of member countries (AEM).

During the late 1980s and early 1990s, ASEAN played an important role in mediating the civil war in Cambodia just as the EU attempted to mediate in the Balkan conflicts of the 1990s. In January 1992, ASEAN members agreed to establish a free trade area and to cut tariffs on non-agricultural goods over a 15-year period beginning in 1993. The ASEAN meeting in July 1994 signalled a recognition of the need for closer internal ties, wider membership and a greater role in regional security in the post-Cold War era. The following year brought the Treaty on the South East Asia Nuclear Weapon-Free Zone. In July 1997 ASEAN formally admitted Laos and Myanmar as members. Cambodia's application for membership was accepted in April 1999; the application had been previously suspended due to concern over the legitimacy of its new government under Hun Sen. The combined gross national product of ASEAN countries in 1999 amounted to US$685 billion, and a total trade figure reached US$720 billion.

Implications for small businesses

While it may seem that the operations of a customs union are remote from those of a small business they have a direct impact on all operations within the union.

In the case of the EU, it is EU law that is superior to national law. In the UK, since the adoption of the Social Charter by the Labour government in the late 1990s, much of UK employment law has been directly influenced by EU law. As will be shown in the case study below, a dispute between two trading partners over one product can have a dramatic effect on unrelated business if sanctions are applied.

The US–EU banana war of 1999

On the face of it there seems little connection between the Scottish cashmere wool industry and Caribbean bananas and yet a trade dispute in 1999 over preferential treatment for the bananas produced by ex-EU member colonies nearly led to the demise of the cashmere industry in the Scottish borders.

The Lomé Convention (now known as the Suva Convention) represents a trade and aid agreement between the EU and certain African, Caribbean and Pacific (ACP) countries, first signed in February 1975 in Lomé, Togo. The first Lomé Convention (Lomé I), which came into force in April 1976, was designed to provide a new framework of cooperation between the then European Community (EC) and developing ACP countries, in particular former British, Dutch and French colonies. It had two main aspects. It provided for most ACP agricultural and mineral exports to enter the EC free of duty. Preferential access based on a quota system was agreed for products, such as sugar and beef, in competition with EC agriculture. Secondly, the EC committed ECU 3 billion for aid and investment in the ACP countries. The convention was of particular importance for those Caribbean countries (formerly colonies of EU member states) that relied heavily on the banana crop for their economies.

The convention was renegotiated and renewed three times.

The emergence of the single European market at the end of 1992 affected ACP preferential access to EU markets. The Caribbean's many smallholder banana farmers argued for the continuation of their preferential access to traditional markets, notably Great Britain and France. They feared that otherwise the EU would be flooded with cheap bananas from the Central American plantations, with devastating effects on several Caribbean economies. Most of the major US banana companies obtained their stocks from Central and South America rather than the Caribbean and had made large investments. Negotiations led in 1993 to the EU agreeing to maintain the Caribbean producers' preferential access. The renewal of this access, at the US believed the expense of its companies in 2000, led to the US to take action at the WTO (see chapter 3). The US was given permission for sanctions to be applied to certain products emanating from the EU.

Among the products that the US decided to apply tariffs to was Scottish cashmere wool – a luxury item whose manufacturers rely on sales to the US market. Thus an unrelated industry was nearly destroyed over a dispute between two trade blocs over an unrelated product. Fortunately a solution was found to the problem and the cashmere industry was saved although it remains vulnerable to future sanctions.

David Ransom (2001) has written an excellent account of the banana war – details at the end of this chapter.

In February 2000, after a quarter of a century of the Lomé Convention being the cornerstone of trade and aid between Europe and the developing world, a new trade and aid agreement was reached between the EU and 71 ACP countries. The treaty, which replaced Lomé, has become known as the Suva Convention, after Suva, the capital of Fiji. The Suva Convention is expected to run for 20 years. Some of the poorer ACP states will continue to enjoy virtually free access to European markets and there will be regional free trade agreements between the EU and better-off developing countries.

CASE STUDY QUESTIONS

1 Why was it considered important that the ex-colonial powers acted to protect their former colonies – some of which had achieved separation by violent means?

2 What motives other than those of fair trade might the US have had for its actions?

3 Is it acceptable to use whole industries and the lives and welfare of the workers in them as political/trading pawns?

Summary and key learning points

- A market is purely the forum for an exchange between parties.
- Geographically markets types can be expressed as the following types: local, national regions, national, supra-national regions, international/global, virtual.
- Customs unions allow countries to come together to remove barriers to trade.
- Some customs unions, the EU being the main example, also include a supra-national level.
- Customs unions provide for expanded markets but also more competition.
- Customs unions are growing and treaties between them are becoming common place.
- Instead of individual countries negotiating trade agreements with each other, they do so through the customs unions they are members of.
- Sanctions that may be applied in disputes may hurt businesses unconnected with the dispute.
- Alan Rugman believes that it is not globalization that is occurring but rather regionalization through the development of large customs unions.

QUESTIONS

1. What is a market?
2. What advantages can a customs union provide for:
   (a) a country and
   (b) a business?
3. How can a business be affected by a dispute involving another product and inter-trading bloc problems?
4. How could a common currency lead to a loss of sovereignty?

Recommended further reading

David Ransom (2001) has provided an account of the 'banana war' in *The No-nonsense Guide to Fair Trade*. Will Hutton (2002) *The World We're In* and Hutton *et al.* (2002) *Why Britain Should Join the Euro* provide an argument for the UK adopting the euro. Alan Rugman (2002) argues that it is regionalization not globalization that is occurring, i.e. the formation of regional trade blocs and customs unions in *The End of Globalization*.

Details of the EU, EFTA, ASEAN and NAFTA can be found on their web sites, details of which are included in the Bibliography.

◼ ☑ 4 A global takeover?

<table>
<tr><td>

Learning outcomes

By the end of this chapter you should understand:

- Why there is opposition to globalization
- Some of the threats that globalization is perceived to present
- How globalization is developing
- Why corporations may move from area to area to gain financial advantages
- The dangers of tax breaks etc. provided by government
- The concept of fair trade
- How customers can influence multinational corporations

</td></tr>
</table>

To the average person in the developed world the riots in Prague, Seattle and Gothenburg at recent meetings of world leaders may seem inexplicable. To the majority of consumers in the developed world, globalization has brought immense benefits not least of which has been the increased access to a huge range of consumer products. Why should we fear something that has brought increased choice?

There exists a body of opinion that globalization is less of a commercial benefit than a dangerous force that is likely to make the majority of the world's population less rather than better off.

The reasons for this divergence of opinion from those who believe that globalization increases individual choice and opportunity across the globe and those who see it leading to greater poverty and oppression may lie in a difference in views about the relationships between individuals, the state and commercial organizations operating within and beyond the state.

At the heart of the issue lies the question of what has generated globalization? Different social theories offer different interpretations of how and why trans-world connections have grown. Liberal economics has, since the eighteenth century stressed the role of relatively free and unregulated market forces especially in a context of technological change. It was as hard to regulate for the early railways as it has been for the Internet. It was only after several accidents that the UK parliament began to lay down rules for the regulation of railways. Marxist political economy, albeit somewhat discredited since the fall of so many communist regimes in the 1990s, highlights the dynamics of the international capitalist system as the engine of globalization. For others, however, globalization is a product of modern rationalism – it is a natural development given the political, social and technological evolution of humankind. The true cause is probably a combination of all of the above.

Next to technology (covered in chapter 8 of this book), regulation has also played an enabling role for globalization. Supra-territorial links would not be possible in the absence of various facilitating rules, procedures, norms and institutions. For example, global communications rely heavily on technical standardization – hence the importance of systems such as WINDOWS as covered in the case study on Microsoft in chapter 1. Global finance depends in good measure on a working world monetary regime. Global production and trade are, it is claimed, greatly promoted by liberalization, that is, the removal of tariffs, capital controls and other state-imposed restrictions on the movement of resources between countries. As will be shown later there those who disagree with this statement claiming that that it is only larger companies that truly benefit. Tax laws, labour legislation and environmental codes can also encourage (or discourage) global investment. Nevertheless it has to be conceded that globalization requires supporting regulatory frameworks.

Capitalism has been a further force for globalization. In the 1850s, Karl Marx noted that nature of the capitalist system was to conquer the globe for capitalist markets. Global markets offer prospects of increased profits through higher sales volumes. In addition, larger production runs to feed global markets promise enhanced profits due to economies of scale – it does not cost five times as much to produce five times as much product. Capitalists also pursue globalization since it allows production facilities to be sited wherever costs are lowest and earnings greatest, i.e. increasing profits and shareholder value.

Other impulses to globalization have come from rationalism as the prevailing modern mode of knowledge. With its secular character, rationalist thought orientates people towards the physical world of the planet rather than spiritual and religious dimensions. With its anthropocentrism (human beings at the centre of the universe), rationalist consciousness focuses on the Earth as the realm of the human species – we have dominion over the beasts of the fields, the fish of the sea etc. With its faith in science, rationalism posits that modern, objective ways of knowing have universal validity and can (and should) unite the world. With its instrumentalist logic, rationalism provides efficiency arguments for overcoming territorial barriers to solve human and social problems. Rationalism provides a knowledge foundation for globalization: a way of thinking that spurs the process. Rationalism ignores the more emotional side of human character and places little emphasis on the importance of spirituality. It is this loss of a spiritual dimension that many find worrying. Rationalism may not be as 'scientifically' grounded in reality as it claims. In *Managing the Human Animal* (2000), Nigel Nicholson comments that while humankind may be in the twenty-first century technologically, we are little above our primate ancestors behaviourally and thus act territorially and instinctively – attributes that are likely to act against a homogeneous world.

Many theorists identify one of these forces (whichever one it is depends on their personal viewpoint) as the primary engine of globalization and treat other elements as having secondary or no causal significance. Other analysts hold that globalization has a multi-causal dynamic involving the interrelation of several forces.

At a time when ethnic divides seem as great as ever there is perhaps superficial comfort in the fact that we all seem to drink the same sodas, watch similar television programmes on similar televisions, listen to similar music and eat foods far more exotic than those enjoyed by previous generations.

To the opponents of globalization, however, the issues are far deeper and centre on the removal of fiscal and political independence from governments and the apparent transfer of power to the larger corporations in the world. To such opponents globalization is more than just similar products being available on a global basis; to them it is actually the integration of the global economy by the dismantling of trade and political barriers and the increasing political and economic power of multinational corporations at the expense of the nation state.

A recent piece of work from the political arena rather than the business or sociology area, *The Shield of Achilles* (2002) by US political analyst Philip Bobbitt has charted the evolution of government from that of dynastic princely states where people owed allegiance to the prince or ruler within whose hereditary possessions they lived, through to the territorial state with fixed rather than dynastic borders. Then came the state nation, prevalent up to the twentieth century where the people served the state followed by the nation state we know today in the developed world, where the state looks after the welfare of the people. In simplistic terms the princely state owned the people, the state nation asked 'what can the people do for me?', while the nation state is concerned with what it can do for the people.

According to Bobbitt we are moving from the nation state to the market state where the state is responsible for opportunities not provision. In effect the market state asks 'what opportunities do you need to fulfil your potential?' Globalization can provide wider opportunities and is thus in tune with the market state idea. Bobbitt does, however, seem to ignore the tribal nature of human groups as described by Nicholson (mentioned above) and thus the nation state is unlikely to wither completely. The market state relishes deregulation and privatization (as does the IMF – see chapter 2). The first proponents of the modern market state were Margaret Thatcher (UK Prime Minister in the 1980s) and her US counterpart President Reagan. As early as 1987 Desmond King was predicting changes in the way that we are governed that were probably irreversible in *The New Right – Politics, Markets and Citizenship* – we were moving close to the market state. Bobbitt makes fascinating reading and is thoroughly recommended.

Think/Discussion point: What do people need from the government in order to fulfil their potential?

An increase in trade should benefit everybody. According to Ellwood, world trade is increasing at around 6 per cent per annum. However, as David Ransom (2001) writing in the same series points out the increases are less beneficial unless the trade is actually fair, which he believes in the vast majority of cases it is not. If the result of an increase in trade is actually a decrease in living standards throughout a proportion of the world due to manufacturers cutting wage rates to gain orders, then the benefits of trade become lost to the very people who should gain – those producing the goods.

From the point of view of an individual citizen, government must seem huge and governments have in fact been growing in size and activity throughout the past 200 years. Governments in the 1800s were small in comparison with their modern successors, as of course were populations. Social policy and intervention were in their infancy and for many people the government hardly influenced their lives directly from birth to death – a majority did not even pay income taxes. A modern government, however, even in most non-interventionist regimes, still has a large direct influence over daily life, not least through direct and indirect taxation and the administration of justice and welfare systems.

However, not all governments and economies are as large as the US or the UK or Germany or France or Canada etc. Ellwood states that of the 100 largest economies of the world, multinational corporations account for 50 per cent. In fact according to the United Nations Development Program report of 1999, the 'economy' of General Motors is larger than that of Norway, a European nation although not a EU member and considerably larger than that of Greece, a country that is a EU member. It is somewhat staggering that not only General Motors but also Ford, Mitsui, Mitsubishi, Itochu, Shell and Mauruberi *each* has sales revenues greater than the GDP of Greece. Perhaps even more surprising is that the sales revenue of the US supermarket giant Wal-Mart exceeded the GDP of Israel (a nuclear power) by about $10 billion in 1997, a figure that will have increased dramatically since Wal Mart acquired the UK supermarket giant Asda in 2000.

Globalization and development

A theory of economic development known as dependency theory emerged in the 1960s to assist in addressing the problems of poverty and economic throughout the less developed world. Dependency theory argued that dependence upon foreign capital, technology and expertise actual impedes rather than accelerates economic development in developing countries.

Prior to the 1960s, the prevailing theory of economic development, known as modernization theory, maintained that industrialization, the introduction of mass media and the diffusion of Western ideas including democracy would transform and enrich (financially) traditional economies and societies. These influences would place poorer countries on a path of development similar to that experienced by Western industrialized nations during the industrial revolution of the nineteenth century.

Dependency theory rejected the central assumptions of modernization theory. In the 1960s advocates of dependency theory – mostly social scientists from the developing world, particularly Latin America, such as Andre Gunder Frank – argued that former colonial nations were underdeveloped because of their dependence on Western industrialized nations in the areas of foreign trade and investment. Rather than benefiting developing nations, these relationships stunted their development. Drawing upon various Marxist ideas, dependency theorists observed that economic development and underdevelopment were not simply different stages in the same linear march towards progress. They argued that, on the contrary, colonial domination had produced relationships between the developed and the developing world that were inherently unequal. Part of the ideas of the imperialists of the nineteenth and early twentieth centuries was to conquer not for territories but for raw materials and also for mass markets for their manufactured goods. Dependency theorists believed that without a major restructuring of the international economy, the former colonial countries would find it virtually impossible to escape from their subordinate position and experience true growth and development, dependent as many of them still are on aid from their former colonial rulers. The other side of this argument is the preferential treatment given to goods from former colonies – an example of which, bananas, was the subject of the case study in chapter 3.

Dependency theorists have argued that developing nations were adversely affected by unequal trade, especially in the exchange of cheap raw materials from developing nations for the expensive, finished products manufactured by advanced industrial nations. They argued that modernization theory did not foresee the damaging effect of this exploitation on developing nations especially when linked to non or only slowly renewable natural resources such as timber. Even the achievement of political independence had not enhanced the ability of former colonial nations to demand better prices for their primary exports.

Dependency theorists have also focused on how foreign direct investments (see chapter 7) of multinational corporations distort developing nation economies. These distortions include the undercutting of national firms leading to either demise or takeover, rising unemployment related to the use of capital-intensive technology and a loss of political sovereignty as governments fear to challenge the multinationals for fear of losing investment.

From the perspective of dependency theory, the relationship between developing nations and foreign lending institutions, such as the World Bank and the IMF – see chapter 2, seriously undermines the sovereignty of developing nations. These countries must often agree to harsh conditions – such as budget cuts and interest rate increases – to obtain loans from international agencies. During the 1980s, for example, the foreign debt of many Latin American countries soared. In response to pressure from multilateral lending agencies such as the World Bank and the IMF, these nations enacted financial austerity measures known as Structural Adjustment Programmes in order to qualify for new loans. These economic policies led to a decrease in the amount of money spent on health care and education, higher levels of unemployment and slower economic growth. The effects on many of them, Argentina is an excellent example, were catastrophic with the poor and middle classes suffering real hardships.

Not all the news has been bleak. There have been successes in some newly industrializing countries of Latin America and East Asia since the 1960s, despite the warnings of the dependency theorists, although world economic conditions have played their part. The rise of some Far Eastern economies, Indonesia is an example, was matched by a rapid decline in the late 1990s due to a downturn in world trade and political instability.

While the gap between rich and poor counties remains great there will always be a degree of dependence. While an ex-colonial ruler may wish to give aid out of a sense of duty or even guilt, many multinational corporations act only so as to maximize profits and enhance shareholder value.

The rest of this chapter looks at some of the issues that have greatly concerned the opponents of globalization. One of the most important of these issues is that globalization is seen by many as actually being Westernization or even Americanization. That many of the largest companies in the world, Shell (Netherlands), Mitsubishi, Toyota etc. are not from the US should be borne in mind. However, many of the largest multinational corporations are from the US and tend to bring US values and practices with them when they expand into global markets. As will be shown in the next chapter the most successful tend to think globally but act locally.

Attracting companies

Just like individuals, countries have to earn money before they can spend it – just printing more currency leads to rampant inflation. In order to acquire goods and services from outside their own borders it is necessary to earn foreign currency. The US, UK, Germany etc., i.e. the developed nations, are able to earn foreign currency using a mixture of exporting raw materials and manufactured goods and by providing services to other countries. Much of the UK's foreign earnings are made up of the invisible exports associated with the financial and banking industries. Many developing countries are more dependent on raw materials and are particularly vulnerable to a fall in prices if they are dependent upon a single resource or crop. Raw materials such as fossil fuels (coal, wood etc.) are either non-renewable or only renewable slowly and overexploitation makes the country poorer not richer. One has only to fly over the Amazon basin to see how much rain forest has been lost – it will take hundreds of years to replace. Earning foreign currency by providing services requires the development of expertise which can take a great deal of time and education and therefore the development of a manufacturing capability is seen as a useful addition to the economy as it lessens the dependence upon a small number of raw materials, crops or a cadre of professional bankers, stockbrokers and traders.

Governments welcome manufacturing companies because they not only provide goods for export in many instances but also because they provide employment and with employment goes a reduction in welfare spending and an increase in tax revenue. No government can afford to ignore the social condition of its citizens for long – to do so is likely to lead to the fall of the government through elections in democratic regimes and revolution in totalitarian ones. A government must be seen to be assisting people with jobs especially if the economy is stagnant and there is high unemployment. High employment rates mean that the government has to do relatively little in terms of welfare assistance but once the unemployment rate begins to rise the population requires action.

This is not a new concept. In the 1930s both Theodore Roosevelt in the US and Adolph Hitler in Nazi Germany began huge public works' programmes to put people back to work in order to beat the effects of the great depression. Modern thinking, however, is that less government intervention not more is what is likely to lead to growth and that job creation is a function of the private not the public sector. One of the criteria for IMF assistance (see chapter 2) is often a requirement that the government undertakes privatization of previously nationalized industries.

Think/Discussion point: What are the reasons given for private companies being better at commercial dealings than government-run organizations?

Private is not always better or more efficient as the Enron and Worldcom scandals of 2002 showed. Private corporations can be as inefficient as any other type.

In order to assist increasing employment it is not unusual for governments to offer considerable inducements for companies to set up operations in an area of low employment. The inducements can range from tax breaks through training and building grants through to the provision of infrastructure construction. It is not just governments in developing countries that offer such inducements. Scotland provided considerable inducements to entice electronic companies to the central belt between Glasgow and Edinburgh. Unfortunately a number of the companies that were persuaded to relocate to Scotland later closed or reduced their operations – some moving to lower cost areas – see later in this chapter. That governments including that of the US are keen to assist business in providing economic growth is shown by the fact that according to Klein (2000), the proportion of corporate taxation as a percentage of total US federal revenue dropped from 32 per cent in 1952 to 11.5 per cent in 1998. Encouraging companies by decreasing taxation presents governments with a dilemma. If corporate taxes fall then how is the shortfall to be made up? Hopefully the loss in revenue will be offset by a fall in welfare spending to assist the unemployed – as more people are in work both the need to spend on welfare decreases and the yield from income taxes should increase. This makes economic sense and provided that wages are sufficient that they do not need any form of government subsidy thus depleting the tax yield, the system may well work. If, however, the inducements are so large that individual taxes have to be increased to make up for a loss in corporate taxes then a vicious circle can begin. It is no use reducing property taxes for a company to relocate if the government then has to raise personal property taxes to a level that nobody who works at the new factory etc. can afford to live in the area. In the developed world an increase in an area's prosperity can lead to increases in housing prices and thus deter those on lower incomes from moving to the area. This has been a major issue in the South East of the UK, especially London where public service staff such as teachers who are on nationally agreed wages cannot afford to buy houses in the area.

The perceived wisdom is that encouraging organizations into an area will rejuvenate the economy and lead to a rise in prosperity not just for the workers at the enterprise but also shopkeepers, bus drivers, electricians, schools, service industries, i.e. the whole community will eventually benefit. Provided that the wages paid are sufficient and that the jobs are permanent, the above is indeed the case. However, where job insecurity still exists and only low wages are paid then general prosperity is less likely to rise and may actually decrease causing the government to subsidize the area out of taxation.

In countries such the UK and other EU members with minimum wage regulations that can and are enforced by the courts this is less likely to happen but then some companies will not relocate to such a jurisdiction claiming excessive regulation. Relocation itself suggests that unless there is a huge increase in demand leading to extra production it is likely that one area's gain has been another's loss as has indeed proved the case. Just because an electronics company moves from Glasgow does not mean that demand for its products has decreased. The demand may have increased but the company may have moved to what it perceives as a more advantageous location in terms of profits and shareholder value.

Ellwood quotes an *LA Times* report that prior to the formation of NAFTA in 1995, the jeans manufacturer Guess? Inc was producing 97 per cent of its product in Los

Angeles. By 1997 this figure was down to 35 per cent with 1000 jobs being lost in LA. The company had relocated mainly to Mexico where it opened five factories. Mexico, also a NAFTA member, has a lower average wage rate and as there will be no import restrictions in moving the product into the US, it made economic sense to relocate production to a lower cost area (also see chapter 10). Corporations are not primarily in the social care business, they are expected to make a profit for their owners – the investors – and that means increasing profits. If the price charged cannot be raised then this means cutting costs.

Export processing zones (EPZs)

A considerable amount of the FDI into developing nations has been into operations in EPZs (export processing zones) – areas set up by governments where raw materials are imported and finished products are manufactured and exported free of any customs duties. Developed from the freeport concept (Hamburg was a well-known European example for many years), EPZs are almost mini-economies of their own. The goods produced vary from consumer electronics to clothing, shoes and sporting equipment. The advantage for the manufacturer or assembler is that they are able to operate free from many of the customs restrictions and regulations they might face in a more traditional environment. Klein (2000) has profiled the operation of such zones in the Philippines and concludes that the ones she studied operate at very low wage rates combined with harsh working conditions. As she points out the EPZs with their modern buildings and well laid out roads and open spaces contrast with the abject poverty of much of the surrounding areas – areas where the workers live but in many cases the neat appearance hides a harsher reality. There appears, from Klein's comments, to be little to differentiate the EPZs from a previous generation of sweatshops in terms of wages and working practices.

One of the major issues facing governments promoting EPZs is that of the 'swallows'. These are companies that move in and take advantage of tax exemptions, grants etc. and then move to another similar area if better inducements are offered. This does nothing for the long-term prosperity of an area or for job security. In fact its effect is very negative as in order to attract another company, even more inducements have to be made and workers may be required to accept even lower wages and longer hours. In turn the government will receive less tax revenue and thus must either increase welfare spending or ignore the plight of its poorer citizens – a recipe for revolution and social unrest.

Think/Discussion point: From a shareholder's financial viewpoint is there anything wrong with the company being a 'swallow'?

Child labour

It is a sad fact that although slavery was supposed to have been abolished in the nineteenth century, actual slavery still exists in Africa where people are kidnapped and sold and to a lesser degree in the employment of child labour for subsistence (or below) wages in many parts of the developing world. Child labour was outlawed many years ago in the developed world. There was an outcry in the UK when EU legislation appeared to ban the delivery of newspapers by youngsters – a lucrative source of pocket money enhancement. Fortunately for both the youngsters, their parents and the newsagents this was not the case. There was an outcry in the US when it was discovered that footballs were being produced in Asia by very young children and then being sold at a premium in the US market. The UN organization and charities such as Save the Children and Christian Aid are making determined efforts to stamp out child labour. As a practice it is counter-productive, for although a child may produce something at a low cost, without education that child is never going to put anything back into society. Unfortunately the illness and mortality rates among child labourers are very high and the human cost of saving a few dollars, pounds, euros, yen etc. is incalculable.

The threat to democracy

The anti-globalization protesters claim that globalization is a threat to democracy. Given the size of nations compared to companies this may seem absurd. However, as was shown earlier many global corporations are bigger than some sovereign nations when measured in economic terms. As they have more resource they can call a louder tune – the old adage 'he (or she) who pays the piper calls the tune' (taken from the story of the Pied Piper) is as true today as it has always been. There have been theories that governments have fallen due to the efforts of large corporations who stood to benefit from a change in regime. As Ransom (2001) has reported it has long been believed that it was United Fruit that orchestrated US government support for the overthrow of the elected government of Guatemala in 1954 – a government that was poised to expropriate 400,000 acres of United Fruit banana plantations as part of its support for better wages and conditions.

The key text in this area is David Korten's (1996) *When Corporations Rule the World*. It is one of those books that should be read by all involved in global expansion. Even if one disagrees with his contentions about the power of global corporations it provides useful background on the beliefs of who those who oppose further globalization.

Anthony Giddens, the Director of the London School of Economics, presented the prestigious Reith Lectures (named for Lord Reith, the legendary developer of the BBC) in 1999. The lecture was published in book form as *Runaway World* (1999). He points that out for many in the developing world, globalization looks very looks like a Western takeover of their culture and traditions and that organizations need to be much more sensitive to local feelings. This is in fact achievable. The early Christian church managed its global expansion by incorporating the customs of other religions – a process known as transmutation. This is why Christmas is celebrated in the middle of winter (the solstice, an important time in many early religions) rather than in March when scholars believe the nativity actually occurred. If organizations move too quickly to make local culture the same as their home culture this is likely to bring about conflict with traditionalists. Much of the anti-Islamic feeling about the US centres on the introduction of US customs and values into traditional Muslim family life. These complaints about Western influence by Islamic fundamentalists extend beyond the religious and political to the commercial icons of the West. Sadly the conflict between values has been claimed as one of the factors that led to the terrible tragedy and crime of the attacks on New York and Washington DC on 11 September 2001 – crimes for which there may be an explanation, however irrational, but certainly no excuse.

Noreena Hertz, writing in *The Silent Takeover* (2001), has shown a concern that the growth in globalization at a time of declining interest in political activity is leading to greater unaccountability of global corporations. The low turnouts in the US 2000 presidential elections, the 2001 UK general election and the 2003 Scottish parliament elections seem to indicate a growing disenchantment or at the least complacency with the political process. The funding of politics is another issue in the globalization debate. Large corporations in the US can and do fund candidates to a high degree. In the UK political donations are controlled but directorships can be offered and one ex-minister was imprisoned for accepting gifts and hospitality from a commercial organization, not declaring it and then seeking to sue a newspaper that reported on the issue. If politics ceases to be 'government of the people, by the people and for the people' (President Abraham Lincoln, the Gettysburg Address, 19 November 1863) but just for special interest groups then the whole foundation of democracy is threatened. Corporations answer to shareholders who have 'purchased' their position, not to voters who have democratic choices.

It is seriously doubtful whether there is a global plot for one or more organizations to take over the world as some conspiracy theorists would have us believe. Such a scenario rightly belongs to James Bond, 007 to resolve. However, global corporations have a duty to ensure that what they do be it in monetary or environmental terms is not only for the benefit of their investors but also for the whole of society, a society that is increasingly global in nature.

> **Think/Discussion point**: Is the idea of a corporation running the world just science or political fiction or could it happen? Would there be benefits?

Ethical investments

That concerns are growing about the behaviour of companies on a global scale has been demonstrated by the increasing popularity of ethical investment funds. Ethical investors are only prepared to put their money into companies, products and countries they approve of. They may eschew totalitarianism, religious persecution, child labour, exploitation, deforestation, tobacco, alcohol etc. This type of fund is a growing area for financial advisors and companies need to consider how such investors might react to any breach of their values. A flood of stocks from investors who disapprove of a company's policies onto the market can have a devastating effect on a company's share price.

In terms of economics, for example, globalization substantially alters the organization of production, exchange and consumption. Many firms 'go global' by setting up affiliates across the planet. Many enterprises also form trans-world alliances with other companies. Countless mergers and acquisitions occur as business adjusts to global markets. Questions of competition and monopoly can arise as a result. In addition, corporations relocate many production facilities as globalization reduces transport and communications costs. This can have dramatic effects on local populations and economies. Globalization also expands the so-called virtual economies of information and finance, sometimes at the expense of the economy of raw material extraction and manufacturing. All of this economic restructuring in the face of globalization raises vital issues of human security related to employment, labour conditions, poverty and social cohesion.

In relation to politics, globalization has significant implications for the conduct of governance. Territorially based laws and institutions through local, provincial and national governments are not sufficient by themselves to regulate contacts and networks that operate in trans-world spaces. Globalization, therefore, stimulates greater multilateral collaboration between states as well as the growth of regional and trans-world governance arrangements like the EU, NAFTA, ASEAN and the UN (see chapters 2 and 3). The resultant situation of multi-layered and diffuse governance raises far-reaching questions about the nature of sovereignty and democracy in a globalizing world.

With regard to culture, globalization disrupts traditional relationships between territory and collective identity. The growth of trans-world connections encourages the rise of non-territorial cultures, for example, on lines of age, class, gender, race, religion and sexual orientation. As a result, identity tends – especially for people who lead more globalized lives – to become less fixed on territory, in the form of nation states and ethnic bonds and more on working relationships. One of the advantages of globalization is that it encourages cultural mixing and even hybridity (British Asians, US Italians etc.), where individuals develop and express a mix of identities. At the same time, other people – including those who have less opportunity to participate in global relations – react against globalization with defensive nationalism.

Think/Discussion point: How do you define *your* nationality (place of birth, domicile, culture, etc.)?

Social transformation does occur with globalization but perhaps not to the degree claimed by its critics. The state (either nation or as Bobbitt (see earlier) claims market) is central to the governance of people and companies. Territorial/traditional cultures survive alongside – and in complex interrelations within – supra-territorial/evolving hybrid cultures.

Not surprisingly politicians of all views have widely differing ideas of how to respond to globalization.

Many advocate what is widely called a 'neo-liberal' approach to globalization. Neo-liberalism builds on the tradition of *laissez-faire* economics and holds that globalization will yield maximum gains when its course is left to uninhibited market forces, i.e. minimum government interference. This is essentially a right-wing view and one shared (for obvious reasons) by many large corporations. Neo-liberals therefore prescribe that globalization should be met with full-scale liberalization, deregulation and privatization as occurred in the UK in the 1980s and early 1990s. According to the neo-liberal view, official measures should be used only to enable – and never to constrain – global market forces (this is behind Bobbitt's concept of the market state). The unbound global economy will then in time generate prosperity, democracy, community and peace for all. This view ignores the territorial and instinctive behaviour of humans as described by both Nicholson (2000) in *Managing the Human Animal* and much earlier by Robert Ardrey (1966) in *The Territorial Imperative*. Both contend that our tribal nature means that evolution has a long way to go before we live in a truly global community – possibly thousands of years.

A second general policy framework for globalization can be termed reformism, or global social democracy. Reformists are in agreement with neo-liberals that market capitalism can, if applied properly and with controls, be a major force for social good; however, they argue that these benefits can only be secured with proactive public policies that steer – and where necessary restrict – global flows. For example, many reformists advocate official measures to protect labour, the poor and the environment from the potential harmful effects of untrammelled globalization – the EU Social Charter is an example. Reformist type programmes generally envision a considerable expansion of supra-state governance through regional and trans-world institutions, and many reformists are concerned to enhance the democratic credentials of these regimes. The debate about an EU constitution that became public in the summer of 2003 is an example of this. The EU is moving from a trade bloc to a democratic supra-national government style of state.

Think/Discussion point: Is 'a European' a nationality, a belief, an ideal or a fantasy?

A third broad political response to globalization might be described as progressive radicalism. These critics reject the structural foundations of contemporary globalization and seek to reconstruct the process on a different basis. For example, global socialists as the inheritors of the Marxist ideal regard capitalism as an evil that no amount of reform can correct. Thus they seek to rebuild globalization with a different, post-capitalist mode of production although they often fail to provide any details on how this post-capitalist system will work. From another radical perspective, global postmodernists treat rationalism as incorrigibly flawed and promote an alternative globalization based on different kinds of knowledge and identity politics.

A fourth approach to globalization can be dubbed traditionalism. This viewpoint regards trans-world connections as being inherently violent: globalization intrinsically undermines cultural heritage, democracy, ecological health, economic well-being and social cohesion. In the eyes of traditionalists, globalization has nothing salvageable and must therefore be reversed. Traditionalist calls for 'de-globalization' have come in a number of forms, including ultra-nationalism, religious revivalism and certain strains of environmentalism. The conflicts, both real and emotional, between the West and many parts of the Middle East and Asia reflect this view.

Broadly speaking, neo-liberalism was the prevailing and largely unchallenged policy framework for globalization in the 1980s and early 1990s. Since the mid-1990s both traditionalist and reformist reactions against neo-liberal globalization have gathered force, though *laissez-faire* tendencies remain very strong at the beginning of the twenty-first century. Meanwhile, progressive radical approaches to globalization have to date attracted little mass following, although they may prove important in the longer term.

Green issues

Deforestation, pollution, global warming, species extinction, genetically modified (GM) foods are all seen as problems associated with globalization. The green lobby is growing and growing fast. The EU is far less keen on GM foods than the US, leading to actions at the WTO. In Scotland the Green Party increased its representation in the Parliament from one member to four in 2003. The public seem to have taken on board the fact that we are share one planet and that its resources are not infinite. Green issues may be the major factor in the growth of globalization in the early years of the twenty-first century.

Fair trade

Fair trade means an equitable and fair partnership between marketers in North America and producers in Asia, Africa, Latin America and other parts of the world. A fair trade partnership works to provide low-income artisans and farmers with a living wage for their work. The criteria set by the Fair Trade Federation (FTF) are:

- Paying a fair wage in the local context.
- Offering employees opportunities for advancement.
- Providing equal employment opportunities for all people, particularly the most disadvantaged.
- Engaging in environmentally sustainable practices.
- Being open to public accountability.
- Building long-term trade relationships.
- Providing healthy and safe working conditions within the local context.
- Providing financial and technical assistance to producers whenever possible.

Fair trade is not just a 'would nice to have' idea but can make hard commercial sense just as is organic farming. Worldwide, fair trade sales total $400 million each year. Unfortunately this is only 0.01 per cent of global trade, however, this percentage is growing and more and more companies are finding it advantageous to state their commitment to fair trade.

Small as the business generated by fair trade organizations in Europe and the US may be, the rapidly growing alternative or fair trade movement is setting standards that could redefine world trade to include more social and environmental considerations. Fair traders believe that their system of trade, based on respect for workers' rights and the environment, if adopted by the big players in the global economy, can play a big part in reversing the growing inequities and environmental degradation that have accompanied the growth in world trade.

Oxfam (see chapter 2) was one of the early pioneers of fair trade more than 40 years ago.

Since its launch in the 1960s, the objective of Oxfam's fair trade programme has been to help the world's poorest communities achieve sustainable livelihoods. The programme itself has had a huge impact and helped many thousands of producers to improve their skills, confidence, business understanding and income.

In 2003 the UK retailer COOP began to stress its fair trade policies for coffee and chocolate in its television advertising.

The future

The future extent of globalization is unclear. In one scenario the twenty-first century will experience a continuation – if not a further acceleration – of recent high rates of globalization. Alternatively, globalization will slow down and stop once it reaches a certain plateau. In another forecast – for example, if globalization is a cyclical trend or succumbs to traditionalist opposition – the future will bring a process of de-globalization that will reduce trans-world connections and take us back to the 1950s and 60s when local economies were far stronger.

At present the forces behind globalization seem to be very strong. Current trends in technological innovations and regulatory developments are assisting a further expansion of trans-world connectivity. Both capitalism as a mode of production that promotes globalization and rationalism as a mode of knowledge that stimulates globalization are today deeply entrenched in the developed world and are being spread, sometimes by imposition, on the developing world. A halt to globalization – let alone a slow down or reversal – appears improbable for the time being.

Implications for small businesses

The movement of a large multinational into an area can greatly benefit small businesses. Local suppliers may find new business and the extra spending capacity of the employees is likely to aid the local economy. However, should the company move the local economy may be depressed with small businesses feeling the pinch first. Multinationals may also offer considerable competition to local operations. Given the economies of scale of larger operations, they may be able to undercut long established local operations.

Cooperation with foreign companies may well present new opportunities for smaller local businesses to expand, franchising being a good example. This is explored further in chapter 10.

The consumer reaction

Nike, under its charismatic CEO Phil Knight, has been one of the brand successes of the late twentieth and early twenty-first centuries. Nike has outsourced much of its production to sub-contractors in developing countries. Named for the Greek goddess of victory, Nike's home is in Oregon and is the largest employer in Portland where the company is a leader in local philanthropy. The high quality of Nike's training shoes and other sportswear products have ensured that the Nike logo the 'swoosh' is recognized and respected throughout the world.

Unfortunately in 1997, according to Klein in *No Logo* (2000), an anti-Nike movement began in the US based on concerns about outsourcing, low wages paid abroad and child labour. The issue reached a stage where some school boards in the US were debating whether to accept Nike donations despite an ever-present need for extra financing. When a company's stores (as happened to Nike according to Klein) are picketed by customers and the nation's youth begins to question whether they should purchase products from companies that are outsourcing and thus denying that youth a possible future job, the companies have to listen. No corporation is actually bigger than its customers.

Nike answered its critics and introduced wage rises and increased inspections of sub-contractors in Indonesia where many of the products are manufactured. Klein claims that the poor public relations were in part responsible for some bad financial results in 1998, something Nike had to take seriously.

It may be that the global consumer, who rightly wants low prices, may have realized that there is a social cost that can be too high to justify. If that is true then global corporations are going to have to consider not only their customer's material needs but also their emotional ones.

CASE STUDY QUESTIONS

1   What factors do you believe have led to a small but growing number of consumers to place ethics ahead of the lowest price possible for a product?
2   Does an organization have any social responsibilities in the areas within which it operates?
3   Should shareholder interests always come first?

Summary and key learning points

- Globalization has opponents who are worried about its economic effects and the decline of democracy.
- Many see globalization as Westernization or Americanization.
- The relocation of companies to lower cost areas despite having received inducements to operate elsewhere can have drastic consequences for the original local economy.
- Unless proper wages are paid, governments may end up having to spend tax revenue supporting underpaid workers.
- Providing inducements in the form of grants and tax breaks is no guarantee that permanent employment will be created.
- Globalization not only impacts on trade but also on culture and values.
- Some organizations, termed 'swallows' move from one low cost economy to another, depriving areas of income and job security.
- Consumer resistance to child labour and exploitation is growing and has led to boycotts.

- Democracy can be threatened if the concerns of special interest groups are put above those of the general population.
- Globalization may be both a threat and an opportunity to local businesses.
- Global organizations have responsibilities to more than just their investors.
- No organization is bigger than its customers – they pay the wages and provide the profits.
- Fair trade is on the increase.
- Globalization is likely to increase.
- While there may be threats to small business there may also be opportunities especially if the local economy is improved by additional earning power.

QUESTIONS

1 Why do some people consider that globalization is not always a benefit?
2 Why might 'swallows' move from one area to another?
3 How can customers make their feelings known about corporate ethics?
4 'One day corporations will rule the world, not governments', discuss this statement.

Recommended further reading

The following texts, also detailed in the Bibliography, provide an insight into the concerns about globalization and related human behaviour:

Ahiakpor J C W (1990) *Multinationals and Economic Development*. London: Routledge.

Ardrey R (1966) *The Territorial Imperative*. London: Atheneum.

Bobbitt P (2002) *The Shield of Achilles – War, Peace and the Course of History*. New York: Alfred A Knopf.

Drainville A C (2003) *Contesting Globalization*. London: Routledge.

Ellwood W (2001) *The No-nonsense Guide to Globalization*. Oxford: New Internationalist.

Giddens A (1999) *Runaway World*. London: Profile Books.

Hertz N (2001) *The Silent Takeover*. London: Heinemann.

King D (1987) *The New Right – Politics, Markets and Citizenship*. Basingstoke: Macmillan.

Klein N (2000) *No Logo*. London: Flamingo.

Korten D C (1996) *When Corporations Rule the World*. San Francisco: Berrett-Koehler.

Korten D C (1997) *Globalizing Civil Society*. New York: Seven Stories Press.

Korten D C (1999) *The Post Corporate World*. San Francisco: Berrett-Koehler.

Nicholson N (2000) *Managing the Human Animal*. New York: Crown.

Ransom D (2001) *The No-nonsense Guide to Fair Trade*. Oxford: New Internationalist.

Sassen S (1996) *Losing Control: The Decline of Sovereignty in an Age of Globalization*. New York: Columbia University Press.

Sassen S (1999) *Globalization and its Discontents*. New York: New Press.

■ ☑ 5 Think global, act local

Learning outcomes

By the end of this chapter you should understand:

- What is meant by thinking global but acting local
- How thinking global but acting local can lead to success
- The success of many multi-nationals in terms of thinking global but acting local
- How the concept can relate to smaller organizations

Think/Discussion point:

Q: When is a Vauxhall Aquila a Suzuki Wagon R?

A: All of the time – they are virtually similar vehicles.

Q: Is a Nissan car made in Sunderland (UK), British or Japanese?

A: It all depends on how you view the product – it is a Japanese make but British built, i.e. it can be both British and Japanese.

One of the case studies in this chapter is on Ford, one of the largest motor manufacturers in the world and one of the first corporations to act globally but think locally. Ford is undeniably a major US corporation but a whole generation of motor cars, e.g. the Popular, the Cortina and the Anglia, were considered in the UK to be quintessentially British. Ford appeared to many in the UK to be a British company – hardly surprising as it acted as if it was by having a major UK manufacturing base that not only produced vehicles for the UK market but also exported from the UK.

To understand the success of companies such as Ford it is necessary to understand a little about how the market in private motor vehicles developed.

The first point to note is that Ford and its competitors are not in the motor car business, they are in the affordable, convenient personal transport business. If public transport improves then that is as much competition to Ford as a new Volkswagen product.

Thinking globally but acting locally allows an organization to appear to be local when it is in fact a global operation.

The chapter is different from the others in this book in that after a consideration about culture it is mainly composed of case studies of organizations that have achieved this aim. Two of the cases are overtly US companies while the third is a

US/UK operation. They were chosen not because of the nationality but because they are exemplars of thinking globally but acting locally.

Why act locally?

Overt, covert and pseudo global expansion

There are two modes by which companies can expand globally. They can either do so overtly or covertly. An overt expansion occurs when customers and suppliers are made immediately aware that there has been a change and that a new player has entered the market either by starting a completely new operation or by purchasing an existing player and changing to the new name and brands. An overt approach is often accompanied by advertising emphasizing the strengths of the new company. The covert approach is to acquire an existing player but to change very little so that it may not be apparent that a new company has entered the market as will be shown in the Carnival/P&O Princess case study at the end of this chapter. There may well be very important commercial reasons for acting in this way. Brand names can have considerable loyalty and changing them may mean the loss of a loyal customer base. General Motors kept the old Rootes Group brand names such as Vauxhall in the UK when they expanded into the UK market.

Ford has always been overt about its expansion in the mainstream market but less so in the luxury end – the Jaguar brand has still been kept.

The process of moving manufacturing into EPZs covered in the previous chapter may often be a case of pseudo global expansion as the company is not attempting to move into a new market for sales but just to cut manufacturing costs. It is a sad reflection on globalization that many quite mundane products could not be afforded by those who produce them and who thus do not form part of the potential market for the product. While a product may be made in a locality it is entirely possible that nobody in that locality actually owns a version of it.

> **Think/Discussion point**: How many people do you believe realize that Jaguar, a luxury product, is actually made by Ford – better known for mass production, family vehicles?

Culture

Culture can be defined as the 'way we do things around here' and differs from place to place across the globe, between ethnic groups and between organizations. There is, fortunately, a wealth of material on managing *cultural differences and* the reader is advised to consult *Riding the Waves of Culture* by Fons Trompenaars, *When Cultures Collide* by Richard D Lewis and *Managing Cultural Differences* by Philip Harris and Robert Moran (details of these texts are given in the Bibliography).

It would be a foolish organization that did not take account of the culture in which it was planning to operate. The issues between some US and some Middle Eastern values were mentioned in the previous chapter. Different cultures have different attitudes to achievement, the application of rules, gender, time etc. all of which Trompenaars has considered in depth. It is interesting to note, however, that many of those protesting about globalization and attending anti-American and anti-Western demonstrations will do so in US company trainers (sneakers) while listening to a Sony® Walkman and drinking a Diet Coke with a Mars Bar as a snack!

There is a whole range of cultural issues that an organization needs to consider if expansion into another area of the world is being proposed. These include:

- What form of hierarchies does the culture encourage
- Attitudes to gender
- Attitudes to age and experience
- Who makes buying decisions
- What is acceptable and not acceptable in advertising copy
- Employment rights and legislation
- Business practices that may run counter to those in the organization's home country.

It may well be that some of the above run counter to the organization's own beliefs and culture. Most organizations based in developed countries have a policy relating to equal opportunities, often to comply with legislation. This may well not always be the norm in other countries. The organization, by being sensitive, can perhaps use its policies to encourage change and enlightenment. Bribery is against the law in most developed countries whereas in some parts of the world 'commission' is the expected way of doing business. More than one CEO has fallen foul of this in doing business the local way and then being criticized and punished at home. As Eddy *et al.* (1976) reported, Dan Haughton, CEO of Lockheed and the company's president, Carl Kotchian were forced to resign in February 1976 (Friday the 13th of all days) as a result of questionable payments to among others Dutch and Japanese government officials during the sales campaigns for the Lockheed F-104 Starfighter and the L-1011 Tri-Star jet airliner.

Advertising can also be another area where culture clashes can occur. In the early days of television a number of US companies, who also operated in the UK, tried to import US advertisements directly onto UK screens only to find out that although the language used might be similar, UK cultural tastes were different to those in the US. Since then there have been examples of advertisements that have been truly global in nature but they have been few and far between. Nike, the British Airways 'Global' advertisement featuring people from all over the world making a globe and the famous 'I'd like to buy the world a Coke' advertisements (covered later in this chapter) worked almost everywhere. Others often need to be customized for the particular culture. Even throughout the English-speaking world there are considerable cultural and subtle linguistic differences. The concept that the US and the UK are 'divided by a common language' is very apt. Christopher Davis (1997) has provided a useful guide to how to avoid the British making mistakes in the US and vice versa in *Divided by a Common Language*, a humorous but useful text for those who live on one English-speaking side of the Atlantic and are working or vacationing on the other. A US advertisement on British television (those of the 1960s featuring Victor Kiam of Remington and the K-Tel advertisements spring to mind) can jar because of the slight difference in nuances and accent. This can lose sales not gain them. Interestingly at least one UK supermarket has used US themes (based on the *Dallas* soap opera) to excite its UK customer base!

Finding out

It is not difficult to discover the cultural norms of an area and it is nearly always worth taking the time and spending the money (it will be an investment) to do so. Suppliers, customers and employees will always be happier with an organization and products or services that they feel comfortable with and the more in tune the organization and what it offers, the more comfortable people will be and thus the more likely they are to give their business to the organization. In a Muslim/Jewish cultural area references to ham, pork and, in the former, alcohol should be avoided in advertising – it never pays to offend a potential customer.

> **Think/Discussion point**: How would you set about discovering the norms and values of another culture?

Culture and the products/services

The same types and often the same brands of products and services are now available on a global basis. However, as George S Yip points out in *Total Global Strategy* (1992), the idea of a completely similar product/service available all over the globe is a myth. There are nearly always local variations as a result of differences and culture. At the simplest level these may be purely linguistic. Coca-Cola, as will be shown later, is one of the most standardized global products but even Coke labels need to reflect the language of the user. It is noticeable that many products now include multi-lingual labels and instruction. Even mundane products such as shower gel on sale in the UK may include labels with English, French, Portuguese, Italian and other European languages (increasingly those of Eastern Europe as the market base expands) on the same label in an attempt to cut costs. Some nations prefer certain colours to others and if this can be accommodated in production costs, all well and good. Using locally preferred packaging shows that the organization has actually been considering the preferences of its customers. It is vitally important that effective market research is carried out to see whether changes need to be made to a standard product. There may well be legislative reasons for doing so. While automobiles now look very similar in most countries, governments have different safety and emission regulations and these need to be catered for. Not all countries drive on the right-hand side of the road, e.g. the UK, Eire, India, Pakistan, Cyprus, Australia, New Zealand and one part of the US still drive on the left (the US Virgin Islands). Modern manufacturing techniques have made it easier to produce left- and right-hand drive automobiles using the same jigs, machine tools and production lines but the issue also affects headlight lens etc. – small points but very important ones.

There may be demographic differences. A product that is dominated by female sales in one culture may be more male oriented in another, small automobiles are a good example. Something that appeals to youth in one place may be initially more attractive to an older age range in another. The mobile telephone market usually starts with the older business sector as the main purchasers with youth following on. The organization must examine such factors so as to decide where to pitch its entry. As a market becomes more mature then it will bring along those who have grown up with the product. In the 1960s, e.g. Coca-Cola was a youth drink. That generation has grown up but still drinks those brands when buying sodas.

McDonalds's (see case study in chapter 10) has become famous for both a highly standardized product and a highly standardized level of service and delivery but even it makes local adaptations. Islamic and Jewish cultures do not eat pork while the French expect alcohol to be served in many establishments that people in the UK do not. Within the standardized product, McDonald's has been able to cater for local variations. The knowledge that such variations are necessary at the outset of an expansion can greatly aid in building a loyal customer base.

It may be necessary to change the name of a product to suit local preferences although the current trend is to adopt names that are culturally neutral. Many of the automobile producers actually make up names, the Ford Ka and the Citroën Saxo being examples, or use numbers or a word that is clearly recognized globally, Mondeo, Neon etc. The UK brand name of the confectionery Snickers was for a long time Marathon until it was realized that UK purchasers would accept Snickers. Organizations need to be very careful that what is acceptable in one language is not unacceptable in another.

Even if the product stays the same, the packaging may change to reflect local culture. Pictures of Caucasian children on a product destined for Asia would be insensitive. US and UK Cornflakes taste the same and the packaging is similar but not quite the same. Kellogg's have managed to achieve what Coca-Cola has; many in the UK think that Kellogg's Cornflakes are a UK product. Perhaps the true indicator of having 'gone global' is that people in a particular market believe that the product/service/brand is indigenous to that market.

According to Yip (1002), there are only 19 truly global brands, the top five of which are: Coca-Cola, Sony, Mercedes Benz, Kodak and Disney. Apparently nearly everybody in the world knows about and recognizes these names. Not surprisingly Levi-Strauss, Kellogg and Ford are also in the list.

Services are one type of economic good that often require considerable variation. Financial services including banking, insurance, investments and pensions are subject to considerable national legislation. The major financial institutions such as HSBC (Hong Kong and Shanghai Banking Corporation) overcome the problem by acquiring local operators and in many cases keeping the original brand names but adapting their services to fit corporate guidelines, although it is noticeable that HSBC are now using their own name in the UK and sponsoring TV drama series to bring the name to people's attention. HSBC are following in the tradition of the original soap operas – so-called because they were dramas sponsored by soap powder manufacturers.

Pricing

The financing of globalization is covered in chapter 7 but the issue of whether to pay global or national rates of pay or whether to charge different prices in different areas belongs to this chapter. Most organizations pay at a level that approximates to local rates. To pay higher rates (say US wage levels in the Philippines) might distort the local economy and cause dissent between those employed by the organization and those not.

As standards of living differ across the world and wages may be higher or lower it should be expected that costs will also differ and thus the price charged. However, as people become more and more mobile they are likely to come across these price differentials. It is already less expensive for UK motorists to order and pay for a new vehicle elsewhere in Europe, because UK prices have traditionally been higher – the EU is currently taking steps to harmonize prices to a greater degree. For those living on the South Coast of England it may be cheaper to take a ferry to the Netherlands, pay to convert a vehicle to right-hand drive, drive it home and still save a considerable sum over the UK price! Seeing something for sale for less elsewhere might lead to customer dissatisfaction – customers rarely think about the link between earnings and prices except in their own area.

Parallel importing

In the 1990s, many companies became concerned about the phenomenon of parallel importing. This was an issue that affected among others the pharmaceutical and the music industries as a result of the lowering of trade barriers especially within the EU.

Many of the concerned manufacturers had been accused of price fixing in the UK by supermarkets and discount retailers who had been unable to obtain supplies directly to sell at a discount. The manufacturers, it was claimed, wished to keep prices at a higher level in the UK than elsewhere.

The prices of many products fluctuate according to supply and demand and may be relatively lower in one country than another, the price of books and compact discs in the US compared to the UK for example.

The supermarkets and discount retailers have dealt with this problem by buying supplies from abroad at local wholesale prices and re-importing them into the UK and selling at a discount. This is a practice known as parallel importing and is a direct consequence of going global and the price differentials that are bound to occur.

In 2001 the UK supermarket giant, Tesco and the US jeans manufacturer, Levi-Strauss became embroiled in a legal argument when the latter tried to stop Tesco selling its product at discounted prices. Tesco were importing the jeans using parallel import methods much to the chagrin of the manufacturer whose regular retailers were charging a much higher price.

Manufacturers claim that the specifications may be different and that this accounts for the differences in price.

The writer of this material heard of a case where a person in the UK once received a series of medicines all in Italian or Spanish packets (the instructions were also in English). The pharmacy (now closed) admitted that they were saving money by parallel importing – what price they charged the National Health Service was a matter not, apparently open for discussion.

Implications for small businesses

While small businesses may not be able to grow like Ford, Coca-Cola and Carnival they should be sensitive if they begin to expand globally. The more than can carry out the idea of 'think global but act local' the more likely they are to be accepted and gain a loyal customer base.

Getting it right

The remainder of this chapter is concerned with examining how three companies have thought globally but acted locally.

Ford

There was a time when each developed country had its own indigenous motor industry and thus to understand how globalization in the industry has come about, a brief history of the sector is required. In terms of Ford the case study centres on how Ford, a US company, made itself into a local UK company from 1911 onwards.

Attempts to find a form of motive power to replace horses as a form of transport stretch back to the end of the seventeenth century. Steam power was the most promising but it was not until the end of the eighteenth century that any degree of success was achieved. Britain had pinned its hopes on steam traction for both public and personal transportation and thus it was in France, Germany and the US that the development of the internal-combustion engine occurred. It was the mid-1880s before the internal-combustion engine could be brought to a level where it could be used in a vehicle capable of running on roads efficiently.

In 1885 and 1887 Karl Benz and then Gottlieb Daimler introduced the first successful petrol-engined cars. The Benz vehicle was much the superior, as it was designed as a whole, using the new technology of the bicycle industry. Daimler's carriage was no more than an adapted horse vehicle. Benz went into limited production of his three-wheeled carriage in 1888 and the modern motor industry was born. However, the Daimler engine was revolutionary and was to change the face of the motor industry.

A crucial event in the history of the motor industry was the 1889 Paris World Exhibition. It provided the world's public with its first view of this new form of transport.

America's first petrol-driven vehicle was made by John W Lambert in 1891 and in 1895 the first American motor-manufacturing company was established by the Duryea brothers, Charles and Frank, whose prototype appeared in 1893. Elwood Haynes, Alexander Winton and Henry Ford were also active in the 1890s.

The demand for motor cars was growing steadily in the late 1890s. The largest European manufacturer, Benz, claimed to have made 2500 cars by 1900, and in the US, Olds had made 400 from mid-1899 through to 1900.

By 1911 over 600,000 cars were on US roads, far more than in European countries – the US lead in the industry was already building.

With its higher per-capita income, efficient mass-production techniques, and dispersed population the US vehicle market and vehicle industry outpaced that in the rest of the world, which by the outbreak of the First World War meant predominantly Europe. By 1914 there was one vehicle for every 77 people in the US, for 165 in Britain, for 318 in France and for 950 in Germany. This also meant that Britain was the largest market in Europe, to which the French were the largest exporters.

Mass production of motor vehicles

Mass production techniques were being used in the UK, Germany and the US from the 1800s onwards as steam presses and convey belts became the norm. Henry Ford did not invent mass production but he was one of its greatest exploiters.

From 1908, when the Model T was introduced, Ford brought together the lessons of over 100 years in a highly efficient manner. He standardized the output of precision-made products, which allowed the interchangeability of parts, and manufacture on moving production lines, with operations divided and simplified at work stations, were combined in the Ford Highland Park plant between 1913 and 1915. Such was the efficiency of the factory system that cars were made at ever decreasing prices – the unit cost decreased and as the price remained stable, profit margins soared. Vehicles left the line every 10 seconds, at an annual rate of 2 million.

As the European countries were at war by then, there was little external competition. Mass production gained a further boost as US industry produced munitions and supplies of all kinds for the allied forces both before and after the US entered the conflict in 1917.

As a result, mass motoring emerged in the US in the 1920s. As European makers, notably Morris in Britain, Citroën in France, Opel in Germany, Fiat in Italy and the Ford plants outside the US began to build large local markets – Henry Ford was quick to see the potential of local manufacture for local markets, as opposed to central manufacturing serving a variety of local markets.

In the 1920s, as Europe rebuilt its industries after the devastation of war, the US and US car plants in Canada made over 90 per cent of world vehicle production. Most vehicles were sold in North America, although exports accounted for 35 per cent of the world vehicle market outside the US.

As early as 1903, the same year Henry Ford founded the Ford Motor Company in the US, two Ford Model A cars were shipped from Detroit to Britain and displayed at the Cordingley Automobile show in Islington. In 1905, the traditional Hackney horse-drawn cab was joined by three Ford Model B taxi cabs – the motor vehicle had begun its take over of London.

The Model T had its world debut at the 1908 Olympia Motor Exhibition and boosted sales of Ford vehicles in Britain to the extent that Henry Ford decided to establish the first Ford factory outside of North America. The first factory was a disused tram works just south of Manchester at Trafford Park, near Manchester Docks and production began on 11 October 1911. Initially static workbenches were used with mass production methods being adopted in 1913 when the plant boasted Britain's first moving production line. Up to 21 chassis per hour could now be produced by just 60 men. Output doubled in the first year and the Model T was the best-selling car in Britain taking 30 per cent of the market. Ford has continued to produce a series of best-selling British cars over the years: the Ford Popular, the Anglia, the Cortina, the Escort, the Sierra, the Fiesta, the Mondeo and the Focus.

During the First World War, Trafford Park also produced light tanks and one-ton commercial vehicles alongside the Model Ts. Double shifts increased the Model T output to 100 per day to accommodate the ever-increasing demand as the vehicle was also used by the military for utility purposes – an early form of jeep.

By the early 1920s it was obvious to Ford that a modern factory designed for operations on a vast scale was desperately needed if supply was to meet demand. Ford management finally decided on a site on the banks of the River Thames near the (then) small village of Dagenham in Essex.

By the end of 1924 Trafford Park had produced Britain's 300,000th Ford and it continued to produce Ford vehicles until the opening of the Dagenham factory in 1931. Ford moved their work teams to the south. Special trains carried 2000 workers, their families and possessions to their new homes and workplace. Many more were hired from local areas thus rejuvenating the local economy at a time of depression. In December 1929, Ford Motor Company Limited (UK) was floated with a capital of £7 million as the hub of a European expansion.

The Second World War brought new challenges for the Dagenham factory. Employment increased from 12,000 to 35,000 as Ford met the demand of 360,000 military vehicles including light vans, army trucks, mobile canteens and Bren Gun carriers. During the war, more than a quarter of a million Ford V8 engines were produced and 95 per cent of Britain's wartime tractors were produced at the Dagenham plant. Ford also returned to Manchester during these war years to establish a factory to build 34,000 Rolls Royce Merlin engines for the RAF's fighters and bombers.

The end of the war saw a huge rise in demand for Ford vehicles at home and abroad. The UK government was keen to export vehicles to obtain foreign currency to aid reconstruction. Indeed home demand was subordinated to exports and potential customers in the UK often had to wait for vehicles (from all UK manufacturers) while export orders were fulfilled. 1947 was the first full year of peacetime production and Dagenham manufactured 115,000 vehicles.

By 1950 Ford had designed an all-new saloon range, the Consul and Zephyr, and they were shown at the Olympia Motor Show in October. By 1953, despite post-war shortages of materials, production had risen to more than 300,000 units each year.

In 1953, Ford set up plants at Doncaster, Southampton, Croydon and Romford in addition to extending Dagenham. Despite its US origins, to the British public it was a British company producing vehicles for the UK market and earning the country export revenues. Thinking globally but acting locally was working. Ford was seen to be as British as Morris, Austin and Vauxhall (actually a US General Motors operation – another example of thinking globally but acting locally).

With demand still increasing for Ford cars, Ford of Britain looked North in 1960 to set up a second car-producing factory. Halewood on Merseyside was chosen for its port facilities and adequate supply of labour. The £40 million factory produced its first car on 8 March 1963. Ford was now in a position to extend its range of vehicles to include an inexpensive, compact, family car – the famous Ford Cortina in which many of the author's generation learned to drive.

The Cortina

Together with the Austin (later British Motor Corporation) Mini, the Cortina was the quintessential British.

The Chairman of Ford Britain, had an early sight of the early prototype at the Detroit facility in the US and immediately ordered the British product development team to proceed with developing a competitor to a rival Ford Germany design, one part of the Ford global operation. The team were successful and the first Cortina went on sale in 1962. By the time the Mark II was introduced, more than 1 million Cortinas had been sold. Dagenham was able to concentrate on the new Cortina model while Halewood took over the production of the ever-popular Anglia 105E. Halewood also produced the Corsair from 1963 until it was eventually replaced by the Capri series in the late 1960s, the last of which emerged at the end of the 1980s, the writer buying one of the final examples. The Capri was a sporting saloon that gained a huge following.

While the UK Rootes Group named its cars the Morris Oxford and the Austin Cambridge, Ford adopted more continental, 'sunny' names – Cortina, Capri, Granada and Sierra.

Expansion in the UK continued as it did in both the US and Germany (where many of the Granada models were produced). A plant in Swansea was acquired in 1965 plus further expansion in the Midlands the year after. That same year Ford established an industry first – a transatlantic computer link, a system that is standard practice today.

Ford also made a major contribution to UK motor sport and rallying with the Cortina special editions, especially the Lotus Cortina being the average buyer's answer to a rally car.

Ford was not without its industrial relations problems during the period but they were the same as those of the other UK motor vehicle, shipbuilding and other heavy engineering companies – they were part of the so-called 'British disease' of the 1960s and 70s and in no way connected to the fact that Ford was a US corporation.

The Cortina, Capri and Escort (a smaller, popular car that also gained a great rally reputation) ranges proved very popular with the British public and in 1976, Ford introduced the Fiesta – the company's first front wheel drive small car. The Cortina, Escort and Fiesta continued to lead the UK best-selling vehicles list throughout the 1970s and into the 1980s. They were cars designed for British families and British roads and very unlike the vehicles produced by Ford for the US market – vehicles that tended to be much larger. Occasionally one could see a UK Ford, often a Capri on US roads and it always drew attention.

The radically different Ford Sierra replaced the Cortina in 1982. It was a bold design move and at the time, its aerodynamic styling was unique. Sierra soon became the benchmark for hatchback family sized saloons and paved the way for the 1993 Mondeo, still one of the most popular family vehicles in the UK but also designed for the more general European market. By this time Japanese vehicles designed for a global market, including that of the US and the rest of Europe, were appearing in the UK in large numbers and other manufacturers were setting up UK and European plants. In part this was to avoid EU import restrictions, the companies also setting up US plants to avoid US restrictions on Far-Eastern vehicle imports. The Japanese were also thinking globally but acting locally.

Cosworth Racing joined the Ford family in 1998 and was followed by the acquisition of AB Volvo (the Swedish car maker, well respected and with good sales volume in the UK) in January 1999. The Automotive Premier Group, covering Jaguar Cars (one of the most prestigious UK marques), Volvo Cars, Aston Martin (one of the most famous UK sport's car makers) and Lincoln was created in March. By acquiring Jaguar and Aston Martin, Ford increased its UK local image. It is difficult to think of Ford in the UK as anything but a UK company despite its US origins.

Not only Ford but also General Motors and Chrysler established operations abroad in the 1930s for the same reason as the Japanese began manufacturing in the US and Europe in the late twentieth century – European governments protected their motor industries from US competition with tariffs and quotas. However, a locally made car, even if made by a US company, was not subject to such restrictions. Provided the vehicles matched local needs, the company had cause for optimism in regard to sales. Ford certainly proved this point in the UK as did companies such as Toyota much later.

By the early 1970s European economic growth and more efficient vehicle manufacture meant that total European car market and car production exceeded that of North America for the first time since the early days of the industry. With tariffs falling throughout the world from the early 1960s; the unsuitability of US style cars – petrol consumption tended to be high given the relative cheapness of petrol in the US – for most export markets meant that this fall was to the initial benefit of first European and then Japanese and other Far Eastern manufacturers. However, around 20 per cent of European car production and sales was accounted for by US firms.

The figures for 1995 show that there were over 625 million cars and commercial vehicles in use in the world. Of these 193 million were in the US, 17 million in Canada, 63 million in Japan and 183 million in Western Europe (Source: Microsoft® Encarta 2002). As regards cars alone, Western Europe, with 162 million in use, exceeded the US, with 146 million.

The motor industry is global in scope. American dominance of the industry lasted from 1910 to 1965 when the US still made 50 per cent of the world's vehicles. Although this dominance no longer exists, the US still leads world production.

In 1902 the German firm Daimler acquired a wholly owned subsidiary in Austria and became the first multinational enterprise in the motor industry. In 1998, Daimler and Chrysler merged. In 2003 the most highly developed multinational companies are Ford and General Motors, followed by the Japanese firms Toyota and Nissan. The European producers are much more closely tied to their region, although Volkswagen of Germany and Fiat of Italy have major operations in South America (the old version of the VW 'Beetle' was still being manufactured in South America in 2003).

Most of the vehicle firms operating in the rest of the world are subsidiaries of the major US, Japanese and European producers. In countries like Malaysia, China and India, production is undertaken by local firms, but invariably with major help from the foreign giant corporations. In the mid-1990s only the Korean firms of Hyundai, Daewoo, Kia and Samsung looked as if they could join the ranks of independent car makers, capable of financing, designing, producing and then marketing their own vehicles. The downturn in the Far-Eastern economies in the early 2000s has meant that they have had to make tie ups with US and European manufacturers in order to survive.

The current market leaders in Europe in terms of market share are: Volkswagen (includes Seat and Skoda) – 20 per cent; General Motors (Opel, Vauxhall), Peugeot-Citroen, Ford (including Jaguar and Volvo), Renault and Fiat, with approximately 12 per cent each; BMW – 6 per cent and Mercedes with about 4 per cent. In total the Japanese have about 13 per cent of European sales and other Far East companies 3 per cent; the Koreans 2 per cent. Daimler–Chrysler and small independents make up about 6 per cent.

Ford has been as successful a British company as they have a US one. Their UK models have been designed with UK tastes and conditions in mind. Ford is part of the UK commercial scenery – that is what thinking global but acting local means.

CASE STUDY QUESTIONS

1 How has Ford demonstrated that it is able to think globally but act locally?
2 To what extent has Ford in the UK been able to develop independently to Ford in the US?
3 Why are premium brand names such as Jaguar kept distinct from the main Ford models?

Coca-Cola

In the early 1980s the author visited the Soviet Union (as it then was) for the first time. At a pavement booth in Moscow he was sold something that looked very much like a bottle of Coca-Cola. The colour was right, the bottle was the right shape, the label even looked right – the taste was not! It was not a bottle of Coke at all but a Russian copy!

Think/Discussion point: Is imitation always the best form of flattery or is it plain criminal counterfeiting?

However, long before the fall of the Berlin Wall in 1989, Coca-Cola was available in nearly every corner of the globe. It is not alone in this in the developed world at least. Last year the author was given a bottle of Highland Spring water in a bar on St Kitts in the Caribbean – he lives 4 miles from the Highland Spring plant. While some soft drinks (sodas as they are known in the US) are only regional – Irn Bru in Scotland is an example – Coca-Cola and its rival Pepsi Cola have conquered the world. No matter what cultural differences and conflicts there may be between groups the chances are that some if not all on each side drink either Coke or Pepsi.

As Mark Pendergrast states in his book, *For God, Country and Coca-Cola*, Coca-Cola is more than a product, it is a global institution indeed perhaps an icon of the late twentieth and early twenty-first centuries.

From its inception in 1885 in Atlanta, Georgia by the morphine addicted Dr Pemberton and subsequent sale as one of the many patent medicines for stomach ailments, Coca-Cola has spanned the globe, being available in nearly every country and indeed bar, café, restaurant and mobile food outlet in the world.

The first versions of the drink may have been addictive in the truest sense of the world containing as has been claimed small amounts of cocaine (Pendergrast, 2000, pp. 88–9) although this has been denied by the company. It must be stressed that since 1903 analysis has shown that Coca-Cola has contained no cocaine whatsoever.

The global interest in Coca-Cola as a product and a company is such that the company spent $15 million on a museum in Atlanta (Georgia) dedicated to the product, a museum that receives over 3000 visitors per day during the tourist season.

A drink that had apparent beneficial properties, a good taste and was inexpensive had all the ingredients for success at the turn of the twentieth century. At the time immigration was swelling the US population (it rose from 50 million in 1880 to 91 million in 1910) and this provided a ready market for Coca-Cola and its rivals of which, at the time, there were many.

By 1895 Coca-Cola had lost its medicinal image and was being marketed using bottles and soda fountains as a pure beverage and by 1900 was available widely across the continental US.

In 1897 the company began sales outside the continental US, firstly in Hawaii, Mexico and Canada expanding to Cuba in 1899 and to the UK in a small way as early as 1900. Despite the fact that there is a perception that

Coca-Cola was brought to the UK by the GIs during the Second World War it had already been in the country for over 40 years.

By 1909 the drink was not only being exported from the US but also bottling plants had been set up in Cuba, Hawaii and Puerto Rico. The idea of bottling in the same area as consumption has been crucial to the success of Coca-Cola as it allows the local customer to identify the product as being more local than it actually is because it is produced by local workers – the very essence of thinking global but acting local. Is a US product made and bottled in Germany, US or German – or does it really matter? There is a paradox here in that Coca-Cola is both local but is also quintessentially a product of the US and thus is identified with US values and even politics and diplomacy no matter where actual production occurs as will be demonstrated later in this section.

The famous shaped bottle was first introduced in 1916 and is still an alternative to can today, although it now more often made of plastic rather than glass.

In 1923 the company decided to expand from the UK into the wider European market and a series of bottling franchises were arranged but unfortunately many of the franchisees failed to ensure the purity of their water supplies causing major problems and embarrassment for Coca-Cola as a number of customers became ill.

Nevertheless in 1932 the UK's first Coca-Cola plant opened outside London at the same time as Pepsi Cola began to become a serious rival. This was ironic as Coca-Cola had the opportunity to buy Pepsi in 1922 but decided not to – one of the great errors of commerce perhaps?

During the Second World War US servicemen took Coca-Cola abroad with them and the company went to great lengths to ensure that supplies of the product reached the troops. It was the movement of GIs in Europe and Asia that really brought Coca-Cola to the wider European and Asian markets. In West Germany after the war, Coke was like chocolate (and cigarettes in Romania prior to the overthrow of the communist regime) almost an unofficial currency. In the 1950s bottling and sales commenced throughout Africa, the West Indies, the Middle East and South America. Tourism was growing and vacationers wanted to see products with which they were familiar. The wording on the label might be in a foreign language but the logo and its colour, the bottle and the contents were the familiar ones from the US – important for US tourists and also to maintain the company image. Coca-Cola did not expand into the communist sphere of influence but in the 1960s rivals Pepsi Cola began to operate behind the Iron Curtain.

It was not until the Japanese government dropped its import controls in 1960 that Coca-Cola could operate there despite a huge US troop presence (the product was available to them from the PX (the military personnel-only retail outlet that sells US products to US service families, essentially a little bit of middle America in Germany, Japan, the UK etc.) but by 1964 Coca-Cola brought off a coup by paying for the Japanese television coverage of the Tokyo Olympics of that year. Almost overnight the Japanese market became second only to that of the US, accounting for 18 per cent of corporate profits.

Unfortunately for the Coca-Cola Company, the cold war, beginning with the Berlin Air Lift in 1948 saw the product being more and more identified with US policy. In the UK a Labour party Member of Parliament actually spoke up against the company and in France the left wing fomented violence directed at the US in general and Coca-Cola in particular as a symbol of 'US imperialism' caused serious disruption.

By operating local plants and providing employment for local people, Coca-Cola was able to weather these storms and by 1965 the product was made available in the Soviet Union. In 1966 Coca-Cola had refused to franchise its operation in Israel but bowed to political pressure and set up a plant. Unfortunately the middle of the 1960s was a bad time for the peace process in the Middle East with war erupting between Israel and its Arab neighbours in 1967. The Arab countries announced a boycott of Coca-Cola unless the company pulled out of Israel. The boycott (costing Coca-Cola $20 million in profits per annum) came into effect in 1968 but was short lived as in Egypt alone it is believed that it led to 25,000 workers laid off, producing tremendous pressure on the government.

In 1971, Coca-Cola became truly a global organization with the famous advertisement, 'I'd like to buy the world a Coke.' Using 30 young people of all races and colours, the advertisement to the tune of 'I'd like to teach the world to sing in perfect harmony' stuck a chord with many young people expressing as it did the ideals of peace and love – and all brought about by Coca-Cola! The advertisement was so memorable that in 2000 it was voted number 16 of the 100 greatest advertisements in a UK poll. Interestingly the advertisement was the first positive image use of non-white faces in a UK television advertisement. The Coca-Cola advertisement was suitable for showing anywhere – it was all-embracing and culturally neutral; exactly what Coca-Cola had been aiming to be as a global product that belonged to everybody.

As the twenty-first century dawned Coca-Cola despite its obvious US origins was a global product manufactured, bottled and drunk all over the world. It may well be one of the most global products ever but its growth has been by thinking global but acting local.

CASE STUDY QUESTIONS

1   In what ways was the Second World War beneficial to the Coca-Cola in a global sense?
2   Is there an irony in a US company sponsoring a global event (the Olympics) in Japan in order to penetrate the Japanese domestic market?
3   Why did the Russians feel the need to imitate the Coca-Cola bottle design and product even if they were not prepared for the product itself to be sold within their borders?

Carnival Corporation

In 2002 the author and a colleague were asked to contribute to a report to the UK Competition Commission regarding the proposed merger between the second and third largest players in the global cruise industry, Royal Caribbean International and the UK company P&O Princess. The merger did not proceed because of a rival bid for P&O Princess by the Carnival Corporation – the largest of the cruise operations.

The Carnival Corporation of the US is an organization that has experienced massive growth. The global cruise market, of which Carnival is by far and way the market leader, increased from 5 million annual customers to nearly 10 million between 1993 and 2000 – 75 per cent of those customers are from the US.

When Carnival Cruises' first vessel *The Mardi Gras* (the ex-Canadian Pacific Liner, *Empress of Canada*) left Miami on her maiden cruise in 1972 she went aground. One competing company even offered its customers a drink named 'Mardi Gras on the Rocks'. Hardly an auspicious start for a new venture.

However, by 2001 Carnival was not only successful it was also the market leader in the fastest growing sector of the tourism industry.

Ted Arison had been a colonel in the Israeli Army and had then been involved in the air charter business. In 1966 he joined forces with a Norwegian, Knut Kloster who had a new passenger ship, the *Sunward* laid up in Europe. The cruise industry was just beginning to boom in the US and Arison suggested basing the *Sunward* at the then small port of Miami. Together Kloster and Arison formed Norwegian Caribbean Line (NCL), a company that became Norwegian Cruise Lines (NCL) eventually being owned by Star Cruises of Thailand.

NCL was very successful but in 1971 Arison and Kloster split up. Kloster remained with NCL and Arison acquired the *Empress of Canada*, a surplus-to-requirements Atlantic liner and renamed her *Mardi Gras*.

Arison grew Carnival by two means. The first was by offering a product to a new segment of the market – the younger vacationer – and secondly by acquiring well-known brands not just in the US but also in Europe thus increasing the customer base.

Carnival's growth

Carnival cruises is just one of the corporation's brands and the growth of the brand has been from one ship in 1972 to 19 in 2003.

Carnival Cruises took a bold step in 1998 when, responding to customer demand, they made the *Paradise* a totally smoke-free ship banning all smoking on board – a move that has been followed by other operators. In 1996 they offered a guarantee to their cruises allowing customers to leave the ship with a refund at the first port of call if they were not satisfied and by 2000 had introduced a cyber café to all the vessels in the Carnival brand fleet.

Horizontal expansion

The Carnival brand appeals to young, US vacationers. But of the 9.5 million people who undertook a cruise in 1999, many were neither young nor from the US. The UK is the second largest market and the rest of Europe provides another major slice. Many of those who enjoy cruises are older in years and the Carnival brand would not suit them. One of the best known brands catering for the more mature vacationer is Holland America Cruises derived from the Holland America Line that operated the Netherlands–US service in the days of the ocean liner. In 1987 Holland America acquired a 50 per cent stake in Windstar Cruises (a company operating large sail-driven cruise ships) and completed the purchase the following year. However, later in 1988, Carnival acquired Holland America giving it a foothold in the premier cruise market for more mature customers. Carnival changed very little. The appearance of Holland America ships especially the livery remained unchanged and they continued under their Dutch names with little reference to the new ownership.

In 1991 Carnival acquired a 25 per cent stake in the luxury operator Seabourn Cruises (operator of a series of small, yacht-like vessels). In 1996 Carnival purchased a 29.6 per cent stake in the UK vacation business of Airtours plc at a cost of $310 million. Airtours were a very new entrant into the UK cruise market with an operation geared to the budget end of the market and linked to their core flights plus hotel package holidays. The Airtours operation already had a stake in the Italian Costa company and its minority stake gave Carnival an entry into the UK market. Spending another $300 million in 1997, Carnival bought out Costa Cruises of Italy, a major player in both the US and European standard cruise markets. In doing so it sold its stake in Airtours and acquired the Airtours (now called MyTravel) stake in the Italian company. Carnival also added one of the Club Med sailing cruise vessels (very popular with young Europeans) to the Windstar fleet.

In the early years of the twentieth century the UK government had kept Cunard (owners of some of the greatest Atlantic liners) out of the grasp of the US financier J P Morgan by providing subsidies on the stipulation that Cunard remained British. This changed in 1998 when Carnival acquired the Cunard cruise operation (including the famous *QE2*).

Thus by 1998, the Carnival Corporation had the following brands:

Carnival Cruises	US	Standard
Cunard	US/UK	Luxury
Costa	Europe/US	Standard
Seabourn	US	Luxury
Windstar	US	Niche sail cruises
Holland America	Europe/US	Premier

By 2001 the acquisitions had added 33 ships plus four building with a combined tonnage of 1,492,000 GRT giving the Carnival Group 44 ships totalling well over 2 million GRT. This makes the Carnival Group easily the largest cruise conglomerate in the world with well over 33 per cent of the global market – a market that is still growing.

Carnival has expanded by acquiring traditional brands and keeping them very much as is. Indeed it is doubtful whether the customers know they are actually on a Carnival owned vessel. Certainly few passengers on the Cunard liner *Caronia* in 2003 were aware that they were actually on a Carnival Group vessel when spoken to by the author who was working on the ship. The ambience was typically British, the ship was registered in the UK and the officers were British – it must have been a British operation. Think global but act local.

The cruise industry, like other multi-segment industries, has a number of distinct customer bases. There are cruises for those on a budget and others that are extremely luxurious – the difference is price. There are also those such as the main Carnival operation that are for younger vacationers and others for those of more mature years. By building their own brand and acquiring others Carnival has been able to achieve massive growth in an industry where building times are relatively long and where the capital investment required is huge.

It has not all been a success. Carnival has tried to acquire other operators, Premier Cruises and Royal Caribbean, but without success. Their Latin America operation and another in the Far East were also lacking in success.

P&O

In 2003 P&O merged with Carnival to form a dual listed company – the combination forming the largest player in the global cruise market.

P&O was founded in 1837 when Arthur Anderson and Brodie McGhie Wilcox (who had been trading as Wilcox and Anderson since 1825) set up the Peninsular Steam Navigation Company, the Peninsular in question being the Iberian Peninsular, to offer a regular steam ship service to Portugal and Spain.

The company was a success and as its routes became extended to India, the Far East and Australia the word Oriental was added to its title the company becoming the Peninsular and Oriental Steam Navigation Company – P&O.

By 1920 P&O had acquired the British India Company, the Union Steamship of New Zealand and the New Zealand Steam Ship Companies as well as holding a majority shareholding in the Orient Line.

P&O policy was for acquired companies to continue operating under their own name and house flag. In 1960 there was a formal merger between P&O and Orient Line (the last of the minority shares in Orient Line were finally acquired in 1965).

P&O wanted to re-enter the rapidly expanding US cruise market in 1974. P&O had attempted to enter the US market earlier but the name, very familiar in the UK, was relatively unknown to US vacation and cruise seekers. P&O acquired Princess Cruises, a US company that had built up a loyal customer base since its foundation in 1965. P&O kept the name of the company and the name of the ships. Princess Cruises became one of the major players under the P&O house-flag but it was some time before the P&O lettering appeared on the sides of the ships. There was no reason for US customers to know that their vacation was actually with a UK company. They dealt with the Princess Cruises office in Santa Monica (Los Angeles), the currency on board was the $US, the entertainment and food were geared to US tastes and the funnel carried the original Princess symbol. At the same time P&O ran their traditional parallel cruise operation for the UK market and in 1983 acquired the cultural cruise operation of Swan Hellenic. In 2000 P&O set up a separate company, P&O Princess to operate the cruise business that by 2002 included P&O Cruises in the UK,

Princess Cruises, P&O Cruises (Australia), Swan Hellenic and Seetours, Aida Cruises and A'ROSA Cruises in Germany – the company having expanded into the German market. In 2001 P&O nearly acquired Festival Cruises, a pan-European operation and in that same year announced a merger proposal with Royal Caribbean Cruises in which P&O would hold 51 per cent of the shares in the new company. The Carnival Corporation (owners of Carnival Cruises, Cunard, Holland America and a number of other cruise lines and the largest cruise company in the world) made a counter bid for P&O Princess (i.e. the cruise operation of P&O and not the ferries etc). The concept that was adopted in 2003 was for a dual listed company whereby Carnival and P&O would retain their identities and brands but would become one company.

Thus the Carnival/P&O Princess merger has seen the operation enter as a local player into the US, the UK, the Italian, the Netherlands, the Australian and the German markets. The purchasing power and the ability to move ships around (two Princess ships were recently transferred to the UK P&O Cruises brand and a Carnival and a Holland America ship rebranded to Costa recently) allows for maximum value and huge flexibility.

Carnival has confirmed its commitment to its UK operations by ordering the world's largest liner – *Queen Mary 2* – introduced in 2004 and another new vessel, *Queen Victoria* for 2005. These will be to all intents and purposes British ships – Carnival thinking globally but acting locally.

CASE STUDY QUESTIONS

1 Why will Carnival Group's biggest ship to date, the *Queen Mary 2*, carry a UK registration and have a British ambience when a majority of the passengers will be from the USA?
2 How does the Carnival Group portfolio especially after the P&O Princess merger demonstrate a commitment to as wide a customer base as possible?
3 What was Arison's secret (clue – the answer lies in the previous question)?

Summary and key learning points

- Make the product appear local even if it is not thus engendering local loyalty.
- Be culturally sensitive when setting up new plants and operations.
- Be aware that local politics can intrude into operations however good the product is.
- If the product is global, develop advertising that is culturally neutral.
- Let acquisitions keep their identity and thus their brand image and customer base.
- Be seen as a local benefactor e.g. Coca-Cola paying for Japanese coverage of the Tokyo Olympics. The company is also involved in many other sporting and cultural activities.

1 What is meant by 'think global but act local'?
2 What are the common factors that have brought success to Ford, Coca-Cola and Carnival?
3 How could a small business 'think global but act local'?

Recommended further reading

For further information about global strategies you should consult Yip's *Total Global Strategy* (1992). Information about Ford and the motor industry can be found in:

Langworth R (1987) *A Complete History of the Ford Motor Company.* New York: Random House.

Studder M (2001) *The Global Strategies of MME and Government Policies: Ford Motor Company and the Automobile Industry in Canada and Mexico.* New York: Routledge.

Waller D (2001) *Wheels of Fire.* London: Hodder & Stoughton.

Wickens P (1987) *The Road to Nissan.* Basingstoke: Macmillan.

Information about the cruise industry can be found in:

Cartwright R and Baird C (1999) *The Development and Growth of the Cruise Industry.* Oxford: Butterworth Heinemann.

Dickinson R and Vladimir A (1997) *Selling the Sea.* New York: Wiley.

■ ⅴ 6 Globalization and the human resource

Learning outcomes

By the end of this chapter you should understand:

- The sensitivity needed towards human relations in globalization
- The need for a global human relations policy
- Recruitment issues
- The importance of national laws relating to employment
- The need for cultural sensitivity
- The issue of wage rates
- The importance of both skills and other forms of training
- The need to develop talent and potential across a global enterprise

Organizations exist to fulfil certain objectives. In the case of commercial organizations these objectives usually centre on profits and shareholder value. There has been much criticism in recent years of the short-term attitude of many Western companies and investors – typically demanding 15 per cent ROI (return on Investment) year on year rather than making long-term investments in the operation. It has been pointed out that many Far Eastern companies and investors have used market share as a better guide to performance, the argument being that high market share (provided it is a large enough market) is likely to be profitable.

To achieve its objectives, whether a certain profit, ROI or market share, an organization needs a strategy. Corporate strategy can be defined as the direction and scope of an organization over the long term: ideally which matches its resources to its changing environment and in particular its markets, customers or clients so as to meet stakeholder expectations. Policies are the organizational procedures and plans for achieving its strategy. It follows therefore that within the corporate strategy, policies and procedures there will need to be a financial strategy, a research strategy and a human resource (HR) strategy etc. Each of these strategies is derived from and nested within the overall corporate strategy.

It is now realized that people form the human/intellectual capital of an organization, defined as the asset value of the knowledge and experience of the employees of an organization.

The sensitivity needed towards human relations in globalization

Despite the high capital cost of much equipment, people are still the largest investment an organization makes. Human relations is about more than just employment patterns and wage rates. It is about developing potential and loyalty. These are important issues with major implications for globalization as will be shown in this chapter.

Records from the past such as the Christian Bible make it clear that the seeking and utilization of personnel from other cultures have never been totally restricted to the members of the particular group in question. The Roman legions were quite prepared to utilize the fighting abilities of non-Roman groups.

Political developments that bring countries into ever closer political and economic groupings – the EU is an example of this as is NAFTA – often have the free movement of people as one of their core concepts. The ability of organizations to hire staff from a larger grouping without the need for complex immigration procedures aids the recruitment of a wider pool of staff and also to expand into new areas of the world.

Language

The major commercial language in the world is English but there are a number of versions of English each with its own grammar, spelling and meaning of many words. Microsoft Word, a word processing program used throughout the world, listed no fewer than 185 separate languages in the Word 20005 spell and grammar check utility. Of these there were multiple versions of French, Portuguese, Dutch, Italian, no fewer than 13 variants of English including British English and US English (Canadian English was also there as a different variant), and no fewer than 20 variants of Spanish plus Catalan and Basque.

The large number of television and movie offerings in the various forms of English mean that most of the time native English speakers are able to cope with the variations. When working with people who normally use another language or even a variant of the manager's own language it is always worth eliciting feedback to ensure that the words have identical meanings to each party. Language can be a barrier to talent but need not be so if both parties take the trouble to understand each other's languages.

Stereotyping

One of the issues that concerns those involved in race relations is the issue of stereotyping. Stereotyping occurs when a simplified conception of behaviour is applied to a whole group or even nation with very little factual evidence. The danger with stereotyping is that a perception that 'all (whoever they are) are not good at a particular skill or activity'. Eddy *et al.* (1976) in *Destination Disaster*, a text about a particular incident in the airline industry, make the point that there were some Western pilots who were prone to making derogatory comments about the standard of English spoken by some Middle Eastern air traffic controllers. While this could be a safety issue, the writers pointed out that it was the Arabs who developed the mathematics that enables us to design and operate aircraft at a time when Western Europe was still in the Dark Ages. It is very dangerous to make assumptions and comments about other races. It is often the case that a particular race or nation shows an above-average skill for something not because it is innate but because it is something that is valued and encouraged by that society.

> **Think/Discussion point**: Be honest – have you ever been guilty of stereotyping?

The need for a global human resources policy

Even the smallest organization in the EU may be employing or dealing with staff from another member country. The EU guarantees freedom of movement and employment (subject to the necessary skills and qualifications) to its citizens. Nor should it be forgotten that we live in a multi-cultural society and that employees may not all share the same culture. In this case the employer (and other employees) need to be sensitive to the cultural norms and needs of those around them – the same applies to customers!

In *The Global HR Manager* (1999), Pat Joynt and Bob Morton have edited a useful volume that considers the issues facing those responsible for HRM (human resource management) or the personnel function in organizations operating on a global basis. They have introduced what they call 'the Seven Cs' of international HRM. The 'Seven Cs' are:

- Culture
- Competition
- Communications
- Competencies
- Compensation
- Careers
- Collaboration.

Culture is covered in the culture section below, competition and competencies under skills development, compensation under wage rates and communications and collaboration in the skills and the talent development sections.

The basic message from Joynt and Morton is that successful global HRM ensures that the policies adopted meet the cultural needs of the employees in each area, provide the organization with competitive advantage (something that the management guru, Michael Porter (1980) has always considered vital for organizational success). Employees also need the necessary skills, competencies, development opportunities and career paths plus decent wages.

Recruitment issues

Setting up in a new area poses recruitment problems. It may well be that the local government agencies are only too willing to assist in the recruitment process.

The alternative is to employ a local agency. When going global it may well be that the skills required are not present but that the potential to acquire them is. Recruiters should look for those not only with the skills but also those with the potential and aptitude to acquire skills quickly.

National and organizational norms

One area of potential conflict that may occur is when organizational norms and practices conflict with national ones. Government policies take precedence in that government's jurisdiction. If the organization cannot live with any restrictions then it must either not move into the area, withdraw or lobby through legitimate means. Circumventing the law through illegal means is nearly always found out.

In the US the constitution and the courts do not intervene greatly in commercial matters except where there is fraud. Other countries are highly regulated. Organizations need to ensure they know what the regulations, rules and practices are before entering an area. A careful study needs to be undertaken to ensure that organizational values will not be compromised by national norms.

The need for cultural sensitivity

Culture can be defined as the 'way we do things around here' and differs from place to place across the globe, between ethnic groups and between organizations.

Unfortunately people often equate cultural differences with one culture being 'better or worse' than another. Nothing could be further from the truth or likely to cause problems. Cultural norms are just different. Expressions such as better or worse are purely subjective. Nevertheless, within the ambit of respecting culture we also need to remain true to ourselves. An organization working in a culture that treats women badly should not shrug its metaphorical shoulders and go with the norm. It should try to accomplish change but do so sensitively.

Think/Discussion point: If you were a manager working in a culture that considered women as second class citizens how would you try to influence your staff that this is in fact counterproductive?

You might well point out sensitively that women are just as productive as men and highlight the achievements of women in other cultures. Groups often receive second-class treatment because they are perceived as a threat. As a manager you will need to show your male employees that equality does not have to be threatening.

It would be a foolish organization that did not take account of the culture in which it was planning to operate. In respect of this material different cultures have different attitudes to employment and career progression and these will have implications for both the development and especially the implementation of an

HRM strategy. The cultural differences that need to be taken into account include:

- **What form of hierarchies does the culture encourage?** In a particular culture it may be necessary to train or even promote a person higher up in the hierarchy before somebody lower down not because that person needs the training or development first but because of his or her position. In a culture that is hierarchical a strategy that offers equal opportunities to all employees may need to be adapted initially and explained carefully to those further up the hierarchy first. While this may well go against equal opportunities policies it may be necessary in the short term. It will be important that senior staff in the new culture buy in to the HRM strategy, something they may resist if their position appears, to them, to be threatened.
- **Attitudes to gender.** Promotions, training and development, job enrichment etc. should be provided in line with an organization's equal opportunities policies. In cases where the culture does not usually provide equal opportunities the organization should be sensitive in the way that it explains why it intends to insist on equal opportunities being applied to all aspects of its operation.
- **Attitudes to age and experience.** There may well be issues not only of the order in which employees are offered promotion or training and development opportunities but also the age and experience of their managers and supervisors. For example many US and European organizations provide job rotation/enrichment opportunities and management development programmes to junior staff who show management potential. There are areas of the world where this would normally be unacceptable given the way hierarchies are arranged in those areas. There are still places where position depends on age rather than ability although this is a practice that is declining. Sensitivity is required especially in convincing senior staff that providing such opportunities to their juniors should not be considered a threat to the senior person's position.
- **Attitudes to the education process.** If employees have been used to an education process that is formal and examination/test based they do not consider more informal training and development programmes to carry much credibility. The organization also needs to do a comparative exercise to achieve compatibility between qualifications across its global network. Even within a single country such as the US or the UK not all university degrees carry the same esteem.

It is not difficult to discover the cultural norms of an area and it is nearly always worth taking the time to do so. HR strategies that can be related to the culture of an area are always going to have a better chance of succeeding than generic ones imposed from corporate headquarters without much thought being given to the cultural differences the organization may find as it expands globally.

The importance of national laws relating to employment

Employment law in the UK and the rest of the EU is very different to that in the US. The UK has minimum wage rates and strict legislation on employment contracts and unfair dismissal. These rules are far less strict in the US but that country has tougher age discrimination legislation (although announcements in the summer of 2003 suggest that the UK will follow suit). Both countries have anti-discrimination legislation in place in respect of race and gender.

The fact that an organization has a standard contract of employment does not mean that it can use it in all areas. It will have to comply with the legislation in the jurisdiction within which it is working. This does not apply to foreign nationals paid elsewhere. There have been cases of foreign domestic staff employed by foreigners being treated very badly in the UK as the issue of their employment has been a grey area especially in respect of diplomats. If a person is not paid in a particular jurisdiction then the employment legislation of that jurisdiction may not apply. There are also tax issues in respect of these matters. Where one is paid and in what currency may determine employment status.

The issue of wage rates

The cheapest staff to employ are slaves. Slavery, thankfully, is now illegal although it still exists in certain parts of the world in either illegal or 'bound servant' forms. Slavery is not only inhuman but also inefficient. One may be able to frighten somebody to do something to an acceptable standard. But unless people are nurtured both physically (with food, shelter etc.) and emotionally (through financial and praise rewards) they will never go the extra mile. No slave ever gave more than necessary to avoid a beating and receive a meal.

Multinational companies often come in for criticism for paying different wage rates for the same job depending on the area it is carried out. Is this really unfair?

Think/Discussion point: If a loaf of bread costs 50p in the UK and 10p in another area with other goods priced pro rata, should workers in both areas be paid at the same level?

There is a difference between equality and equity. Equality means that all people would be paid the same for the same work in every part of the globe the organization works in. Equity means that they would be paid wages that allowed them the same buying power etc.

Paying above the local rate to a slight degree may well aid recruitment but rates that are too high may lead to distortions in the local economy. Local authorities and government publish information about wage rates and these are readily available. Multinationals should not use their dominant position to influence local rates. If they push the rates too high then other, smaller local companies may be unable to retain staff and be competitive. Rates that are too low lead to the problems of the government having to subsidize workers as mentioned earlier in this book.

Compensation in HR terms refers not only to salaries but also to other benefits. Training and development (see later), whether it leads to increased pay levels or not, has to benefit both the organization and the individual and may form part of the total remuneration package. Child care, housing and transport may also need to be considered. If the area the company is moving into lacks these facilities then they can be provided as part of the compensation package. It may also be possible to allow the wider community access – this gains good publicity and good publicity is free advertising. In the nineteenth century it was not unusual for companies (Lever Brothers were a well-known example) to build their own communities complete with schools, clinics and entertainment facilities. This is a role that was later taken over by government agencies to a large extent. There may well be a need for organizations expanding globally on a large scale to consider the benefits of such an approach especially if moving into a less-developed area.

> **Think/Discussion point**: Should companies be required to provide infrastructure improvements for the wider community?

In the UK more and more planning applications are requiring companies to provide roads and in the case of housing developments, schools, shops and health centres.

The importance of both skills and other forms of training

One of the reasons for a company moving into a new area in addition to gaining new markets or financial inducements relates to the skills base available. India has attracted a number of new companies due to the high quality of its education. Renowned universities attract new business into their environs. Cambridge in the UK has become a 'Mecca' for high-technology companies due to the high international reputation of its research work.

It may be necessary to set up a company training scheme prior to the operation beginning. This is what Tom Peters (1987) reports that Nissan did in Smyrna, Tennessee. The company spent $63 million (including a $7 million state grant) training 2000 workers. That equates to well over £30,000 per worker. As Peters reports it not only gave Nissan an opportunity to cut down on learning curve errors (these can be very costly) but also acted as an important motivational factor as it stressed the company's policy of investing in its work force. Spending that amount of money shows commitment to the future and that the company sees its workers as an investment.

A company that moves into an area and is unwillingly to invest in its work force should be viewed with suspicion. Either it does not care about quality or perhaps it does not plan a permanent presence.

Skills

A skill is the ability to do something in a satisfactory or more than satisfactory manner. Competencies are an agreed set of standards that detail tasks a person should be able to undertake, the range of situations to which they apply and the knowledge and understanding that relates to them. They provide a means of measuring skills. Core competencies are those skills that represent the fundamental expertise within the organization.

A skills gap is the gap between the skills a person has and the skills that he or she needs to carry out a task. When an organization considers moving into an area as Nissan did in Smyrna it may discover that the necessary skills are not available. By carrying out a training needs analysis (TNA) – a systematic review of the current skills base against organizational requirements – it is possible to measure the size of the skills gap.

Training

Training is concerned with ensuring that a person knows, understands and can carry out the specific instructions concerned with the mastering of a particular task or set of tasks.

The training and development strategy of the organization indicates the direction and scope of the training and development opportunities developed and provided by the organization for its employees and other concerned partners. Ideally this matches the training and development provided to both the needs of the organization and the individual in order to ensure that the organization can respond to changes in its external environment. The policies and procedures generated by such a policy need to be flexible enough to ensure that adequate training can be provided wherever the company decides to operate. Even opening new retail outlets will bring with it the need for product training for sales staff. It may also be necessary to provide training for those agents, retailers, franchisees, service agents etc. who are not part of the organization but have a direct link with customers. It is no use introducing a new vehicle to the Indian market unless there are trained mechanics able to carry out repairs etc.

Training can then be provided either by the company itself using formal courses and coaching or in collaboration with outside institutions. Coaching – the process in which a more experienced person works on a one-to-one basis with a less experienced one to improve the latter's performance – is a useful way of introducing staff from more established parts of the organization. Provided there are no language problems they can be brought in on a short-term basis to act as coaches and mentors. This not only passes on skills but also helps integrate the new operation into that of the corporate body. Not only can coaches and mentors pass on skills but they can also aid the passing on of corporate values and norms.

In terms of cost–benefit analysis – the standard business decision-making tool used to investigate the desirability of an activity or project by comparing the costs likely to be incurred with the benefits that will accrue using a financial basis – properly designed and delivered training is an investment not a cost; it pays for itself and then some.

Competencies – implications for training and development

All of the staff of an organization regardless of where they are based need to be able to demonstrate the core competencies that the organization has deemed essential.

One of the first steps an organization should take when moving into a new region is to put in place training and development based on the core competencies.

Organizations often find it useful to link training and development in core competencies with work on the organizational culture and aims as part of an induction package to the employees in the new area. The sooner these staff members 'buy in' to the organization's values, the sooner the new operation will begin to make an effective contribution to the organization's operations.

E-learning – the delivery of learning packages using linked computers – has simplified the training process in many ways as packages can be put together and even linked to corporate HQ. While there may still need to be actual on-the-job training it may well be that there are areas where e-training (procedures, form filling, simulations etc.) can be highly beneficial and cost effective.

Communications

As covered above a training and development strategy can often include components that not only develop the individual but also aid communication and networking across the organization. Bringing people together for training and development allows them to build and increase their network.

Employee development

Development is a process in which learning occurs through experience and where the results of the learning enhance not only the task skills of the individual but also his or her attitudes. Development is linked more to education (the broadening of the knowledge and skills base of the individual and indeed the group with the objective of the individual functioning in and being a benefit to the society he or she lives in – not normally an organizational responsibility) and empowerment (the process of releasing the full potential of employees in order for them to take on greater responsibility and authority in the decision-making process and providing the resources for this process to occur – definitely an organizational responsibility).

Training and development does not exist in a vacuum but that it should be tied to organizational strategies. Organizations train and develop their employees so that the organization can gain competitive advantage over others working in the same field.

Training should be challenging and involve the individual in gaining an overall view of the organization. Development does not need to consist purely of organized courses: job rotation, visits to other plants, a stint at corporate HQ, working with suppliers etc. all form part of a development programme. The aim is to gain a more rounded employee who is able to contribute above and beyond mere skills but can aid decision-making and help grow the organization.

For those in developing countries where educational opportunities might be scarce but aspirations high, the use of development programmes can be a powerful motivator as both the organization and the employee gain from the experience to a high degree. Development programmes also provide an excellent retention incentive. It always costs more to acquire a new employee than to retain an existing one.

An employee who sees that there is investment in his or her development will see the benefit of staying with the organization.

> **Think/Discussion point**: Is training and development a cost or an investment?

Competitors

An understanding of the competition and how competitors are training and developing their people is vital for the drawing up of a training and development strategy. In cases where an organization is moving into a new geographic area it is useful to consider how more established players in the market deal with training and development and what skills they believe are necessary at the present and will be necessary in the future.

The wider community

The individual needs to see the personal benefit he or she will receive from the training and development. If organizations move into less developed economies, the benefits staff can receive from training and development opportunities can stretch beyond the organization and into their wider lives. In areas where further and higher education opportunities are limited, the benefits to the organization of having an effective training and development strategy can include the attraction of high quality staff. These people may well be motivated by the opportunity to access training and development as well as for the monetary compensation in the form of wages.

Careers – implications for training and development

Training and development should form a part of an individual's strategy for his or her career progression. While new blood is always to be welcomed in an organization it needs to be balanced by those employees who have progressed from within the organization. Growing, especially globally, provides a flow of new people into the organization. The latter will have a clear understanding of the organizational culture while the former bring fresh ideas and thinking. A balance between 'picking your own' and 'growing your own' is always to be desired.

Organizations moving into new areas will wish to engender employee loyalty and this can be assisted by a training and development strategy that presents the employee with a career development path within the organization.

Collaboration

Throughout the world there are colleges, universities and training providers that know and understand the local conditions. In the first instance an incoming organization can form productive partnerships with training and development providers. The organization can benefit from their local knowledge and local providers are likely to have more credibility with the new employees.

A further form of collaboration involves collaborative training and development activities conducted with both the organization's staff and staff from key suppliers and even customers. The need to have service agents etc. trained has already been mentioned. Training and development often provides opportunities for staff from suppliers and customers to work with the organization's staff in a relationship that is based on communal learning rather than commercial issues.

The arrival of an organization into an area may well be regarded with suspicion. However, if the organization shows that it will provide not only direct economic benefits to the area but will also increase the training, development and career prospects for local inhabitants then it is more likely to be welcomed. This benefit to the organization highlights the importance of the training and development strategy and its role within the overall expansion strategy of the organization.

The need to develop talent and potential across a global enterprise

Talent is something the vast majority of managers claim they are looking for when appointing staff but often having found a talented person, that same majority of managers fail to manage the talent in a manner that is both beneficial to the organization and to the talented person his or herself.

Talent can be described as 'ability – a natural ability to do something well'. The word can also mean ancient money from the Latin *talentum* – connected to the idea of desiring things.

To be realized talent also needs supporting roles and an audience. As the author has written elsewhere (Cartwright, 2003), a hermit may possess great skill and aptitude but without other people around him or her, the only talent that can be displayed is that of living and managing on one's own. This is undoubtedly a talent of sorts but as humankind is a social animal it is a talent that is only useful in certain extreme cases.

Bruce Tulgan (1996) has written of the issues involved in managing the disenfranchised underachievers dubbed 'Generation X' who succeeded the post-war 'Baby Boomers' who dominated the workplace of the 1980s and 1990s. While mainly a developed-world phenomenon they are increasingly to be found in other areas. Generation X has had the advantages of greater educational opportunities than their predecessors and are much more likely to negotiate their work tasks, conditions and remuneration than those who have gone before them. They are not more talented than their predecessors but they have far more opportunities to display their talents.

Tulgan argues that the talents of Generation X and their willingness to challenge orthodox employment practices are leading to a revolution in such practices – a revolution that is talent driven.

As has already been covered in this chapter anybody recruiting globally or expanding into new areas of the world needs to recognize that different parts of the world may well have different attitudes and value systems.

Gender, social structure and disability can often be the most pertinent in restricting the opportunity for talent to be displayed.

It may be very difficult for a manager from the US or Europe to appreciate the different social structures operating in a very diverse country such as India where the caste system still exists and may have implications for organizational hierarchies.

In many parts of India organizations operate on a purely Western model but it is still possible to find more remote areas where other social systems are prevalent. In these areas talent may not have had an opportunity to be displayed. It is not that there are no talented people of a lower caste rather that the system does not facilitate them in displaying their talents. Once they are given opportunities there are just as many talented people as in any other group.

The issue of gender and the place of women can be very problematic for managers in certain areas. The glass ceiling can and does inhibit talent. This is a personal issue for the female in question but also a loss to the organization. It is amazing that there are still organizations that assume that only men can do certain jobs. Such organizations do their staff and their shareholders a grave disservice in under utilizing the talent they have. Luckily there is now much sex-discrimination legislation but it should not be necessary. No organization should set out to restrict its access to talent. There are still parts of the world where women are banned from work and even driving. While such areas are declining in number they still exist and may present a cultural dilemma for a manager from the West or a Western organization imbued with concepts of equality.

Think/Discussion point: Have you either experienced or seen the glass ceiling in operation?

Similar attitudes may exist in respect of race and disability. There are societies that may not provide opportunities to those with a disability or of a certain race despite the wealth of potential talent and ability.

Talent as an investment

It was only towards the end of the nineteenth century that universal education came to be accepted in both Western Europe and North America. Prior to the industrial revolution and the need for technically educated employees, education was the preserve of a small minority of society. Education for the masses was discouraged as it was believed that it might lead to revolution. While much of the world now has universal education at least at a primary (elementary level) there are still places where the use of child labour (as discussed in chapter 4) means that education does not reach all of the society and thus much talent remains undiscovered.

One of the main issues that Bruce Tulgan (1996) has confronted has been the balance between the relative power of the talented employee and the organization. He has argued that as workforces become better educated and talent provided with increased opportunities to be realized so the talented individual has gained greater power over the organization. Whereas at one time the majority of workers were put in fear of dismissal, in the more 'talent-rich' environment of the twenty-first century it is the organization that has the fear of its talented workers leaving for better conditions etc. This has implications for how organizations should invest in individuals who may well leave. The concept of a lifetime of employment with one organization is disappearing fast throughout the world even in Japan where it was the norm for many male Japanese workers. In such a situation investment in individuals made sense but does it still make sense when the individual may leave? Tulgan believes that it does although the onus is now on the organization to capitalize on the talent within its workforce with greater urgency. The change in the balance of power also affects the way employees can negotiate their conditions of employment.

Using a global diversity of talent

As an organization expands globally it needs to consider how it will:

- Recognize talent
- Recruit talent
- Develop talent
- Channel talent.

Talent is an attribute that needs direction if it is to be used constructively and effectively. The increase in an organization's talent base coupled with properly constructed development programmes can provide organizations with considerable competitive advantage.

Implications for small businesses

The first implication for small businesses is that talent and skills should not be ignored just because of the nationality, gender, race, disability etc. of the applicant. It is skills, potential and ability that are being recruited not a particular type of person.

When moving into a more global environment even if it is only with a product rather than a full operation it is important to ensure that a full service infrastructure is in place. This may well entail product training for local agents.

Small businesses can also rotate job assignments to ensure that all staff are aware of the full range of business activities and what the contribution of individual efforts make to the overall business.

Kodak

Kodak is a name recognized across the globe and is almost synonymous with both the movie industry and still and cine photography. George Eastman, the founder of Kodak, was born 1854 in upstate New York. Leaving school at 14, Eastman had little grounding in science and technology.

The 1860s saw a considerable growth in what was then the new art (and science) of photography in part due to a desire of the soldiers fighting the US Civil War to provide a photographic image for their loved ones and carry an image of their families into battle.

In 1884 Eastman patented the first film in roll form (the derivatives of which are still in use today) to prove practicable. In 1888 he perfected the Kodak camera, the first camera designed specifically for roll film. It is believed that he just made up the name Kodak as a suitable and scientific sounding brand name. In 1892 he established the Eastman Kodak Company, at Rochester, New York, one of the first firms to mass-produce standardized photography equipment. This company also manufactured the flexible transparent film, devised by Eastman in 1889, which proved vital to the subsequent development of the motion picture industry; an industry that was to grow in leaps and bounds in the early years of the twentieth century. Eastman was associated with the company in an administrative and executive capacity until his death in 1932. Eastman was one of the outstanding philanthropists of his time, donating more than US$75 million to various projects.

As a global company Kodak is known for its large investment in its human resource. The investment in its people is seen as an integral part of the company's strategy of remaining in the forefront of the photographic and allied industries.

Kodak operates a huge range of development programmes and training opportunities. In addition to programmes for existing staff, Kodak also provides internships for students at colleges and universities. These internships generally last for 10 weeks and are available to those registered on relevant degree programmes from bachelor degrees to doctorates.

A core value stated by Kodak is the respect, integrity and opportunities provided for personal development within the organization. Each employee at Kodak works with his or her supervisor or manager to develop an Employee Development Plan (EDP). The EDP is designed to assist the employee in meeting personal goals within the context of the business needs of Kodak.

The company also operates Kodak Rotational Programs on a global basis. These are available for engineers, image scientists, software researchers and development and production staff.

The programmes are intended to:

- broaden the individual's understanding of Kodak's business opportunities
- establish a personal network of resources to support the individual's career
- enhance the individual's social and leadership skills.

and consist of a personalized employee development plan, job assignments, events and classes.

Personalized employee development plan

This individualized plan is intended to assist the individual to develop the skills and competencies necessary to succeed in global manufacturing at Kodak, including core and specialized training based on individual areas of interest and specific work-related assignments. Core training includes:

- A general Kodak orientation
- Manufacturing process overview through tours and training
- Quality, reliability and lean manufacturing (important Kodak values)

- Education on Kodak processes
- People and leadership skills.

Job assignments

A series of job assignments enables the individual to develop and apply the skills necessary for effective technical contributions and manufacturing leadership. Each assignment is in a different technology or business so that all participants experience diverse global manufacturing opportunities. Assignments increase in complexity, opportunity, responsibility and account-ability over time. Participants select assignments with advice and support from mentors and the individual's managers within the organization.

Events and classes

Formal training is provided using specific events and classes. These form an integral part of the programme.

Networks

Another vital component of the Kodak training and development strategy is the formation of a series of global employee networks. These networks include the 'Empower Network' designed to assist employees with disabilities enhance their skills, knowledge and abilities and the 'Asia Pacific Exchange (APEX)' to aid recruitment and retention of Asian and Pacific Islands employees.

The whole philosophy of training and development at Kodak is based on mutual benefits for both the company and the individual. The rotation concept not only provides development opportunities for the individual participants but also invigorates the organization as the individuals bring their increasing experience and expertise to different areas of the corporate operation.

Kodak maintains close links with colleges and universities (following the tradition set by George Eastman). By doing so the company is able to tap into the knowledge and expertise in the universities and provide additional educational opportunities for Kodak employees.

In all of the training and development offered at Kodak it is possible to trace a direct link with the overall strategy of the company and its desire to be at the cutting edge of technology. Such a vision needs a heavy investment in people as well as machinery and research.

CASE STUDY QUESTIONS

1 Kodak makes a point of stressing the mutual benefits of its training policy – how do both parties in the process benefit?
2 What are the advantages of job assignments in development programmes?
3 How can Kodak benefit from internships where the intern does not pursue a career with the company?

Summary and key learning points

- Multinational organizations need a global HR policy nested within and contributing to the overall corporate strategy.
- Recruitment may need the assistance of local agents.
- Sensitivity needed towards human relations when undertaking globalization.
- The importance of national laws relating to employment cannot be understated – they must be followed.
- There is an issue of paying different wage rates in different areas – equity rather than equality.
- Skill and other forms of training need to be provided not only for new staff but also for agents, retailers etc.
- The need to develop talent and potential across a global enterprise gives the organization a much larger talent base.
- Development programmes also motivate and help retain staff.
- No potential talent should be ignored for reasons of race, gender or disability.

QUESTIONS

1 In what ways should companies expanding globally show cultural sensitivity?
2 'Development is about more than just skills' – discuss this statement.
3 Why do multinational organizations need a global HR strategy?
4 How can global HR issues aid small businesses?

Recommended further reading

Managing across cultural differences is covered in:

Harris P R and Moran R T (2000) *Managing Cultural Differences.* Houston: Gulf.

Lewis R D (1999) *Cross Cultural Communications – A visual Approach.* London: Transcreen.

Lewis R D (2000) *When Cultures Collide.* London: Nicholas Brealey.

Trompenaars F (1993) *Riding the Waves of Culture.* London: Economist Books.

Trompenaars F and Hampden-Turner C (2000) *Building Cross Cultural Competence.* London: Nicolas Brealey.

Tulgan B (1996) *Managing Generation X.* Oxford: Capstone.

Tulgan B (2001) *Winning the Talent Wars.* Naperville, IL: Nicholas Brealey.

Bruce Tulgan has written about Generation X and managing talent in:

Tulgan B (1996) *Managing Generation X.* Oxford: Capstone.

Tulgan B (2001) *Winning the Talent Wars.* Naperville, IL: Nicholas Brealey.

Further information about general global HR strategies can be found in:

Harris P R, Moran R T and Stripp W G (1998) *Developing the Global Organization – Strategies for Human Resource Professionals.* Houston: Gulf.

Joynt P and Morton R (eds) (1999) *The Global HR Manager.* London: Chartered Institute of Personnel and Development.

⊻ 7 Finance and globalization

Learning outcomes

By the end of this chapter you should understand:

- What FDI is
- Why it is important
- How FDI is attracted
- The consequences of government control
- The effects of tax, interest and exchange rates on FDI
- The importance of stable regimes when attracting FDI

It is said that 'money makes the world go around'. Whether this is true or not it is certainly a fact that the free movement of capital around the world is what drives globalization.

This short chapter seeks to look at some of the actors that influence companies to invest in global operations. For details on FDI statistics the reader is encouraged to consult national web sites and *The Global City* (2001) by Saskia Sassen. This chapter does not pretend to be a treaty on global finance.

Huge sums of money move around the globe every second. It is not dollar bills, sterling or euro notes that move but electrons. Money moves electronically in huge amounts.

Think/Discussion point: Does anybody know how much money there is in the world?

More and more companies are seeking to invest and set up operations in areas where the financial regime is liberal and allows them to maximize profits and shareholder value as was shown in chapter 4. There are those who believe that this is at the expense of workers' rights and welfare.

Foreign direct investment (FDI)

One of the main drivers of globalization has been foreign direct investment (FDI). FDI is defined by the IMF in terms of an investment that is made in order to acquire a lasting interest in an operation that is in an economy other than the investors. The IMF further notes that the investor has a wish to become involved in the running of the operation in which the investment is made. FDI is about operation rather than investment purely for dividend payments.

Foreign Direct Investment (FDI) has surpassed a trillion dollars by 2003.

Think/Discussion point: Can you imagine one trillion dollars?

Cross-border mergers and acquisitions, including the purchase by foreign investors of previously nationalized state-owned enterprises, are providing ever higher volumes of direct foreign investment.

Not all multinationals prove competent at turning around previously state-run enterprises. In July 2003, Connex South Eastern lost its franchise to run a part of the old British Rail network due to poor service.

FDI is forming a global marketplace for companies as much as for products. Companies are being bought and sold across borders on a large scale. FDI by companies is the largest source of external finance for much of the developing world having replaced bank loans. The case study on Carnival/P&O in chapter 5 showed examples of US FDI in Italy (Carnival acquiring Costa) and UK FDI in the US (P&O's purchase of Princess Cruises).

Governments in both the developed and the developing world recognize the importance of attracting FDI.

Think/Discussion point:What advantages do governments gain from FDI?

FDI to developing countries rose in 2000 to $208 billion (from $179 billion in 1998), while FDI flows into developed countries (the US, UK, Germany etc.) climbed to $636 billion (from $481 billion in 1998).

What was interesting in 2000 was that FDI outflows from developing countries last year almost doubled, to $66 billion. This indicates these countries' desire to access markets in the developed world. It somewhat negates the arguments of the anti-globalizationists that globalization is a way for the developed world to exploit the poor when companies from the developing world are investing in richer countries in order to access more sophisticated markets.

The selling of foreign affiliates by transnational corporations (TNCs) in 1999 increased from $3 to $14 trillion between 1998 and 1999, according to the UN. There is a huge trade not just in products but in actual companies themselves.

The privatization of many Latin American services that used to be government controlled including electricity services in El Salvador, Guatemala and the Dominican Republic; telecommunications providers in El Salvador and Guatemala; and airport concessions in Costa Rica and the Dominican Republic has proved a golden opportunity for FDI just as it did when the UK followed the same path in the

1980s. As far as FDI into South America is concerned, it has been large North American and European companies that have invested the largest amounts.

In 1999 record levels of FDI poured into Brazil, Argentina, Chile and Bolivia driven by the long-term growth prospects and major privatization.

In contrast, FDI flows to Central and Eastern Europe and to Africa have remained relatively modest perhaps due to worries about return on capital and political/social instability. It will be interesting to see how much more Latvia, Poland and Hungary attract after their accession to the EU.

Why is a rise in foreign direct investment around the world important?

In order to compete businesses are having to spread their investments all over the globe to access markets, technology and talent. The increase in FDI is a clear indicator of the trend towards globalization. FDI includes corporate activities such as businesses building plants or subsidiaries in foreign countries, and buying controlling stakes or shares in foreign companies. It does not include short-term capital flows, such as the portfolio investments of 'emerging market' mutual funds where the investment is for shorter term gain.

Foreign direct investment has been on the rise around the world since the 1900s, as was shown in chapter 1 when considering J P Morgan. It is its scale that has increased dramatically over the last decade or so. The US, as the world's largest economy, sees far greater FDI activity than the other major industrialized economies in sheer dollar terms – not just US firms investing in other countries but also considerable investment by foreign companies into the US. Britain is the largest foreign direct investor in the US.

Think/Discussion point: Why might a developed country such as the US attract FDI? (clue – size and NAFTA)

The UN Conferences on Finance for Development have argued that private (individuals and corporations rather than governments) international capital flows, particularly FDI, along with international financial stability, are vital complements to national and international development efforts. Others have also emphasized the importance of private sector investment for development, both domestic and foreign.

FDI and poverty

A key issue is whether FDI can contribute to the objective of reducing poverty. This will depend on how the gains from FDI are distributed, among sectors, workers and households. As discussed in chapter 4, if the only benefits of globalization are to shareholders and not to employees than the issue appears fraught with social and political dangers. Evidence on the effects of FDI on income distribution and poverty in developing countries is lacking. In principle, there is, unfortunately, no direct link between FDI and poverty reduction.

There are three possible indirect links:

- If FDI contributes to export growth, productivity growth and finance for the balance of payments, it supports increases in national income that offer the potential to benefit the poor.
- If FDI increases employment it may help some to moveout of poverty. Well-developed linkages with local suppliers may increase employment of various skill groups.
- Foreign firms may pay higher wages than local firms for workers with similar qualifications (see chapter 6). This can, of course, impact on other local firms who may not be able to afford the higher local rates without becoming uncompetitive.

The poorest countries, such as those in Africa (that receive a very small proportion of FDI), appear the least able to derive growth benefits. It is a false assumption that FDI will contribute to poverty reduction through fostering growth in poor developing countries.

If the foreign investment represents additional investment in a country then it should provide increased employment in that country. This benefits workers and the economy in general thus, in theory benefiting the whole population.

However, as increasing amounts of FDI are for mergers and acquisitions, such as buying privatized firms, this may not necessarily increase employment. If foreign firms are more capital rather than labour intensive, employment levels will actually fall even if the income of those still in employment rises. The actual decrease in employment caused will place a strain on the government's welfare agencies.

However, if an incoming foreign firm has used FDI to improve the efficiency of a local business, that business may be so competitive as to drive out the competition and employment in both the sector and the wider economy. Unfortunately there is little evidence of the total employment effects of FDI, partly because such effects depend on the country, sector and time framework.

Think/Discussion point: Are there steps a government can take to ensure that FDI leads to relatively permanent jobs and prosperity? What might be the implications of taking such steps? (clue – FDI loves deregulation)

Attracting FDI

No country appears immune to the lure of FDI. Britain has made a great point of stressing that the restrictions and taxes on companies undertaking FDI are better than in other parts of the EU. Tax breaks, EPZs etc. were discussed in chapter 4. In the UK the corporate tax rate used to be 52 per cent, now it is 30 per cent – a powerful incentive to invest in the country.

Ellwood (2001) makes the point that governments should be discerning in the FDI they accept, going for quality rather than quantity. Long-term FDI that leads to a higher skill base and relatively permanent jobs may be better than a larger amount of shorter term FDI that provides little if no lasting benefits.

Portfolio direct investment

Companies are not the only possible investors in foreign operations. It is also possible that individuals will want to invest in such undertakings. This is often less easy to do as many countries have strict regulations about the amount of investment a non-national can make in either an individual enterprise or a particular sector. Governments have, as an example tended to regulate the amount of control individuals can have over media concerns.

While very wealthy individuals may acquire a portfolio of small holdings in foreign concerns, those with less personal wealth may well choose to invest their money in share (stock) portfolios based on foreign holdings. Most of the world's investment houses have FDI portfolios where the investor can, for example acquire a North American or an Asian portfolio. The investment house will work within the particular region to put together a portfolio that is designed to provide maximum growth for its clients.

Capital

Capital is not money as such but the collective term for a body of goods and monies from which future income can be derived. Generally, consumer goods and monies spent for present needs and personal enjoyment are not included in the definition of capital as they are not investments. Thus, a business regards its land, buildings, equipment, inventory and raw materials, as well as stocks, bonds and bank balances available, as capital.

In accountancy, capital is defined as the stock of property owned by an individual or corporation at a given time, as distinguished from the income derived from that property during a given period. A business firm accordingly has a capital account (frequently called a balance sheet), which reports the assets of the firm at a specified time, and an income account, which reckons the flow of goods and of claims against goods during a specified period.

The forms of capital can be distinguished in various ways. One common distinction is between fixed and circulating capital. Fixed capital includes all the more or less durable means of production, such as land, buildings and machinery. Circulating capital refers to non-renewable goods, such as raw materials and fuel, and the funds required to pay wages and other claims against the enterprise.

Frequently, a business will categorize all of its assets that can be converted readily into cash, such as finished goods or stocks and bonds, as liquid capital (often referred to as liquid assets). By contrast, all assets that cannot be easily converted to cash, such as buildings and equipment, are considered frozen capital. This is as true in the domestic situation as it is in business. If you own your house it is an asset but if you need money quickly it is unlikely that a house sale will be the answer – it is not a liquid asset as its value cannot be realized quickly. It is possible to borrow against it.

Another important distinction is between productive capital and financial capital. Machines, raw materials and other physical goods constitute productive capital. Claims against these goods, such as corporate securities and accounts receivable, are financial capital. Liquidation of productive capital reduces productive capacity, but liquidation of financial capital merely changes the distribution of income.

Medieval economies engaged almost wholly in subsistence agriculture and were essentially non-capitalist. It was not until trade began to revive in the West during the time of the Crusades (commerce following hard on the heels of war – not an unusual occurrence) that capital became important. The revival was accelerated worldwide throughout the period of exploration and colonization that began late in the fifteenth century as discussed in chapter 1. Expanding trade fostered greater division of labour and mechanization of production and therefore a growth of capital. The flow of gold and silver from the New World facilitated the transfer and accumulation of capital, laying the groundwork for the industrial revolution. With the industrial revolution, production became increasingly dependent on the use of large amounts of capital. The role of capital in the economics of Western Europe and North America was so crucial that the socio-economic organization prevailing in these areas from the eighteenth century through the first half of the twentieth century became known as the capitalist system, or capitalism.

In the early stages of the evolution of capitalism, investments in plant and equipment were relatively small. As industry developed and grew, however, industrial, or fixed, capital – for example, capital frozen in cotton and steel mills, factories, railways and other industrial and transport facilities – became dominant. Late in the nineteenth and early in the twentieth centuries, financial capital in the form of claims to the ownership of capital goods of all sorts became increasingly important. By creating, acquiring and controlling such claims, financiers and bankers exercised great influence on production and distribution. After the Great Depression of the 1930s, financial control of most capitalist economies was superseded at least in part by state control. A large segment of the national income of the US, Great Britain and various other countries flows through government, which as the public sector exerts a great influence in regulating that flow, thereby determining the amounts and kinds of capital formed.

The argument of the anti-globalization lobby is that governments are losing control of the flow of capital through their economic systems and as such are giving power to the multinational corporations who control the capital.

Flow of capital

No individual or company will wish to invest money in a place where they cannot retrieve it. If governments wish to attract FDI then they need to ease any restrictions there are on the flow of capital in and out of their jurisdiction. The only restrictions should be those preventing money laundering and the proceeds of criminal activities leaving the country.

It is obviously better for any single economy that it sells as much as possible outside the economy or attracts net FDI so that money flows in rather than importing goods from outside, which then have to be paid for. The relationship between the level of imports and that of exports is known as the balance of payments. The imbalance is critical. Too many imports and too few exports and the economy will have trouble earning its way. The other way around can lead to actions against the economy and tariff wars. Following the Second World War and its immediate aftermath, Japan became a major exporter of vehicles and fast-moving consumer goods (televisions, hi-fi equipment etc.) while placing considerable barriers on imports often using quality standards as the mechanism. Japan's positive balance of trade led others to adopted strict controls on Japanese manufactured goods by introducing tariff barriers against them. In turn this led to Japanese FDI in the UK and US thus allowing them local, tariff-free access to Europe and North America.

As more and more governments have relaxed exchange controls especially to attract FDI, it has been easier to buy and sell foreign currencies. Fortunes have been made (and lost) in trading on the foreign exchange markets and in trying to anticipate movements of one currency against another. Companies will not want to invest (as stated above) in countries that restrict the ability of a company to move money in and out.

Companies also require as stable as possible exchange rates as they will not wish to lose money in currency transactions. This is one of the reasons given by a number of multinationals operating in the UK for the UK to join the euro (see chapter 4) – they would benefit.

Foreign exchange is a commodity like any other, and its price fluctuates in accordance with supply and demand: exchange rates are published daily in the principal newspapers of the world. When the exchange rate is floating, free of government intervention, the rate of exchange, or the price of the currency of one country in terms of that of another, will depend on overall supply and demand and on the relative purchasing power of the two currencies, that is, on the competitive position of the two countries in world markets. Gold and wealth tend to flow from countries that buy more than they sell abroad. At times, speculation in foreign exchange by dealers, brokers or others becomes a major influence on exchange rates. However, governments are often not prepared to allow their currencies to float freely. A leading example of an alternative to floating was the European Exchange Rate Mechanism (ERM) that existed until the 1990s (see chapter 3). Under this system individual governments pledged to keep their currencies within a specified 'band' around a central parity. Up to 1992 the system appeared to be working well with most currencies fluctuating within relatively tight bands of ±2.25 per cent. However, the concerted speculative attacks of currency speculators resulted in some countries leaving the ERM and others loosening their bands to ±15 per cent. These events raised doubts as to the ability of ERM members to keep their currencies in line, although ultimately they did nothing to delay the introduction of the single European currency (the euro) in January 2002. Countries now realize that defending a currency against speculative attack – in terms of lost foreign currency reserves – especially in liberalized international financial markets can be very expensive.

Government control

When the foreign exchange needs of a country exceed total receipts from abroad, and it has little gold and is unable to receive foreign credits, the exchange value of the currency of the country tends to decline. Under these conditions, the government has the alternative of allowing freedom of transactions in foreign exchange and permitting its currency to depreciate, or of abandoning free transfer of currency by the establishment of exchange control. The aim of such control is to limit the demand for and to increase the supply of foreign exchange in order to maintain a stable exchange rate. The UK used this mechanism in the 1960s and early 1970s. Such actions do little to attract FDI due to the restrictions placed upon the movement of capital in the form of money.

In addition to exchange rates another key indicator in attracting FDI relates to interest rates.

Interest rates

The repayment of loans to both individuals and organizations comprise (with the exception of certain strict Muslim economics where interest is against Islamic law) the repayment of the capital sum borrowed and an additional amount known as interest. Interest represents the earnings made by the lender and the payment for the tying up of the capital.

The minimum level of interest charged is normally that of the base rate of the relevant central bank. This rate is normally set by the central bank or the government as part of the control of monetary policy.

The higher the interest rate, the less individuals and organizations will wish to borrow and the more they will want to save. Thus money will effectively be taken out of the economy and tied up in savings. The higher the rate the less incentive there is for FDI as the company will have to pay a higher rate for any borrowing that is required. It is not surprising that there is always a wish to save at the highest possible interest rate and to borrow at the lowest. In order for banks and other financial institutions to make a profit it is self-evident that they must lend at a higher rate than they pay to savers. In effect banks take in money from savers on which they will pay interest and then lend it at a higher rate to somebody else, the bank receiving the difference.

Rates can vary according to circumstances. In general terms, the higher the risk of non repayment or the shorter the loan repayment period, the higher the interest that can be demanded. It costs far less, in interest rate terms, for a person to buy their house on a 25-year mortgage than it would to borrow the same amount over a series of shorter time periods. Even if repayment is not made, the fact that the collateral for the mortgage is the house itself, this can always be repossessed by the mortgage lender and sold to repay the capital. If a country wishes to encourage a company in it may arrange loans at very advantageous rate on the premise that the increase in employment and subsequent tax revenue will make up the difference.

Tax

Companies are usually taxed on profits and locally on buildings etc. In order to encourage FDI many governments and local authorities offer tax breaks to companies as an inducement to invest. As discussed in chapter 4, this may bring a company into an area but the advantages will only be seen if profits are such as to attract enough tax and if wages are high enough to contribute to the tax revenue of the government. If they are not then the government may be losing out as it pays more in welfare than it raises in tax despite having attracted investment. Corporations want to pay as little tax as possible and thus are likely to move to areas where such inducements are made. Whether it is possible to ensure that the inducements remain in place in the long term is problematic.

Tariffs

Despite the WTO's wish for a removal of tariffs, they are still with us. A country in a customs union can offer a powerful inducement to FDI as it allows the company access to other members of the union free of tariff barriers. This accounts for the FDI of Japanese car manufacturers into the UK as it allowed them to overcome EU tariff barriers against foreign imports. In a similar manner, many of them also set up in the US where they now benefit from being manufacturers in a NAFTA member.

Stability

Above all, FDI requires stability. The more stable a regime is, the more likely it is to attract FDI. There is no point investing heavily following inducements if a revolution is going to change the conditions offered. Stability is a precursor to high levels of FDI just as it is to decreasing levels of poverty.

Implications for small businesses

While it is unlikely that small businesses will be conducting major FDI it is still necessary to know if FDI is planned for an area. A major inflow of investment can lead to opportunities for smaller organizations to partner with the newcomer. Building projects always need subcontractors etc. There are many ways such as this that small operations can be beneficiaries of FDI. The issue of incoming organizations paying higher wages has already been discussed in chapter 4.

Canon

The name of the Japanese electronics company, Canon, is known throughout the world for a range of cameras, photocopiers, printers etc.

The corporate philosophy of Canon is *kyosei* meaning living and working together for the common good.

Canon began operations as the Precision Optical Instrument Laboratory in 1933, adopting the Canon trademark in 1934. The name was changed to the Canon Camera Co in 1947 and again to Canon Inc in 1969.

The company believes in developing *kyosei* not just in Japan but also in the countries where its products are sold. Canon believes it should establish good relations, not only with its customers and the communities in which they operate, but also with nations, the environment and the natural world. This has important implications for its investment strategy. This involves considering the level of environmental management and to undertake environmental activities to contribute to the society. In order to achieve this Canon has embarked upon a programme to raise the awareness of all employees regarding the importance of the environment and to encourage them to take the necessary environmental measures at the workplace and at home. In Japanese culture there are not the clear distinctions between work and home prevalent in the West. This is an example of green concerns in action.

Canon's global business development is aimed at the technology increasingly in use in homes, offices and industries throughout the world. The company has a global diversification strategy establishing a "Three Regional Headquarters System", based on the Americas, Europe and Japan + Asia. Canon Group consolidated net sales were approximately ¥ (yen) 2940.1 billion (US$24,501 million) in 2002, of which about 75 per cent was generated outside of Japan.

Canon undertakes production plus research and development across the globe using FDI to establish production and research facilities. Some examples are provided below.

In North America, Canon U.S.A., Inc., the Group's headquarters in the Americas conducts research and development functions while integrating regional operations from development to production. Canon Development Americas, Inc. is responsible for a wide range of activities and is developing leading-edge technologies and products. Another Group operation is Canon Virginia, Inc., which has a production system enabling quick and flexible responses to local market needs. Note that all of these operations are within NAFTA so that the products are in fact local. Canon had over 10,000 employees in the region in 2002.

In Europe Canon had nearly 12,000 employees in 2002. There are production facilities in Germany and France, as well as research and development centres in the UK and France – EU members so the products are local.

There are other operations in Australia and other areas of the Far East in addition to Japan.

A major FDI was the commencement of Canon's operations at its new plant in China. Located north of Shanghai in Suzhou, a historical and cultural centre on the Chang (Yangtze) River, the new plant has 85,000 square metres of floor space, making it one of the largest production facilities in China.

The Suzhou plant is concentrating on manufacturing colour network digital multifunction devices (digital MFDs) and monochrome digital MFDs. Further ahead, it is expected to play a pivotal role among Canon Group members and other elements of the production network infrastructure.

With the completion of this facility, Canon now have a formidable production network throughout Asia-Pacific, extending from Dalian in China, to

Taiwan, Vietnam, Thailand and Malaysia. In pursuit of an optimal Asian production network, Canon is seeking a balanced mix of operations in multiple countries, without overemphasis on a particular region.

In the Americas and Europe the company is aiming to set up further new frameworks for local research and development, production and sales and marketing. Canon is aiming to optimize its production system on a global scale – not just in selected regions. At the same time the company has programmes in place to train employees not just on products, production and sales but also on their responsibilities to the environment (see the beginning of this case study) – perhaps this is the optimum model for FDI.

CASE STUDY QUESTIONS

1 Why has Canon been sensible not to emphasize on particular regions for its FDI but to spread its investment across a wide global range?
2 What are the advantages and disadvantages to setting up local R&D operations rather than centralizing all such activities?

Summary and key learning points

- FDI is a major means of attracting money into a country.
- FDI is as important as bank loans.
- Attraction of FDI requires liberal tax regimes.
- Capital does not flow when governments impose currency restrictions.
- FDI may not result in increased employment and thus personal tax revenues may fall.
- Individuals can invest in foreign undertakings using a personal direct investment portfolio available from investment houses and banks.

QUESTIONS

1 What is FDI?
2 Why is FDI important to both multinationals and government?
3 What are the factors that help attract FDI?
4 How might FDI increase rather than alleviate poverty?
5 Why are developing countries investing in developed ones – what do they gain?

Recommended further reading

The following will provide detailed extra information for this chapter:

Sassen S (1990) *The Mobility of Labor and Capital – A Study in International Labor and Investment Flow*. Cambridge: Cambridge University Press.
Sassen S (1996) Losing Control: *The Decline of Sovereignity in an Age of Globalization*. New York: Columbia University Press.
Sassen S (2001) *The Global City*. Princeton, NJ): Princeton University Press.
Sassen S (2002) *Global Networks, Linked Cities*. New York: Routledge.

■ Ⅵ 8 Global communications and the impact of e-commerce

Learning outcomes

By the end of this chapter you should understand:

- How information and communication technology (ICT) can aid all sizes and types of business to become more global in their operations
- The importance of the right type of communication
- The limitations of ICT
- The importance of careful web site design and currency
- How ICT can aid service, retail and manufacturing sectors
- The need for efficient delivery systems
- How organizations such as Amazon have used ICT to grow a global business

Technological innovation has contributed to globalization by supplying the infrastructure and means for trans-global world connections and networks. In particular, developments in means of transport, communications and data processing have allowed global links to become denser, faster, more reliable and much cheaper. Physical transport is as important as the Internet, as while there are goods and services that can and are delivered electronically, large-scale and rapid globalization has depended on a host of innovations relating to coaxial and later fibre-optic cables, jet engines, packaging and preservation techniques, semiconductor devices, computer software and so on. In other words, global relationships could not develop without the physical tools to effect pan-global contacts.

It is rapidly becoming the case that next to people (chapter 6) information is becoming one of the most valuable assets an organization possesses. Thanks to ICT – the linking of computer, video and telephone technologies.

The global acceptability of credit/debit cards and the technological developments now mean that thanks to the Internet:

Any business, of any size, anywhere can become global

Prior to considering how businesses can use ICT to become global it is useful to consider how the technology itself has developed. The telephone has been with us throughout the twentieth century with the television becoming a mass-market product from the 1950s onwards. Digital technology that produces better audio and video quality was developed in the 1990s.

The Internet

The Internet began with the linking together of a series of computers in the US DARPA (Defense Agency Research Projects Administration) to form what became known in 1969 as ARPAnet and was designed to protect military communications in the event of a nuclear attack – a very real fear in the cold war political climate of the time. The US military were aware that its communication network was vulnerable to attack. Initially the system used three university hosts in California and one in Utah. Later in the 1970s the US academic community set up a purely civilian network funded by the NSF (National Science Foundation), which linked an increasing number of US and foreign universities via NSFnet. For the first time academics and researchers could communicate text via a new medium, electronic mail, a name rapidly contracted to email.

As students from these institutions began to take up positions within companies they brought the idea of email with them. It was not long before large commercial organizations in the US, beginning with the computer companies such as IBM and Hewlett-Packard, began to talk to each other via email linking their systems to the NSFnet.

In 1993 Marc Andreesen and his group at the University of Illinois introduced the first web browser software (Mosaic), which was a software application for the UNIX operating system but later adapted for Apple Macintosh and Microsoft Windows. NSFnet gradually became less relevant as a series of commercial ISPs (Internet service providers) entered the market. By the middle of the 1990s, organizations in both the public and private sectors were not only using email but were also beginning to design and post their own web pages. By 1993, the WWW (World Wide Web) had been brought into existence.

For non-computer specialists one of the main implications of the Internet has been for communication. For organizations the Internet and email have revolutionized both internal and external communication. While the earliest computers required a knowledge of commuting, today's machines require only the necessary knowledge to operate the particular application, the vast majority of which use normal languages and pop-up menus rather than complicated computer codes.

The power of ICT is less in the attributes of the individual components, computers, telephones, radio transmission, cameras etc., but in the synergy that can be obtained when they are used in conjunction with each other and the components linked together in a network. While there is only one link between two computers, as Figure 8.1 shows, the number of links increases dramatically as the number of machines increases.

The more computers a single computer is linked to, the greater is the amount of information it can access. The user does not need to rely solely on information stored within his or her computer but is able to access information stored on all the linked computers.

Place two dots on a piece of paper and connect them with a straight line:

Two computers produce one link.

Three computers produce three links.

Four computers produce six links.

Five computers produce 10 links and six computers 15 links as shown below

Computers	2	3	4	5	6	7	8	9	10
Links	1	3	6	10	15	21	28	36	45

Figure 8.1 **Linking computers.**

ICT has provided leaders with almost instantaneous contact with members of their teams no matter how far away that member is. The contact is almost instantaneous because team members are human and need to sleep and eat etc. and so cannot be available for communication 24 hours per day as the computer can be. The ever-increasing availability of broadband is cutting down on Internet connection and download times to a considerable degree.

It is unusual that a model railway magazine carries information about non-model items but the July 2003 edition of *British Railway Modelling* reported that Hatton's (a model shop in Liverpool) had been highlighted by Royal Mail in a case study on how the Internet can help small businesses. Hatton's email its global customer base with new offers on a regular basis and has reaped the rewards of growing a global business from small premises.

The next section considers the implications of how ICT aids globalization including specific case.

Communications

It is worth noting that in the 1760s news of the Stamp Act took six weeks to reach the American Colonies from London. In 2003 the world was able to watch US troops enter Baghdad and UK troops take Basra in real time.

Whether it is the use of the telephone, email or videoconferencing, communicating across the globe has never been easier.

Written communication

Letters and documents are still used. The 'fax' can send an instant letter. There are still times when formal documents (especially contracts) need to be initialled and signed by the respective parties and where even facsimile copies are unacceptable. However, today much commercial communication over distance is electronic rather than physical.

Face-to-face and remote communication

Even the telephone and videoconferencing, impressive as they may be, are no substitute for face-to-face communication. Videoconferencing, as those who use it regularly know, is an imprecise medium for passing on body language clues to the recipient, as covered below.

The telephone

A traditional 'telephone call' can be thought of as a letter in real time. The development of and the growth in use of the facsimile (fax) machine in the 1980s was in fact just that – a real-time method of sending documents. Written material does not allow for the easy transmission of feelings although it is a permanent record. The telephone call on the other hand does allow for some expression although voices may be distorted. More than one operation involving selling over the telephone has 'smile as you dial' displayed in big letters for the sale staff, because just as eyes can pick up body language clues our ears can detect the difference in speech patterns of somebody who is smiling or not as different muscle groups are used and this alters the tone of voice.

No longer are people restricted to land telephone lines. The latest generation of mobile telephones work abroad (in many cases) and can also send text messages and even pictures – keeping in touch has never been easier.

Email

Email, the latest alternative to the telephone, for all its uses tends to be a very curt method of communications. There are protocols for expressing emotion but the use of symbols for a smile has nowhere near the impact of an actual smile.

There has also been an issue as to the number of emails people receive. It is so easy to send a copy to all the people on a mailing list but is it really necessary to email the person next to you?

Videoconferencing

The use of videoconferencing as a device to link sites has grown rapidly in recent years aided by the availability of PC to digital cameras using Windows software and operating through the Internet. However, even with the best definition available the body language clues are hard to pick up (see case study later). The pixel definition of even the most expensive technology is nowhere near as good as the human eye although definition is improving by millions of pixels per month. There tends always to be a minute time lag (only nanoseconds) between the systems and this further confuses the interpretation of the visual clues by the brain.

Broadcasting

Videoconferencing as described above or audioconferencing can be used by managers to address large groups across the globe. There is virtually no area of the world that is not under the footprint of a telecommunication satellite. The former does allow for basic feedback in that the broadcaster can see the reactions while only roars of approval or disapproval (or stunned silence) are available using the latter. Never the less they do provide means by which the leader of a large group can address the group either together or apart. Broadcasts by leaders and politicians have long been used to provide reassurance or reports – the annual State of the Nation report by the US President or the Monarch's Christmas Broadcast in the UK are examples.

Such communications are unfortunately one way and thus do not provide for any meaningful feedback.

One of the areas in which the Internet has proved to be a boon is in the area of corporate dissemination and the ability to form diverse multifunctional teams. Colin Hastings (1994) and his colleagues in the UK have stressed the importance of managing 'the team apart' in their work on superteams. ICT can help ensure that all members of a team or project group are as informed as quickly as possible about developments. Black, Morrison and Gregersen in their study *Global Explorers* (1999) quote a manager of an oil company who stresses the need to communicate the leader's competence and priorities very quickly. Obviously a face-to-face meeting with the team is the best way to do this but it is not always possible. Managers need to use all the means of communication at their disposal to ensure that not only their priorities but also their vision and means of operating are communicated to all who need to know.

The Internet and travel

The more global an organization becomes, the more expensive in terms of both time and money sending people around the network becomes. ICT can assist in removing the need for unnecessary travel. However, as the anthropologist Desmond Morris has pointed out in *The Human Zoo* (1969), leaders of all primate groups (humans are biologically primates) need to go around to their extreme subordinates from time to time reassuring them that the individual is important. A chief executive or manager who is only known through emails, letters or videoconferencing is likely to be perceived as remote. Barrie Pitt, in his analysis of the final year of the First World War, *1918 – The Last Act*, reports the devastating effect the reluctance of senior officers to visit the troops in the allied front line had on morale. It was not just a need to see them sharing the danger but their remoteness was interpreted as callousness. In cases where there is both bad news (redundancies etc.) and good news (praise, new orders and the like), a personal visit will repay the cost in time and money by providing a degree of reassurance in the first instance (it shows they care) and further boosting morale in the second. In *Thriving on Chaos* (1987) Tom Peters stresses the importance of management by wandering around (MBWA), something that is difficult to achieve via a TV screen. Even if it is only an annual visit, executives and managers should try to visit as much of their global network as possible. It is important that not only employees but also key suppliers and customers are included in this process. In the 1990s British Airways (BA) held a series of events entitled 'Winning for Customers'. The entire airline's staff were brought to London for the one-day customer care seminars but so were key suppliers – the reasoning being that those suppliers were a strategic part of the customer value chain. While the exercise was costly, BA was one of the few profitable national airlines in the 1990s and the networking that was developed at these face-to-face sessions proved invaluable.

The Internet has also made travel arrangements easier to make, examples of which are covered in the retail section below.

Finance

As covered in a previous section financial flows are carried out electronically rather than physically moving money around. The financial issues in receiving payment can be greatly simplified by ICT. Even the smallest business can arrange secure payment by credit card. Customers can be assured that their credit card transaction is safe provided the URL (uniform resource locator) has an 's' (for secure suffix, i.e. https: and there is a padlock shown on the lower right-hand side of the web page).

Are you a collector of teddy bears? If so there are a number of companies that make and despatch celebration bears (wedding, bar mitzvah, Christmas, passing exams etc.) around the world. One of these is the Vermont Bear Company in the US. Pay by credit card and some time later your bear will arrive.

ICT and electronic transfer of funds have mad intercountry cash transfers easy – so easy in fact that chasing money laundering is a major priority of many law enforcement agencies and an operation that is proving very difficult to police.

Banking itself has become online and organizations can have instant access nearly 24 hours per day to their account details and balances.

The retail aspects of finance and ICT are covered in the next section.

Retail

As has already been mentioned, no retail (or manufacturing – see later) business is too small to be global. All that is required is a telephone line (preferably broadband), a computer, a modem, a web site and credit card use facilities with one's bank.

The major outlay, apart from the capital costs of computers etc., is the need to have a web site professionally designed and then hosted on a machine that is running continuously. ImageData Corporation in the US and Pinbrook Designs in the UK are just two of the many excellent companies that offer such services. Their details (as examples of the type) can be found in the Bibliography. Those requiring a web site design and hosting service should discuss their needs with a number of such providers in order to find the one that most meets the perceived current and future needs.

Marketing

Marketing is not just about selling it is also about finding out as much s possible about the customer. ICT allows customer preferences to be tracked to see their spending and lifestyle patterns. Cookies, which are small programs that web sites leave on a computer, mean that the customer can be recognized and greeted personally. The more one knows about the customer the better one is able to meet his or her needs. Such information is even more vital in a global market as there may never be a face-to-face meeting between customer and supplier.

Language

Not everybody speaks English. A good web site is responsive to the likely customer base and will be offered in a variety of languages. Many Japanese and Chinese web sites may start off in the native language but there is nearly always an English version available at the click of a button. Going global means recognizing and accepting the use of other languages. The customer's language is the one that matters – not the web site owners!

Visuals

The Hatton's model railway retail site mentioned earlier provides not only details of products but also a photograph – all important when the customer cannot touch the product.

Operating a retail operation via ICT means that it is possible to have a 24-hour operation. While real people may be needed to answer queries, many of the problems of time zones are removed.

More and more specialist retailers are operating national and increasingly international operations using the Internet as a marketplace. Everything from reading glasses to home appliances, to motor cars, to books and software can be purchased on the World Wide Web.

Currency

As used below the term currency refers to the information posted on the web site rather than payment details. It is important that the site is kept up to date – nothing annoys a customer like believing they have found what they want and then discovering that it is no longer available. Close coordination between the web site owner and the hosting/design company is important.

Domain names

In order to possess a web site it is first necessary to obtain a domain name, i.e. the name of the site. The author has bought www.roger.cartwright.net. There are a number of companies to be found by searching under 'domain names' on the Internet who will check if the name you require is available.

A domain name identifies and locates a host computer or services on the Internet.

The Domain Name Service (DNS) allows Internet hosts to be organized around domain names: for example, amazon.com is a domain assigned to the Internet book, music and electronic seller Amazon with the suffix 'com' signifying a commercial organization. Logging on to www.amazon.com will take you to the main Amazon site in the USA. There are also a number of other Amazon sites located in different countries as illustrated in the case study at the end of this chapter.

The suffix .com is called a generic top-level domain name, and up to 2001 there were:

.com (company/commercial organization)
.net (Internet gateway or administrative host)
.mil (military)
.org (non-profit making organization)
.edu (educational institutions)
.gov government agencies)
.ac (further and higher educational institutions in the UK)
.co (some commercial organizations in the UK or New Zealand)

As a result of the rapid growth in Internet use, seven new names – .biz, .aero, .coop, .info, .pro, .museum and .name – are now being used.

In order to increase the number of domains available, there is also a discrete code for each country although this is not always used especially where the .com and the later domains are concerned. Examples of the country codes are:

.au Australia
.ca Canada
.de Germany
.fr France
.jp Japan
.nl Netherlands
.ru Russia
.uk United Kingdom

As covered above, secure credit card payments make it easy for the retailer to ensure that goods and services are paid for. This allows for the retailer to not only ensure prompt payment but to manage cash flow.

Delivery of product/service

Products and services retailed using the Internet come in two forms:

● Those that can be delivered online
● Those that need physical delivery.

Those that can be delivered online

Software and banking services are examples of products and services that can be downloaded directly from the Internet. In the case of software, the customer just pays and downloads. This facility is especially useful for obtaining software updates especially for programs such as virus checkers.

Those that need physical delivery

Flowers, books, electrical appliances, motor cars and holidays cannot be delivered online, only ordered. It is important that the retailer has adequate delivery methods in place to ensure that the customer receives a prompt response. How amazon.com has achieved this is shown in the case study at the end of the chapter. Delivery from abroad is likely to take longer than the customer may be used to and it is important to give an indication of delivery times. Most retailers operating online make arrangements with parcel delivery companies and courier firms to ensure that deliveries are prompt and that goods are delivered in good condition.

Service

In many cases customers not only buy a product they also expect a degree of service. If a motor car is ordered and bought over the Internet the owner will expect that service arrangements will be in place. The same holds for electrical goods.

It is also important that there is an easy-to-use complaints procedure and a returns policy that costs the customer as little as possible in both time and money. Many global products come with world-wide guarantees but there is still a grey area as to precisely which jurisdiction applies consumer protection legislation if goods are sent from one country to another. Payment by credit card eases this problem as the major credit card companies provide a degree of protection for their cardholders.

Providing the same level of personalized service over the Internet as can be provided in a face-to-face situation is difficult. By using 'cookies' it is possible to provide a personalized greeting as amazon.com does. It is also possible to do what local shopkeepers have done for generations – provide suggestions based on previous purchases.

Manufacturing

While the above use of ICT has concentrated on retail, manufacturing has also benefited from the abilities of ICT to link people in real time.

The Boeing Aircraft Corporation headquartered around Seattle (WA) is one of the world's two largest airframe manufacturers – the other is Airbus Industrie in Europe.

By the early 1990s Boeing had an excellent record of producing civilian jet airliners. The Boeing 707, 727, 737, 747 (Jumbo), 757 and 767s were familiar sights on the runways of the world's airports. Their main US rivals, Lockheed and

McDonnell Douglas, were unable to compete with Boeing (McDonnell Douglas being acquired by Boeing in the 1990s) and only the European Airbus Industrie were selling an equivalent volume of airframes.

It was deemed that the airline world was ready for a large twin-engined airliner capable of performing on long-haul sectors. The use of two engines cuts the costs of both purchase and operation considerably but requires a high degree of reliability. The 777 was the first airliner to be built to gain ETOPS (Extended Twin-engine Operations) by the FAA (Federal Aviation Administration) from its introduction. A twin-engined airliner offering a range of 5500–7000 nautical miles and carrying 300–400 passengers was likely to be very attractive to the world's airlines especially as it was predicted to be very fuel efficient.

A modern airliner is a highly complex machine requiring a considerable number of carefully engineered components. Manufacturers such as Boeing now contract out a great deal of the component manufacturing not only within the US but also across the globe. There is the advantage that the contractor has to bear the start up costs (as will be discussed in chapter 10) but the disadvantage that Boeing has to make its proprietary information available to an organization that may be also working with a competitor or may actually become a competitor in the future (this has always been a worry for US companies partnering with those in the Far East). Nevertheless it has proved more effective for companies such as Boeing to work this way and involve others in the process.

For the 777 the manufacture of components was spread across the world to a degree never before utilized. Parts were produced not only in the US but also in Italy, Japan, Australia and the UK.

Eddy *et al.* (1976) report that when Lockheed and Rolls-Royce were collaborating on the Tri-Star in the 1960s and 1970s, an airline that used the Rolls-Royce RB211 engine, Rolls-Royce engineers were to be seen flying across the Atlantic to take metal ducting designed in Derby to Burbank to see how it fitted on the aircraft and how it would perform. This was both time consuming and expensive. Boeing decided to find a better way. Airliners can be described as thousands of components all flying in formation – Boeing had to ensure that the components were of the right quality and that they fitted exactly no matter where they were made. The key to this lay in ICT.

Modern technology allowed Boeing to link its designers to the contractors and even to the actual machine tools that were being used to produce the parts.

One of the problems in designing something as complex as an airliner is that of interference – two components trying to occupy the same space. In the days of two-dimensional drawings this was an all too frequent occurrence.

Computer-aided design (CAD) can produce drawings in three dimensions and thus show the relationship in space between components.

Boeing put together a massive amount of computer power in a system known as CATIA (Computer-graphics Aided Three-dimensional Interactive Application) and EPIC (Electronic Preassembly in the CATIA). EPIC allowed a computer model of the finished aircraft – a virtual airliner – to be produced.

CATIA was linked to component manufactures so that the specification of parts designed on the system were immediately available to them and could be fed, if necessary directly to the machine tools.

Aircraft design is a process rather than event and there are often many design changes. Before systems such as CATIA these might be posted, faxed or even hand delivered. With the system used by Boeing, everybody concerned with that component would know of changes as soon as the new design was on the system. The time savings were immense.

As EPIC could spot any interference it meant that the finished product was much more likely to fit together properly. The whole process was documented for an excellent book, *21st Century Jet* by Karl Sabbach, and also for a joint US/UK television series.

Each component or major group of components was the responsibility of a DBT (Design Build Team) that could include remote members as the Internet and ICT made email and videoconferencing an easy and useful tool.

No longer did designers have to take their drawings or models to a colleague on another floor or even another city or continent to see if it was okay. The whole process could now be carried out over a network of computers.

The DBTs also formed a forum not only for discussion but also ownership of a component. By using the technology to involve team members at remote locations, everybody was involved. This is an important motivational point often neglected when subcontracting. The further away the subcontractor's staff are, the less likely they are to feel part of the team and thus to own the project.

While Boeing set up a special bank of computers to handle the huge amounts of data, smaller projects can use these concepts with linked PCs over a local (LAN) or wide area (WAN) network.

By feeding information form CATIA into EPIC, it was possible to see exactly how the airline would appear and this also made the task of simulating its performance easier. In fact so good was the design that the 777 was even more fuel efficient than predicted and it did become the first airliner to achieve an ETOPS rating at its introduction.

What can be applied to an aircraft can be applied on a smaller scale to any manufacturing process. Computer-aided design linked to partners and their machinery can cut errors considerably and provide a higher quality product. While the parts may need to be shipped from different parts of the globe, the design work can be undertaken electronically.

It is even possible for remote control of processes. This is especially applicable to hazardous activities etc.

Just in time

The delivery of components just in time for them to be fitted on an assembly line has become the norm in modern manufacturing. Just in time saves the organization the costs of holding stocks, costs that include paying for the goods before they are needed, insurance and storage. ICT can assist a global just-in-time operation by ensuring that production in one part of the world commences with just enough time for the process to be complete and the components delivered. The wider the network, the more danger there is of a part going astray so it is necessary to have careful monitoring and control of stock and component movements.

Training

Training was covered in some detail in chapter 6. ICT can aid the training process using computer-based packages that can be accessed from anywhere within the organization's global network. In the days of laptops and Internet cafes there is no reason why employees cannot undertake a degree of training anywhere. While there will always be, as stated in chapter 6, a need for on-the-job training, there are many aspects of training, especially simulations that can be carried out as simulations.

Partnerships

Chapter 10, a chapter considering how businesses can grow globally, has a section on growth through partnerships, franchises, agencies etc. All of these benefit from the immediacy of communication and information that ICT can bring.

Home working

One of the great advantages (or possible disadvantages) of ICT is the ability to work from home. There are many in the service sector who can carry out much of their work with a computer and a modem. There is the loneliness that can occur when one is not interacting with others on a regular basis but the possibilities for small, one-person, global empires to start up from an attic bedroom exist as they have never done before.

Implications for small businesses

Provided that a small business has access to a computer and a telephone – global expansion is possible. There needs to be a reliable delivery service and it pays to use professional web hosting and design services.

Payments can be taken via credit card and web sites need to be kept up to date.

Manufacturers and component suppliers can integrate design and production processes using ICT.

Amazon.com

Globally, Amazon.com is probably one of the best known names of the new dot com companies that seemed to spring up (and sometimes disappear just as quickly) at the end of the 1990s and into the early years of the new century. Amazon has revolutionized firstly book sales, then software and music sales in the US, the UK, Germany, Canada, France and Japan.

The founder of Amazon.com is ex-Princeton graduate Jeff Bezos, the son of a Cuban immigrant to the US. After graduating from Princeton, Bezos became involved with the computer side of the banking industry and began to see the potential of the Internet for commerce. It is now generally agreed that the birth of the World Wide Web was in 1993 (Spector, 2000) but even before that a number of proactive entrepreneurs were registering web site names. Among them were a very small number of booksellers, the first being Computer Literacy. Research that Bezos carried out for his then employer in 1994 showed that Internet usage was growing at the time at an incredible 2300 per cent per annum. Bezos considered exactly which products/services would be best to offer using the Internet as the supplier–customer interface. His choices included software, clothing and books. His research indicated that books, a product going back centuries, were a very good choice for retailing through the most up-to-date medium of trade.

The book trade has always been fragmentary with a large number of publishers in different countries together with retail outlets ranging from small, independent one-site operations to national and latterly international chains. In the US even the largest of the publishers, Random House, had less than 10 per cent of the market and that the two largest retail chains, Barnes and Nobel and Borders (who also have a large UK operation) accounted for less than 25 per cent of the $30 billion of adult US book sales in 1994. Since then children's book sales have grown considerably, fuelled by the Harry Potter phenomenon. Despite its fragmentation, however, book selling is big business as reading is a popular activity – in 1996 global book sales netted $82 billion. In the UK the 1990s saw a deregulation within the industry with the scrapping of the net book agreement that had fixed prices. Booksellers could now discount and the major chains did just that, three for two deals etc. on novels becoming increasingly common. In the US this trend had been led by Crown Books in the 1980s.

The major problem that traditional bookstores have is the need for space for selling and warehousing. Even the largest store in the US or UK could only carry a small percentage of the 1.5 million English language books in print at any one time and thus many books had to be ordered in forcing the customer to wait. Waiting for a novel is one thing, waiting for a book needed for study or business can be a major issue.

Bezos realized that a virtual bookstore using the Internet could place no limit on the number of titles available to the customer. His operation could acquire stock direct from the publishers or from one of the small number of book distributors. The Internet technology would make the customer's task of searching for a title relatively simple and a check could be kept on customer preferences so that recommendations could be made, thus personalizing the service to the same level as possible when using a small independent book store on a regular basis. There it is the owner who knows the customer; in the Bezos' vision it is the computer. The key issue would be that of speedy delivery of the book to the customer.

Moving to Seattle, Bezos spent much of 1994 meeting people and learning about the book business. As has been stressed in this material, he conducted a thorough analysis of the market and the competition.

In November 1994, Bezos and his associates began the Amazon.com operation in a converted garage in a section of Seattle. Using the database of 'books in print' and information from the Library of Congress (look at the front of nearly any book in the English language that is likely to reach the US or UK markets and you will find Library of Congress and The British Library statements that the book is included in their catalogues).

The company was launched to the public in 1995 by which time it had acquired a database of more than one million titles. An ordering system, customer identification system, distribution and the all important credit card facilities had been established. No longer need those with access to the Internet (a growing percentage of the US population) travel to a bookstore. No matter how remote they were, they could browse the book lists online and order with confidence. The only thing they could not do was to scan the shelves and the pages of the books on them. However, more and more information about content is available in the media, on the Internet and on the Amazon.com site itself so that virtual browsing has become more of a reality.

From the beginning, Amazon.com discounted its best sellers by 10 per cent with some titles discounted by up to 30 per cent. The way the Amazon.com/co.uk etc. site works provides a degree of a personal relationship and that entering the site (provide the 'cookie' has not been deleted from the PC) elicits a personal welcome back and news of the latest releases in the customer's particular areas of interest based on previous purchasing patterns.

Like the vast majority of the early dot com operations Bezos lost money – $303,000 in 1995. However, even so early on in the history of the company over 2000 people per day were visiting the site and within two years this would increase to 80,000.

By 1996 Bezos had acquired sufficient venture capital to expand the Amazon.com operation and the company had increased to 150 employees and more importantly, $16 million in sales – prompting an approach from the major bookseller, Barnes and Noble, although no deal materialized. Also in that year an associates programme was launched whereby the owners of other web sites could direct their visitors to Amazon.com and receive a small payment if this resulted in a purchase.

In 1997, Amazon.com made its IPO (initial public offering). Despite the fact that the company was still losing money, £3 million in the first quarter of 1997, sales had boomed and investors considered Amazon.com worth buying and the IPO was oversubscribed. The opening price was $18 and after an initial rise and fall ended the year at $52 – not bad for a company that had only made losses.

Global expansion

In 1998 Bezos began talks with Bertelsmann AG, the German media giant that already had a small Internet book-selling operation BOL. This led to nothing but Bertelsmann later acquired 50 per cent of the Barnes and Noble online operation – competition was growing. Amazon then acquired a UK online operation and a smaller online bookshop in Germany. This gave Bezos an entry into the lucrative UK and German markets. The UK was important, as London is a large publishing centre for English language books. Most of the major publishers operate parallel UK and US operations publishing simultaneously in both countries. With further expansion into Canada it can be seen that with the exception of Germany, Bezos was moving into the global market for English language books – the biggest of the world's markets. Many of the textbooks used in Africa and India are in English.

These moves led to formation of Amazon.co.uk in the UK and Amazon.co.de in Germany. Amazon customizes its sites for national preferences. A small example of this is that the customer loads their purchases onto a shopping cart on Amazon.com but into a shopping basket on Amazon.co.uk (Americans and Canadians use shopping carts in supermarkets while the British refer to a shopping trolley). On the UK site US published and supplied books are dual priced in dollars and pounds sterling.

This expansion has led to certain copyright problems. US copyright law bars the importation of copyrighted books for commercial resale (but not for private use). Bezos considered that a US citizen buying from Amazon.co.uk (easily accessed from the US) was just the same as flying to London, buying the book and bringing it back to the US. This argument is still underway. Certainly users of Amazon.co.uk have no difficulty in acquiring US books through the site as the writer can testify. The decision to expand into the UK and Germany was sensible as much of the British Commonwealth will happily buy from the UK and Central Europeans are accustomed to doing business with German companies. With its local distribution systems, Amazon.co.uk and its German counterpart have grown rapidly to become an established part of the local book-buying scene.

By 1999, Amazon as a group had expanded into CD and DVD sales through its online Zshops and in 2001 started to sell electronic items including cameras. In 1999 total sales were $2.6 billion and again in 2001 Amazon acquired the Borders online operation.

By 2001 the global expansion had included two further very important markets – France and Japan.

In addition to the associates programme, where writers can link their web sites directly to Amazon, the company has also begun to offer second-hand sales either using dedicated booksellers or even private individuals. Amazon takes care of the payments and the seller agrees to despatch the material within one or two working days.

Horizontal expansion

From books it was a natural expansion beginning in 1999 into music and then software. The next move was into software delivery although using physical delivery rather than online and then into electronic products, digital cameras etc. The UK began to offer this service in April 2003 with Canada, Germany and Japan following over a period of just a few months.

Harry Potter

The Harry Potter books have made the Scottish author J K Rowling a multi-millionaire. Children have queued for hours waiting for bookstores to open at midnight in order to obtain the latest instalment of the boy wizard's adventures. Advance sales have been the highest ever recorded.

In January 2003 *Harry Potter and the Order of the Phoenix* became the number one Amazon best seller, months before it was actually launched in June 2003. It was one of the first English language books to make the French number one spot.

Amazon teamed up with the distribution giant Federal Express (FedEx) and the US Postal Service to deliver no less than a quarter of a million copies to US homes on the same day the book was available in bookshops. This was a massive undertaking.

There is no doubt that despite the problems of the dot.com companies and the time it takes to move into profit, Bezos has provided the world with an effective means of buying an old product – the humble book, as important today as it has been throughout history for the transmission of knowledge, culture and ideas and for providing sheer pleasure through reading. Amazon has used ICT to move into new global markets, adapting its local web site to meet the needs of the local customers. Amazon is not only an example of how to use new technology to sell an old product but also of how to think global but act local as described in chapter 5.

CASE STUDY QUESTIONS

1 Why was Bezos astute to choose an old product for a new form of selling?
2 How important is it to use the customer's language nuances, e.g. shopping cart in the US (amazon.com) and shopping basket in the UK (amazon.co.uk)?
3 Amazon's expansion into music and then electronics is a natural progression for a bookseller – do you agree?

Summary and key learning points

- Information and communication technology (ICT) can aid all sizes and types of business to become more global in their operations.
- It is important to understand the limitations of ICT.
- Face-to-face communications are still important.
- ICT can link retailers to a global marketplace.
- Delivery systems need to be in place to respond quickly to customer demand.
- Professional help should be sought in designing web pages.
- Web pages need to be kept current.
- business can become global even if operated from home.

QUESTIONS

1 'ICT replaces the need for managers to make site visits' – discuss this statement with reference to the importance of face-to-face communication.
2 Why should professional help be sought in the design and hosting of web pages?

3 How can payments be made securely when undertaking e-commerce?
4 How can ICT help an organization think global but act local?
5 'Home working will one day replace the office' – what are the implications of this statement?

Recommended further reading

General information on the digital marketplace can be found in:

Aldrich D F (1999) *Mastering the Digital Marketplace.* Chichester: Wiley.

For information about Amazon.com:

Saunders R (2000) *Amazon.com.* Oxford: Capstone.

Spector R (2000) *Amazon.com – Get Big Fast.* London: Random House.

For information about the Boeing 777 and the design/manufacturing process see:

Sabbach K (1995) *21st Century Jet – the Making of the Boeing 777.* Basingstoke: Macmillan.

◼ ⋁ 9 The global customer

Learning outcomes

By the end of this chapter you should understand:

- The meaning of 'the customer is always right'
- The global nature of business
- The removal of monopoly status from many organizations
- The lifetime value of the customer
- Thinking global but acting local is a good customer strategy
- The value chain
- The importance of branding
- The types of loyalty
- The importance of consistency

'The customer is always right' has entered common usage both by customers and those who seek their custom. Like many well-known sayings its origin is not completely straightforward. It has been attributed to Lord Sainsbury in the UK but also to a Philadelphia department store owner, John Wannamaker, who is reputed to have first used the phrase as early as the 1860s.

The customer is not always right. The customer makes mistakes, has false expectations and may even be rude. Nevertheless the customer is the only person other than share and stockholders who brings money into an organization. Having a declining number of customers is equal to a declining income – thus a declining organization!

Think/Discussion point: As a customer are you always right?

The modern marketplace is increasingly becoming global. ICT, as shown in the previous chapter, means that geographic barriers no longer limit customers and potential customers. Goods can be acquired from across the globe at the keystroke of a computer connected to the Internet. The impact of the Internet on customer relationships was discussed in detail in the previous chapter, suffice to say it is a massive impact.

The customer at the centre of an organization's objectives

While a commercial organization might have its core objective as maximum profit and increasing shareholder value, unless the customer is at the centre of the operation neither of these two objectives can be fulfilled to their maximum.

Competition

The 1980s and 1990s saw the breaking up of many monopoly situations across the world. As competition increases so also does the bargaining power of the customer. There are increasingly fewer and fewer organizations that can hold their customers hostage. Once customers discover that they have bargaining power they are increasingly demanding greater quality and value for money. The concept of the customer at the centre of an organization's activities is now at the core of the philosophy of more and more commercial organizations.

There are two major reasons for an acceptance of poor customer service:

- No choice
- Attitudes.

If the customer has no choice or relatively few choices and wants the product then they may have little alternative but to accept poor service and even an inferior product. This was the situation in many communist economies prior to the 1990s. What the break up of those systems showed was that a situation of no choice has a relatively short life cycle. Monopolies, situations where one organization provides the sole source of supply and can therefore provide the barest minimum of service and quality if they desire, can only be continued through active government intervention against competition. Monopolies are legislated against in the UK (and the rest of the EU), the US and many other countries. Governments have realized that a lack of choice leads to dissatisfied consumers and dissatisfied consumers can display their frustration through the ballot box.

While governments wish for competition to increase customer choice, drive prices down and quality up, organizations, while espousing the ideal of competition publicly, often try to achieve as near a monopoly situation as possible. For the supplier a monopoly is the ideal situation as it gives them total control of the market and prices. For the customer as much choice as possible without destroying the market is ideal. Competition usually means lower prices and higher quality. It is important that there is some form of control of competition. All organizations need a critical mass of customers to survive. Too many organizations chasing the same number of customers could lead to a situation where the market is so divided between them that no organization actually has enough customers to survive. The author has illustrated this numerically in a companion volume to this text (Cartwright, 2000, *Mastering Customer Relations*).

Customers seem to be best served by organizations that are either big enough to offer such economies of scale so as to be able to compete on price or small enough to offer a personal, exclusive service. Supermarkets have developed rapidly in the UK as have the smaller, more specialized food shops and delicatessens. It has been the middle of the size range organizations that have been squeezed, in many cases, out of business.

> **Think/Discussion point**: Are there medium sized organizations in your area that have been unable to compete with national or global competitors while smaller organizations have been able to find a niche within which they can survive such competition?

Public and private sectors

There are four basic types of organizations, defined by ownership and prime function (for profit and not for profit as the terms are generally understood) as shown in Figure 9.1.

In terms of size, the current position in the UK is that the for profit/private ownership and the not for profit/public ownership sectors are in fact by far the biggest components in terms of economic activity. The former includes the majority of all commercial activities and the latter the entire public sector including national and local government, the National Health Service, education and the armed forces. Prior to the 1980s, the for profit/public ownership sector was very large and contained some huge monopoly or near monopoly organizations. These included the steel, coal, gas, electricity and ship-building industries, railways, British Airways and other nationalized concerns including major car manufacturers. Under privatization these industries have moved into the for profit/private ownership quadrant and become open to global competition, mergers and takeover.

The importance of good customer relations was first realized by those areas of the private sector that had immediate, face-to-face contact with paying customers, examples being the retail, hotel, transportation and entertainment sectors. Many of

	Public ownership	Private ownership
For profit	Nationalized industry	Commercial organizations
Not for profit	National/local government	Voluntary sector

Figure 9.1 **Typologies of organizations.**

Table 9.1 Previous and current ownership of some UK operations.

Company	Previous name	Sector	Ownership
Corus	British Steel	Steel making	UK/Netherlands
English, Welsh and Scottish Railways	British Rail (part of)	Rail freight haulage	US (Wisconsin Central)
Thames Water	Thames Water Board	Utility	German

the operations in these sectors were already operating on a global basis so realized the importance of the global customer and the wealth of choice he or she had. Today all private companies who rely on profit need to be conversant with the factors leading to good customer relations especially as global competition increases. It was the private sector that first felt the blast of global competition – competition that has almost entirely destroyed for example the German camera industry and has led to most UK car manufacturers being in foreign hands. In the public sector, comprising more monopolistic situations, globalization was slower to have an impact but nevertheless, as will be shown later there has been one.

It might be thought that customer service is less important commercially in the public sector. However, customers are also voters and thus the customer is able to express an opinion (albeit every few years) on the standard of service received from the public sector. Most sections of the public sector have now developed customer care programmes and the necessary training for staff. As funding from central government has been targeted so as to follow the individual, so local government, the education service and the National Health Service have seen, perhaps more transparently, the value of the individual to their growth and budgets. While such organizations do not measure success by profits, government has begun to apply strict performance targets and monies are contingent on achieving those targets, one of which is invariably customer satisfaction. Such target-driven performance has been criticized as being too simplistic and the UK government announced in 2003 that it was seeking alternative means of measuring public sector performance perhaps because many of the targets had not been met. It may be that they had been set too high in order to garner public support but failure to meet them was politically unacceptable – if you can't meet the target then political spin seems to suggest that you change it or scrap it!

Examples of the global expansion into what was the UK for profit public sector are shown in Table 9.1.

As soon as the government privatized these key industrial sectors they became open to foreign direct investment (as discussed in chapter 7) and as can be seen in Table 9.1, many UK household names including utilities are either wholly or partly in foreign ownership.

The changing attitudes of customers

Customers are becoming used to choice and quality. Today's customer challenges and wants to know the why and not just the how. The medical and legal professions, local and national government, newly privatized industries and education have all been required to become more responsive to the needs of their customers.

In 1982, Tom Peters and Bob Waterman published *In Search of Excellence*, their study of successful US companies and made the point that closeness to the customer and active listening to customers were key attributes for successful companies. A similar study in the UK by Clutterbuck and Goldsmith drew remarkably similar conclusions. In *The Winning Steak* (1983) and *The Winning Streak Mark 2* (1997), a study of successful UK companies showed that success was closely related to the care given to the customer.

Loyalty, satisfaction and delight

Customer driven v. product led

There are two extremes to a relationship with the customer and indeed to marketing as a whole. An organization that adopts a *product-led approach*, develops products and systems that are suited to the organization. Henry Ford expressed this approach well in the 1920s when he offered customers a Model T Ford in 'any colour as long as it's black'. Such an approach can work in a situation where there is no competition and demand exceeds supply. It is noticeable that modern vehicle manufacturers, having listened to their customers, develop a whole range of variations and options around the same model and are thus able to adopt a much more *customer-driven approach* – you can have almost any colour you like and if it is not a stock colour it may be available if you pay a little more.

It is not only in terms of the features of physical products that a customer-driven approach is manifested. Service features such as opening times, new means of communications and even the provision of disabled and mother and child parking spaces demonstrate a commitment to putting the needs of the customer before those of the organization. The use of the Internet for delivery of products and services provides a convenient 24-hour option (see chapter 8).

Think/Discussion point: Which is more likely to survive competition in the modern global environment, a product-led or a customer-driven organization?

Value added

A person's house is not worth what they might believe it is or even what an agent claims it is. Its value is either the cost of rebuilding (the insurance value) or what somebody else is prepared to pay for it.

Each step of the process of delivering a product/service be it building a vehicle or processing a loan or dealing with a planning application carries a skill/time cost and a monetary amount of added value that the customer is prepared to pay. This is known as a value chain with the costs of the product building up at each step together with a contribution to the added value. The costs of each step of a process consist of a series of factors:

cost of raw materials
+
labour
+
contribution to the overheads of the organization
+
extra costs (marketing, distribution etc.)
+
costs of ongoing servicing etc.
+
added value to the customer

Costs can only be covered and a profit made if the value to the customer (i.e. the price he or she is prepared to pay) is more than the cost of production/delivery. The larger an organization is, the easier it is to cut down costs through economies of scale. Global organizations have an advantage in this regard.

As profit is the difference between the total costs of the product/service and the price paid, it is easy to see that added value and profit are closely linked.

Many, many organizations can satisfy their customers. It is only those few that are prepared to really put the customer at the centre of their operations that are able to truly delight the customer. Satisfaction is better than dissatisfaction but even the use of the word in English suggests that there is far more that could be done. Satisfaction is only a step on the road to delight. Chapter 4 considers customer loyalty and it is not satisfaction but delight that secures long-term loyalty. In emotive terms satisfaction is what the customer expects, delight is what provides a warm glow. Delight, from the customer's point of view, could be described as receiving more than the minimum expected added value. Delighting a customer actually adds added value to the relationship between the supplier and the customer.

Customer service and the bottom line

Market share, as stated earlier, is one of the aspects of an organization's performance given considerable weight by investors. This is obviously only a factor with private, for profit organizations but it is an important one as the effect of a drop in market share on investor confidence can be quite dramatic.

Customers who defect from an organization do not disappear into thin air; they tend to go to a competitor. Thus the market share of the original organization decreases at the expense of an increase in the market share of a competitor. This in turn influences investors. On a global scale investor confidence is all important. A defecting customer (especially as customers tend to tell their friends, colleagues and relations when they defect) can begin an avalanche that can have a dramatic effect on investment.

Lifetime value of the customer

One sale does not a loyal customer make. The aim of any organization should be to retain the customer for as long as possible. A weekly shopping basket may be £60, little to a major supermarket chain. Over a year that is £6052, over 20 years it is £62,400. Multiply that by the number of customers and one can see why the US giant Wal-Mart was so interested in the UK supermarket Asda, a company with a nationwide operation and a huge customer base. While there have been those who have criticized Wal-Mart in the US (notably Bill Quinn in *How Wal Mart is Destroying America (and the world)*, 2000), the organization has grown rapidly. Wal-Mart had begun its global expansion – as the company saw it bringing lower prices to a wider customer base – when it entered Mexico in 1991. The purchase of Woolco's Canadian operation in 1994 brought Canada into the Wal-Mart empire and operations in Argentina and Brazil were acquired in 1995. Wal-Mart entered the potentially huge Chinese market in 1996.

Weftkauf in Germany was acquired in 1997 giving Wal-Mart a European foothold that was to be strengthened in 1999 when it acquired the Asda Group and its 229 stores in the UK. Asda (as Associated Dairies) had been a founder and major player in the UK supermarket business together with Tesco, Sainsbury and Somerfield. Bill Quinn (no lover of Wal-Mart) has described this as a Wal-Mart invasion of Britain.

Quinn is highly critical of Wal-Mart's expansion. However, it is a fact that consumers want discounted products and Wal-Mart supplies them. In 1999 Wal-Mart was ranked No. 1 Corporate Citizen in the US, No. 7 in *Fortune* magazine's Most Admired Companies in the World and No. 6 in overall corporate reputation in the US according to Interactive Inc.

Modern hypermarkets may, as Quinn points out, destroy the business of local retailers but they are what customers want. It is difficult to blame a single company for responding to demand. In building large out-of-town facilities in the UK, Wal-Mart (through Asda) are following the pattern laid out by Tesco.

In 1998 Wal-Mart's annual charitable contributions totalled $102 million, the company having made a $551 million operating profit the previous year.

Products from around the globe

One of the things that has changed over the past decades is the range of global goods to be found on local shelves. No longer are foreign delicacies and clothes a speciality purchase. The global customer knows what is out there and wants it as locally as possible. This has major implications for small businesses – see later in this chapter.

Year long

Fruit and certain other delicacies used to be seasonal. The global customer today wants such products on a year-round basis and organizations need to respond. As more and more people are able to take foreign holidays, the more they want the products they have seen, eaten and drunk when they return.

Loyalty

What does the term loyalty mean to a global customer?

People were once loyal to their local shop. Has loyalty disappeared? The answer is no but it has changed. People are loyal based on service and quality rather than location.

David Clutterbuck and Walter Goldsmith in *The Winning Streak Mark 2* (1997) make four very important points that impact on the current state-of-the-art of customer relations:

- The best customer is usually an existing customer.
- Organizations should focus on developing a talent for focusing on the customers the organization really wants to keep.
- Building firm relationships with customers.
- Putting competitive advantage before cost.

As an organization expands its customer base it will acquire new customers. These customers need to be retained. It is also important that in expanding globally, previous customers do not become forgotten about. If this happens they may become disillusioned and defect.

Wind (1982) examined customer loyalty and postulated that there are five classifications of customers or potential customers in respect of loyalty:

1 Current loyal customers who will continue to use the product or service.
2 Current customers who may switch to another brand.
3 Occasional customers who would increase consumption of the brand if the incentive were right.
4 Occasional customers who would decrease consumption of the brand if a competitor offered the right incentive.
5 Non-users who could become customers.

There is also a final category that can be described as non-customers as they are:

6 Non-users who will never become customers.

A sub-category of type 5 could be non-users who have never had the opportunity because the product or service has been unavailable in their area. Thanks to globalization this is becoming rarer.

There is also a final category that relates to the think global but act local concept already discussed within this material. These are customers who do not know they are customers for a particular product or brand.

Brand names

For many similar products it may be only the brand name that distinguishes between competitors and a well-known brand name becomes, in effect, a very valuable USP (unique selling point).

Branding is one of the most important concepts of contemporary marketing. As the Canadian writer, Naomi Klein (2001) has pointed out in her extremely thought-provoking book, *No Logo*, for those organizations that have contracted out the vast majority of their manufacturing, their brands are all that they actually have of value.

In the modern world it is actually brands that customers relate to rather than products. Klein shows the importance of the brand by stating that when Philip Morris purchased Kraft for $12.6 billion in 1988, the actual worth of Kraft was about $2.1 billion and the value of the brand $10.5 billion, i.e. they paid six times the paper worth of Kraft to acquire the name. One can only guess what the worth of Nike or Coca-Cola would be.

Sir Richard Branson of the Virgin Group makes no apology for the use of Virgin as a brand attachment to his enterprises. Branson is one of the most entrepreneurial people to come out of the UK and is unique in being a role model for the young. The name Virgin in front of something says a great deal about that product and its quality.

Brands can become very vulnerable to any customer dissatisfaction either with the brand itself or the manner with which it is produced. Nike has suffered from picket lines after it was shown that it was using very low paid individuals in the developing world to produce goods at the expense, some in the US believed, of US workers who could have been employed on similar tasks. A good brand name needs to keep its image.

More and more it is not the product or service that is promoted and advertised but the brand. Brands are what people buy into and are far more than just a mere product.

A number of years ago, a Snickers chocolate bar in the US was known as a Marathon in the UK. The famous VW Golf was the Rabbit in the US. Recent trends have been to adopt global brands but to use words and phrases that have universal appeal and no negative or abusive connotations.

Branding is an important part of the relationship between an organization and its customers. Brand loyalty can be quite high and the basic concept is to encourage the customer to identify with a particular brand. There are many, many brands of washing powder on the UK market but most are made by just two or three companies. Chocolate bars of different brands fill the shelves but there are only a few major manufacturers. Certain VW, Skoda and Seat cars look very similar, this should be no surprise as the brands are all owned by the same group. The fashion industry has produced the concept of displaying the brand as part of the customer's image.

Once a brand gains a reputation for quality then its position is strengthened. The more global the reputation, the greater the strength. Quality is not the only reason for brand success: fashion, as discussed above, may play also a part. It is difficult to tell whether different 'trainers' for children sold in a shoe shop are actually worth the large differentials some brands are able to gain. In this case the name itself is more important than the product, hence the problem of pirate copies mentioned earlier. Branding and the loyalty of a customer to a particular brand is an important weapon in competition and takeover attempts may be purely to acquire a particular brand.

The popularity of particular brands can be culturally and geographically specific. Brands that sell well in Scotland, for example the soft drink, Irn Bru, may be much less popular in England and Wales. Even names can be problematic. The Fiat Ritmo motor car of the 1980s was marketed as the Strada in the UK as research showed that the name Ritmo would not be acceptable to UK buyers, research at the time suggesting that the name conjured up an image of a lawnmower! As discussed above the famous VW Golf was for many years the Rabbit in the USA, an acceptable title there but not so in the UK and the rest of Europe.

Generic branding

A phenomenon of recent years has been the proliferation of so-called 'own brands' appearing on supermarket shelves. These are products that the supermarket has packaged for them by a supplier but branded as though they were the supermarket's own. In the early days of mail order in the US, organizations such as Sears would have products made for them and then branded with the Sears' name. Contemporary own-brand products are often cheaper than the well-known brands especially where staple products such as baked beans etc. are concerned. Whether the quality differs or not is a matter for the individual customer to decide. Some own-brand products have a reputation for very high quality.

Organizations such as the Goldstar conglomerate from South Korea owed much of their success in the consumer electronics sector by supplying generic products for the retailer to brand as its own.

Where the product is a generic one, the quality standards are dictated by the retailer as it is they, under UK legislation, who are responsible for the standard of goods sold. If a retailer allows its name to appear on a product then any deficiencies will be interpreted by the customer as being the fault of the name on the box, i.e. the retailer and not the actual manufacturer whose name is only likely to appear in very small print if it is mentioned at all.

Badge engineering

Branding and generic branding are legitimate business activities. What is perhaps less legitimate, although legal is the practice of badge engineering, something that the car industry has been accused of in the past. Badge engineering is basically charging different amounts for identical products. Identical that is except for the brand name. As certain brand names command more perceived value, customers are more likely to pay a premium for a product badged with that brand even if it does not differ from a similar product badged with a less popular brand.

Counterfeiting

It has become so much a part of image that some people are now prepared to buy something that they know is a fake just for the brand name. That this is dishonest and devalues the brand seem not to bother them. As long as others believe they are promoting a certain image – then this, they say is OK – of course it is not. Naturally the holders of the brand name take a very different view and are determined to stop others cashing in on their good name with imitations.

Types of loyalty

It is important to distinguish between loyalty to the generic product, the brand and a particular supplier.

Many people are loyal to coffee as a beverage. There are also those who are only occasional coffee drinkers and those who never drink coffee at all, perhaps for medical or religious reasons. Those who drink considerable amounts of coffee can be described as having a generic product loyalty. Within that group there will be some that buy just the cheapest coffee or drink whatever is available. For them Cartwright (2000) introduced the term *A-loyal*. They are loyal to the generic product but not to a particular brand. They will not care where the product comes from or who produces it. Within the group of those who are product loyal there will be those who have a particular *brand loyalty*. They always buy a particular brand or at least a brand from the same producer.

Supplier loyalty

Many customers are creatures of habit. Not only are they loyal to particular brands, they are also loyal to particular suppliers. There is a customer type known as a hostage (Jones and Strasser, 1995), i.e. somebody who has no choice but to be a customer of a particular brand or supplier. Such a situation could occur in a small community where there is only one shop selling perhaps just one brand of a particular item. A customer who is without transport could be forced, if they really want that item, to be loyal to that one brand and that one supplier. The term introduced for this is *pseudo-loyalty*. A statistical analysis of the customer base would show considerable loyalty but it is pseudo-loyalty because given the opportunity the customer might well choose another brand from another supplier. The introduction of large edge-of-town supermarkets throughout the world has provided a dramatic illustration of pseudo-loyalty as smaller shops saw customers they had previously thought of as extremely loyal defecting to the supermarkets in large numbers lured by lower prices and increased choice. The Internet and the opening up of the global marketplace as discussed in chapter 8 is reducing the number of hostages.

Customer behaviour

This chapter has introduced a number of terms that can be used to describe the degree of loyalty a customer has to a particular generic product, brand or supplier: A-loyal, and pseudo-loyal. In effect they describe a variety of customer behaviours. The wok by Jones and Sasser in the US cited earlier has also considered customer loyalty and in particular why apparently satisfied customers defect to another supplier or product. The answer is that mere satisfaction is no longer enough for an increasing number of customers. As quality and choice increase, delight becomes the customer goal rather than just satisfaction.

Delighted customers do not defect unless they cease to become delighted or are even more delighted by the offering of a competitor.

The bonds of loyalty become strengthened over time as each good experience builds on the previous one. This means that a competitor will need to provide considerably more delight in order to woo a customer and that may well not be a cost-effective method of gaining new customers. In the next chapter the means by which companies can grow globally are explored. One of the advantages of takeovers and mergers is that there is a ready-made customer base. A new company moving into a new area may need to build up a loyal customer base from scratch – a time-consuming task that may involve enticing customers away from established competitors. When P&O acquired Princess Cruises in 1974 (as referred to earlier in this book) the company not only acquired the Princess ships, it also acquired a large and loyal US customer base. For that reason the organization took time in presenting its new identity. To all intents and purposes, as far as Princess customers were concerned they were still customers of the same company.

Jones and Strasser have concluded that as soon as there is increased competition then the level of satisfaction required to retain previously 'loyal customers' increases. They point out that while in monopoly/oligopoly situations it is the customer who has restricted choice as soon as competition opens out it is the suppliers who have only one real choice. They must provide their existing customers with higher and higher levels of satisfaction. The easier it becomes to switch, the more likely it is to happen.

Banking is an example of people apparently remaining loyal even if service levels decline. Until recently, in the UK at least, it has also been relatively complicated to switch to another bank. Banks are now making it much easier for customers to change to them by easing the complexities that the customer could experience. This is, of course, a two-edged sword. If you make it easier for somebody to switch from a competitor to you, your competitors will make it easier for your customers to defect to them. As foreign banks have also moved in it has been important that existing customers are not put off by the thought that they are in fact banking with a foreign operation. For example the Midland Bank in the UK was acquired by the International Hong Kong and Shanghai Banking Corporation (HSBC – whose slogan is 'the world's local bank') in 1992. HSBC only replaced the Midland logo with its own slowly. HSBC operates commercial and personal banking services in Europe, the US, Asia, South America and Australia. In fact the bank has 1720 UK offices – its second biggest operation after the US with 2246 offices. The Scottish Clydesdale Bank was acquired by the National Australia Bank Group in 1987 while the National Westminster (NatWest) Bank is owned by the Bank of Scotland.

Similar issues relate to changing one's email and Internet service provider (ISP) as this may require a new email address. People will have to be informed and so it is easier to remain with the current provider even if the service levels are not as good as those of a competitor. There appears to be a threshold of service below which customers will switch but above which they may be reluctant to do so no matter what inducements the competitor makes.

When the UK government deregulated telephones, gas and electricity in the 1990s the various suppliers made it relatively simple for customers to switch provision. British Telecom, as the UK market leader for telephone services, also made it easy and cheap for defectors to return.

The importance of total satisfaction (or delight) against mere satisfaction was demonstrated by the example of the reprographics giant, Xerox, as profiled by Jones and Strasser (1995). They found that delighted Xerox customers were a staggering six times more likely to give repeat business to Xerox than merely satisfied customers. As it is unlikely to cost six times more to delight a customer than to merely satisfy him or her, then the financial advantages of delighting the customer seem self-evident.

Jones and Strasser have developed terminology for types of customer behaviour that can be linked closely to the development of the global customer as shown below.

Apostles

The apostle is delighted with the service or product. This is of course good news for any organization. Apostles, in effect, carry out a marketing function for the organization. They are highly loyal and delighted and they tell their friends and relations. It will be hard for a company moving in to an area to entice away a competitor's apostles. If, however, a merger/takeover is the means of entry then the company may retain existing apostles provided that there is no diminution in service or quality.

Loyalists

Loyalists form the most important component of the customer base. They are akin to the 'Cash Cows' described by the Boston Consulting Group to describe those products that form the basis for organizational success. Loyalists require much less effort on their behalf than apostles do and yet are very loyal customers coming back time and again. Loyalists provide the stability and objectivity required for sustained growth and thus are what an incoming organization will be seeking. In the case of a merger/takeover loyalists form useful members of focus groups as they will not be afraid to tell the truth as they see it but they will be objective in doing so and that will provide useful data for the organization.

Mercenaries

Mercenaries are the hardest customers to deal with and possibly the fastest growing group of global customers. Mercenaries go for the cheapest or the most convenient option. They are difficult to deal with because they may well be satisfied and even delighted but they are not loyal. Mercenaries may be brand loyal but not supplier loyal. They may well move from brand to brand or supplier to supplier. If asked why they moved the answer may be in terms of cost or convenience but it may well be just a desire for a change. Most of the time the mercenary is looking for the cheapest or most convenient option. The Internet has provided the mercenary with a powerful search tool.

The problem for an organization is whether to expend energy or indeed money on trying to turn a mercenary into a loyalist. The organization will need to satisfy the mercenary even if no repeat business is expected as they will tell people about bad products and services but unless they are very delighted it may well be that they will continue to shop around. From the organization's point of view it is important not to pander too much to the mercenary. Too big a discount on the first transaction may well mean that they will always want such levels if they return but they are just as likely to go down the road and quote your discount to a competitor in the hope that it will be bettered. The problem of course is that the mercenary is difficult to spot during the first transaction. It is only when they reappear demanding higher discounts etc. (or fail to reappear at all) that their nature becomes apparent.

Hostages

Hostages appear to be very loyal but that is only because they have no choice. If a town only has one cinema then it will receive the vast majority of the cinema trade. An organization will not know whether its customers are loyalists or hostages until a competitor or a substitute enters the market – more and more likely as the marketplace becomes global. Even in local economics the hostage situation can be easily seen. A small town supermarket offered very little in terms of both product and service and yet apparently had a very loyal customer base. It was only when a large mega-supermarket opened up some miles away and offered either Internet shopping and home delivery (for a small sum) or a free bus service that the loyal customers were shown to be hostages – they defected in droves.

Hostages have no choice: there is only one convenient shop, one local supplier, one hospital to go to etc. They have no choice but to demonstrate attributes of loyalty even when dissatisfied hence the use of the term pseudo-loyalty for this type of behaviour.

The time for an organization to assess the loyalty and the satisfaction of its customers is not when a competitor opens up but before then. Hostages will leave as soon as they have an opportunity if they are dissatisfied. Even satisfied hostages may leave for a while in order to assess a new competitor. The original supplier will have to hope that the original product/service was of sufficient quality to tempt them back. It is too late to offer discounts and/or enhancements after competition starts. Hostages will ask, and rightly, 'why are you offering this to me now and not before?'

Defectors

Dissatisfy even a loyalist often enough and they may well defect from the organization. Once a customer has defected and given their custom to another organization it may well be difficult to recover the situation as they will begin to build up loyalty bonds with their new supplier or brand.

Organizations need to ensure that complaints are dealt with in an expeditious manner so that any temporary dissatisfaction does not become permanent and thus lead to defection. One organization's lost customer is a gain for a competitor.

Organizations that maintain close contacts with their customers may well detect defection at an early stage and be able to win the customer back. More and more suppliers maintain loyalty schemes that allow them to have regular contact with customers.

Terrorists

The terrorist in customer relation's terms is the worst nightmare an organization can have. Just as the political terrorist acknowledges no rules, neither it appears does the customer relation's terrorist.

Terrorists were often apostles until they were let down and the situation was not recovered. They are not so much dissatisfied with the organization, product or service as at war with it. They have a desire for revenge and retribution. Many of those who appear on consumer affairs television programmes have been previous apostles. On being let down, they have no problem in letting the world know about it. The Internet is full of web sites from those who have been let down by an organization.

The longer a situation remains unresolved the angrier the terrorist becomes and sometimes their actions may be extreme, irrational and even criminal. The threat of a court appearance for harassment or breach of the peace in respect of their relationship with an organization may well have an unexpected and negative effect. Court means publicity and by the time a customer becomes a terrorist, putting the problem right is no longer enough, they want to see the organization humiliated.

The best method of dealing with this type of terrorist is to do what should never be done to a political terrorist – give them what they want and more if necessary and hope that they either become loyalists and apostles again or go away. The organization may consider concentrating on cutting its losses rather than trying to win back the custom. Terrorists are not de-loyal or even disloyal, they are anti-loyal – to use a metaphor, love has turned to hate!

Jones and Strasser's work is useful in that it provides an easy-to-understand explanation of why mere satisfaction is no longer enough to generate loyalty. Loyalty must be earned and should never be taken for granted. It can be purchased as part of goodwill but needs positive action if it is to be retained.

> **Think/Discussion point**: How genuinely loyal are you to the suppliers and products that you use on a regular basis (be honest) – are you a hostage?

Consistency

As global customers experience global products and services they expect a high level of consistency. While different countries may require different specifications for the same product (cars are a good example) or different packaging, the levels of quality and service should be consistent. The subject of the case study below, McDonald's, has become a byword for consistency of product and service throughout the world. The global customer expects the same levels in Barbados as in Brisbane and in Birmingham no matter whether the purchase is a hotel room, a burger or a computer.

Consistency is all the more important in franchise operations such as McDonald's, a point that is picked up in the next chapter when considering how to grow globally.

Implications for small businesses

Whether considering global expansion or not there is a key lesson for all businesses: good customer relationships are no longer desirable – they are essential. One of the Golden Rules for Customer Service developed by the author and his colleague George Green in their 1996 text *In Charge of Customer Satisfaction* was: 'Look after your customers because if you don't somebody else will.'

Increasingly that somebody else will not be an organization down the road or in the next town but one from another country altogether.

Commercial history is full of organizations that did not take heed of similar advice. Loyal customers may just be hostages.

McDonald's

Fast food and burgers may not be everybody's ideal meal but for those in a hurry and families, fast food outlets allow for value-for-money meals while out shopping or sightseeing.

In 1954 Ray Kroc used all his savings to become the exclusive US distributor of the Multimixer® milk shake machine. He was informed of a hamburger stand in California that was operating a number of the mixers and set off to investigate. The stand was run by Dick and Mac McDonald. He convinced the brothers to expand and offered to run the expanded outlets for them.

He opened the first McDonald's restaurant in Des Plaines, Illinois in 1955. By 1965 Kroc owned the operation and the company made its initial public offering in that year. By 1985 it was added to the Dow-Jones 30-company industrial average.

Kroc realized that he could not operate the growing number of outlets and so turned to franchising. Franchising as a means of achieving global growth is covered in detail in the next chapter.

The important consideration for this chapter is that franchisees need to maintain a consistent standard. McDonald's franchises operate to a carefully written set of procedures that ensure consistent quality no matter where the outlet, be it a restaurant, a 'drive thru', attached to a petrol station etc. is.

Regional differences to cope with local tastes (think global – act local) are allowed: McDonald's outlets in Germany serve beer, in the UK they don't. In Israel all produce is guaranteed 100 per cent kosher.

McDonald's has always been a franchising company and has relied on its franchisees to play a major role in its success. McDonald's remains committed to franchising as a predominant way of doing business. Approximately 70 per cent of McDonald's worldwide restaurant businesses are owned and operated by independent businessmen and women – MacDonald franchisees.

The franchising system is built on the premise that the Corporation can be successful only if the franchisees are successful first. Success for McDonald's Corporation flows from the success of its business partners.

McDonald's looks for potential franchisees who are people with good 'common business sense', a demonstrated ability to effectively lead and develop people, and a history of previous success in business and life endeavours. A restaurant background is not necessary. McDonald's does not franchise to corporations, partnerships or passive investors, only to individuals.

McDonald's is, by choice, an equal opportunity franchiser, with a proven track record of franchising to all segments of society. In the US, minorities and women currently represent over 34 per cent of franchisees and 70 per cent of all applicants in training.

The McDonald's arches are now a familiar sight all over the globe. The first restaurant to open in the UK was in Woolwich, southeast London on 1 October 1974. Today there are over 1200 restaurants employing around 68,000 people throughout the UK. The years of opening in just some of the 118 countries McDonald's outlets can be founded are listed in Table 9.2.

Table 9.2 McDonald's global expansion.

Country	Year of opening
Japan	1971
Germany	1971
Australia	1971
UK	1974
Brazil	1979
Saudi Arabia	1983
Russia	1990
Israel	1993
South Africa	1995

Germany and Japan were natural targets for global expansion given the numbers of US troops and their families stationed there during the 'cold war' era. Other expansions have followed political changes – the demise of communism, the ending of apartheid in South Africa being two examples.

The outlets may vary from new buildings to old traditional ones (the conversion of a railway station in Budapest to a McDonald's was very well done) but the arches are all the same – almost. The city fathers in the ancient cathedral city of Canterbury in the UK refused to have full size arches and a smaller version was installed. What does not change is the consistency of product and the consistency of service – both key 'ingredients' to the way in which McDonald's has been able to grow a loyal global customer base.

CASE STUDY QUESTIONS

1 To what extent has global consistency been the major factor in the success of McDonald's?

2 How important do you believe local variations to meet cultural norms are in an operation as vast as McDonald's?

3 Food technologists play an important part in the success of McDonald's, to what degree are those who study global political social trends just as important to the success of the organization?

Summary and key learning points

- The customer is not always right but is always important.
- Customers are used to global products in local situations.
- The removal of monopoly status from many organizations has led to opportunities for expansion from outside.
- Today's customers have far more choice.
- The lifetime value of the customer is what matters not just the first purchase.
- Thinking global but acting local is a good customer strategy.
- The value chain must always be less than the customer is prepared to pay or there will be no profits.

- Branding is very important and may need to be country/region specific e.g. VW Golf/Rabbit.
- There are different types of customer loyalty.
- Today's global customer tends to behave in a more mercenary manner.
- Consistency of quality and service across a global operation is of critical importance.

QUESTIONS

1 'Globalization has increased the number of mercenary customers' – discuss this statement.
2 What is meant by value when referring to customers?
3 Why is consistency so important across a global operation?
4 How has privatization and the removal of monopolies aided globalization and customer choice?

Recommended further reading

The following will provide useful extra information:

Alsop R (1999) Brand loyalty is rarely blind loyalty. *Wall Street Journal*, 19 October.
Cartwright R (2000) *Mastering Customer Relations*. Basingstoke: Macmillan.
Cartwright R and Green G (1997) *In Charge of Customer Satisfaction*. Oxford: Blackwell.
Clutterbuck D, Clark G and Armistead C (1993) *Inspired Customer Service*. London: Kogan Page.
Clutterbuck D and Goldsmith W (1983) *The Winning Steak*. London: Orion.
Clutterbuck D and Goldsmith W (1997) *The Winning Steak Mark 2*. London: Orion.
Clutterbuck D and Kernaghan S (1992) *Making Customers Count*. London: Mercury.
Gale G T and Wood R C (1994) *Managing Customer Value: Creating Quality and Service that Customers Can See*. New York: Free Press.
Harvey D (2002) *Customers – the Hidden Threat to your Business*. Oxford: Capstone.
Jay R (2000) *Smart Things to Know about Customers*. Oxford: Capstone.
Jones T O and Strasser W E Jnr (1995) Why satisfied customers defect. *Harvard Business Review*, Nov–Dec, 88–99.
Seybold P B (1998) *Customers.com*. New York: Random House.

For information about McDonalds consult:

Kroc R (1990) *Grinding it Out*. New York: Saint Martin's Press.
Love J (1995) *Behind the Arches*. New York: SOS Free Stock.
Watson J L (ed.) (1998) *Golden Arches East: McDonalds in East Asia*. Stanford, CN: Stanford University Press.

☑ 10 Growth and globalization

Learning outcomes

By the end of this chapter you should understand:

- The means by which organizations can undertake globalization
- The means by which a global business can grow
- The importance of partnerships in the globalization process
- Agencies, franchising, alliance, mergers and takeovers
- Subcontracting
- The importance of planning and analysis

Growth is something that all organizations, whether they are operating for profit in the private sector or are in the public domain of operations, can achieve.

How organizations can grow to enter a more global market

There are a number of methods for organizations to grow either by expanding themselves – organic growth, by partnerships and alliances (covered later) or by mergers and acquisitions. In practice it is often a combination of these methods that is used. The use of ICT to allow a small business access to a core global market place was discussed in chapter 8.

Organic growth

An organization can either grow within its current market and product portfolio or it can begin to diversify. The major problem with remaining in the same position and just expanding the customer base is that this can limit opportunities. There may be customers located further away but logistics then become a problem. Most organizations growing organically do so by diversifying. Even so, diversifying globally presents far more problems than doing so on a local basis.

Diversification

There are three main methods of diversifying organically:

- Expanding the portfolio
- Horizontal diversification
- Vertical diversification.

Each of these will be examined in turn and the issues that arrive when attempting to use the particular means on a more global than local basis discussed.

Expanding the portfolio

Expanding the portfolio often involves developing a family of products or services. Much of the success in selling cars and breakfast cereals enjoyed by the major manufacturers comes from the families of models that they offer their customers. This allows the customer to either choose the equipment level of a certain model to suit the amount they are prepared to pay or to trade up to a more expensive model made by that manufacturer – or have some variety at breakfast. The importance of this portfolio family is that it keeps the customer with the organization as their needs change. While the brand may differ, the profits still go to the same destination.

Often adding a new model can allow the organization to appeal to a new customer base. By introducing their smaller US vehicles, the Neon and the PT Cruiser to their European market in addition to the large four-wheel drive vehicles previously available in Europe, Chrysler has been able to gain a footing in the lucrative European saloon car and MPV market in its own name while building on the Daimler reputation for quality. To do so, however, meant altering the specification of the vehicles to one that was more suitable for European customers. Much of this concerned cosmetic items such as replacing chrome trim with black or wood effect. For the UK it was also necessary to offer right-hand drive.

To enter into a new market in this manner requires local expertise and this is where the role of the agent and partner (see later) becomes so important. The more complex the product the harder it is to break into a new area without full sales and service backup.

Horizontal diversification

Horizontal diversification is growth into related areas. Canon (see Chapter 7) offers printers, scanners, photocopiers etc. The technological link between these is fairly obvious. Together they form part of the equipment used in most offices and increasingly at home. There are advantages (often financial in the form of discounts) in using one supplier for all of one's needs in a particular area.

The growth of supermarket operations (such as that of Wal-Mart profiled earlier in this book) is an example of horizontal diversification. This has been a method of growth for a considerable period of retail history as new lines are added to the stock offered. The expansion into groceries, consumer electronics, cleaning services and even banking is a natural method of growth for the supermarket operators. The advantage to the customer, the USP (unique selling point), is that everything is conveniently under one roof.

By bringing in new products from across the globe, it is possible for a local operation to offer a degree of globalization. Where the organization wishes to operate or manufacture on a more global basis it is often possible to start small and then add new lines as the operation progresses. A factory that has opened making training shoes may then add T-shirts or footballs to its production lines.

> **Think/Discussion point**: The Carnival Corporation covered as a case study in chapter 5 is a classic example of horizontal diversification along a customer base. The organization has a product for a whole range of differing types of customer over a diverse geographic range.

Vertical diversification

Vertical diversification occurs when the organization grows by developing or acquiring other parts of the supply chain. Thomson, the UK package holiday giant, started with the sale of holiday packages. The next move was into charter airline operations (Britannia Airways), thus allowing Thomson considerable flexibility in transporting its customers to their destinations. Thomson Holidays has expanded and is now a part of the World of TUI, the largest tourism and services group in the world, employing 80,000 people in 500 companies around the world.

The group employs 17,500 people in the UK, Ireland, Sweden, Norway, Denmark and Finland and has customers in all these areas. This has added considerably to what was a purely UK customer base. It should be noted that with the exception of Norway, all of the expansion has been in EU countries. Furthermore there are Celtic/Anglo-Saxon/Scandinavian cultural links between all of the new customer bases meaning that the customers are likely to share similar values.

Agents

In law an agency is a voluntary relationship between two parties whereby one, the agent, is authorized by express or implied consent to act on behalf of the other, called the principal. The agent can affect or conduct the legal affairs of the principal with others, as in the case, for example, of the agreement known as power of attorney. The authorized acts of the agent are thus considered to be the acts of the principal, who is entitled to the benefits, if any, from these actions. The relationship differs from that of master and servant in that the agent is the representative, as well as the employee, of the principal. The easiest way to introduce a product or service into a new area, especially abroad is through an authorized agent. Most car sales are made through agents. The relationship between principal and agent is not only a legal one but also needs to be one of trust. Much of the success of the expansion will depend on the agent. It is the agent who the customer will come to associate with the product or service.

In the UK it is the vendor of a product who carries the legal liability for the performance of the product. If a washing machine breaks down in the UK it is the retailer who has to put things right. If the service from the retailer is poor the customer will blame both the retailer and the manufacturer. Principals need to lay down very strict performance criteria for their agents.

Any person who has legal capacity to make contracts can appoint an agent. A corporation or a partnership, as well as an individual, can be either principal or agent. Obligations of the agent vary according to the particular legal contract and agreement with the principal, who is generally required to act by specific instructions and is held responsible for wrongful acts of the agent only when they fall within the scope of the legal contract. The agent, besides being paid for services, is entitled to reimbursement for particular expenses.

Appointing an agent costs money but relieves the organization of having to establish a presence from scratch. The agent will have local contacts and can smooth the path for the introduction of the product/service and can help bring the name of the organization to the potential customer base.

Appointing an agent is an excellent way of testing out a market as it requires little capital investment and is an easy arrangement to withdraw from.

Franchising

McDonald's major franchise operation was the case study in the previous chapter. The majority of fast-food restaurants and many branches of retail chains are franchises. The term also applies to instances where a patent holder licenses a foreign manufacturer to make its product, for example, many alcoholic drinks, especially beers are not only made in their countries of origin but also by franchisees in a number of other countries. The terms on which a franchise is granted may involve an initial payment by the franchisee to the franchiser, with future payments based on the franchisee's turnover. Attached to the franchise will be certain conditions, for example, that the franchisee buys supplies only from the franchiser, that the franchise operation meets the same standards and follows the design of other franchises, that the franchisee has exclusive rights to sell the franchiser's goods in a specific area and is not allowed to sell them outside that area. The terms are also likely to state that the franchiser will not give a franchise to anyone else to set up, say, a restaurant or shop within a certain distance of the franchisee's shop or restaurant. As with McDonald's most franchisers set very strict standards for franchisees to ensure consistency.

The advantage to the franchiser of operating its business through the method of granting franchises is that, without making all the necessary capital investment, it can expand its business without losing control. The advantage to the franchisee is that of being able to trade under the name of an already well-established brand, without having to spend time and money developing a new business and establishing a successful brand name. The franchisee also develops valuable business experience. Although he or she may not have total control over the business and may have to make a large investment, trading based on an established name can begin very quickly.

As with any business arrangement it is important for both franchiser and franchisee to pay as much attention to the qualities of each other as to the terms of the franchise arrangement. Potential franchisees need to be confident that the profits projected by the franchiser are realistic, and that the franchiser will supply and service the franchise operation efficiently, and will fulfil other conditions of the contract. This is not usually a problem when dealing with major franchise operations.

In terms of globalization the advantage for the franchiser is that the organization's name becomes known very quickly and that the franchisee, as the operator of the business, knows local conditions and can speak the language. It is little wonder that franchising is now forming a major part of global expansion. Hotels and even airlines are now franchising their operations. Holiday Inn and Marriott are two of the hotel groups that have a number of global franchises. British Airways has franchised some of its operations. The aircraft and crew are in BA livery but the operation is run by a franchisee albeit to BA standards.

Franchise operations are advertised on a regular basis and exhibitions are held where franchisers and potential franchisees can meet.

Think/Discussion point: Franchising minimizes the financial risk for both parties – this is why it is so attractive. For a minimum stake, the franchisee becomes part of a larger organization.

Subcontracting

In *No Logo* (2001), Naomi Klein claims that Nike is a 'product-free' brand. She does not mean that Nike has no products, it has very successful ones. Rather she means that Nike does not actually manufacture any of its own products – all manufacturing is subcontracted. This was one of the issues against Nike that was referred to in chapter 4. Klein claims that Nike has developed a cheap method of manufacturing a product to which the brand name alone adds the value, i.e. it is the Nike name rather than the product that the customer values. While there may be some truth in this, if the product was not up to the standards the customer expects, then the brand would soon lose its value.

Provided that there are strict safeguards on both quality and employment practices, subcontracting to other areas, especially EPZs (see chapter 4) can be a highly efficient method of growth. The organization is able to use local companies to carry out the manufacture to the required specification. This is exactly how Boeing sourced the pats for the 777 jet airliner covered in chapter 8. ICT has made this even easier.

The issue that Klein raises of loss of manufacturing jobs in the organization's home area is important and one of the criticisms of NAFTA – US manufacturing jobs migrating to Mexico. According to Klein Levi Strauss downsized its US manufacturing base by over 16,000 jobs in 1997 with the manufacturing being replaced by subcontractors around the world. If those subcontractors pay low wages then the problems covered in chapter 4 will multiply.

Subcontracting is as old as manufacturing. The difference with today's subcontracting is that in many cases it is the subcontractor who makes the whole product rather than just components. Klein states that there are 52 EPZs in the Philippines employing nearly half a million workers. If those jobs are as a result of growth that is good news; if there have been half a million lay-offs elsewhere than that is very bad news indeed.

The UK retail giant, Marks and Spencer, used to source most of its St Michael branded clothing in the UK – no longer is that true, the company now has 1500 suppliers in over 70 countries. The company claims that it is determined to provide good working conditions for its employees and the employees of its subcontractors.

In the late 1990s the competitive market in clothing forced M&S to work with suppliers to establish overseas manufacturing facilities. Today, 80 per cent of the company's clothing is manufactured overseas but the importance of supplier relationships remains. The top 15 clothing suppliers account for 92 percent of M&S business, many of which are UK companies but whose factories and sourcing are overseas.

Mergers and acquisitions

The simplest way to grow quickly is to acquire an organization already operating in a particular market. Being acquired can itself also lead to growth. As Anslinger and Copeland (1994) have shown this can be a very effective way of achieving growth quickly. The acquisition of Sunglass Hut by Desai Capital in 1988 led to Sunglass Hut growing from fewer than 200 outlets in the US to over 800 throughout the world and a 37 per cent return on investment – over double the figure usually expected. Both the acquirer and acquired can benefit from each other. The former gains market entry and the latter often requires capital to fund its desired growth – the takeover of Princess cruises by P&O already referred to in this book being an example.

Entrepreneurs tend to like new projects and are often willing to sell their creations once they have established a market presence. The entrepreneurial character is often such as to wish to move on to a new challenge and thus the sale of a creation is not as traumatic as might be imagined.

Not all acquisitions are welcome and governments usually have policies on mergers and acquisitions to prevent a monopoly situation developing. In recent years government legislation has been extended to supra-national bodies such as the EU. However, for organizations that wish to grow and have the finance to acquire others, acquiring an established operator provides a means of entering a market and hopefully retaining the customer base that the acquired organization has built up.

Mergers tend to be more of an agreement between equals rather than a purchase – less of a takeover and more of a pooling of resources. They are often undertaken to exploit synergy and provide the means by which both organizations can effectively double in size by combining resources.

There are considerable advantages to becoming bigger, not least of which is the ability to buy using economies of scale and to rationalize managerial and logistical operations to cut overall costs. There is little point in doubling in size or revenue if costs go up by more than double.

Alliances

Alliances are formed when the parties concerned recognize that they can achieve better results in conjunction with another organization than on their own.

Nominally the parties remain independent but often it is the case that if one of the partners has more power and influence than the other that independence can

Table 10.1 Alliances 1914–18 and 1939–45.

	Alliance A	Alliance B
1914(17)–18	Britain, France, US, Japan, Italy, Russia	Germany, Turkey, Austria
1939(41)–45	Britain, France, US, Russia	German (and Austria), Italy, Japan

be threatened. An alliance between a supplier and a major customer may lead to the supplier becoming totally dependent on that customer. In 1999 there was considerable concern that its owners, the German BMW concern, would close the Rover car plant in the UK. Not only would this have affected the workers at Rover but also those in the many suppliers to Rover in the area, so dependent were they on the Rover business. As it was BMW sold Rover to new owners (for £1) but retained the brand and production of the new 'Mini'.

Alliances may just be for the duration of a single project: the partners setting up a new temporary company for the project. The building of the Channel Tunnel being an example of such a set of alliances.

Alliances are formed between competitors who come together for expediency. It is said in politics and military circles that there are no such things as allies – just those whose interests coincide at that particular time. One only has to look at the major partners in the alliances in the two World Wars of the twentieth century to see the transitory nature of alliances. See Table 10.1.

The strategic needs of both Italy and Japan changed between the wars and they thus found themselves fighting their old allies. There are those who believe that if the great powers had not agreed a treaty limiting naval strengths in the early 1920s there might have been a US–UK naval war in 1928!

Think/Discussion point: Alliances do not require friendship only a degree of trust and a common goal.

A business plan

Whatever methods an organization uses to expand, it will need a business plan. Philip Walcoff (1999) makes the point in his *Business Planning for Growth* that a proper plan is a prerequisite for successful growth. A business plan will provide a focus for growth. Unfocused growth is nearly always transitory as it lacks direction.

It is well known in the armed forces that no plan ever survives the first encounter with the enemy. Plans are not static documents but dynamic pointers to a direction. Plans that are adhered to slavishly without regard to the external environment are probably as bad as no plans at all. The plan is the first step along the road of growth. Thereafter it should be monitored and changed as necessary.

A plan also allows the organization to show others – investors, bankers etc. – how it intends to grow, the steps that will be taken and the resources needed. There is nothing like putting a plan down on paper (or PC) to help clarify the mind. Global expansion is likely to involve a number of key players as discussed above – they will want to see evidence of proper planning. One cannot just move a product or manufacturing into an area without careful analysis and planning.

Analysis

As part of the planning process it is vital that the organization has an ongoing process of analysing both the internal and external environments.

The organization needs to know what is happening in the outside world especially in the key PESTLE areas, i.e.

- Political
- Economic
- Social
- Technological
- Legal
- Environmental.

It is an analysis of these factors that will provide an indication of the opportunities for growth and the threats that might confront the organization.

An enlarged version of this type of analysis can be found in *Mastering the Business Environment* (Cartwright, 2001). Needless to say the legal analysis may well require the use of local experts. Employment and health and safety legislation varies greatly from jurisdiction to jurisdiction and can be a minefield for the inexperienced or those who expect their national laws to apply.

These are then fed into a SWOT analysis:

- Strength
- Weaknesses
- Opportunities
- Threats.

The strengths and weaknesses are internal to the organization whereas the opportunities and threats are derived from the PESTLE analysis.

This type of analysis should be conducted on an ongoing basis as the environment in which the organization operates is likely to be subject to changes itself.

Organization structure

It is a feature of organizational growth that the structure of the organization needs to change as it becomes larger especially if it expands globally.

The structure of small organizations may be very simple indeed – one person in charge and a small number of employees. Communication tends to be direct and immediate – people can talk to everybody else face to face. This simplicity and the effectiveness that goes with it may not be possible as the organization grows and the gap between those at the top of a developing hierarchy and those further down becomes larger.

Span of control

As organizations became larger during the industrial revolution, business organizations began to discover a fact that had been known to military commanders for centuries. There is a limit to the number of people who can be effectively supervised by a single individual. Armies, for time immemorial, have been arranged in sub-platoons, platoons, regiments, brigades etc. led by increasingly higher ranking individuals. The number that can be supervised by one person is somewhere around 10 – not a large number. Just like military formations, organizations have developed supervisory/managerial structures based on this 'span of control'.

The globalizing organization needs to address the setting up or adaptation of existing supervisory/managerial structures. As the organization moves into a multi-site operation so it will be necessary to clarify the relationships between the central headquarters' function and those of the various sites. Such matters should be given careful consideration. The relationships are very important to the success of the growth process. The correct degree of autonomy needs to be given to managers to allow them to make decisions. Peters and Waterman (1982) have described the importance of what they termed simultaneous loose–tight properties where the headquarters keeps a tight rein on the vision and financial control while allowing managers to make decisions as close to the point of the customer interface as possible.

Organizational structures should be designed around the needs of the customers and processes. There is no right or wrong way to structure an organization – it is a case of what works best in the particular circumstances.

Implications for small businesses

Small businesses that wish to expand globally can do so in a number of ways. One of the easiest is either as an agency, franchise or partnership with a larger, more experienced operator. Becoming an agent can provide a useful means of building a wider global network. Franchising provides the benefits of big company support with the comfort of managing a small business.

Starbucks

Just a few years ago few people outside of Seattle had ever heard of Starbucks coffee.

Washington State is far from the seat of power in the US. However, the State and its major conurbation, Seattle, is home to some of the best known global names in commerce, three of which – Amazon.com, Microsoft and Boeing – have become household names and received a number of mentions in this text. Seattle is also the home base of Starbucks – a US and increasingly a world icon for coffee drinking. Starbuck was the name of Captain Ahab's first mate in *Moby Dick*.

Once just a single outlet on the Seattle waterfront, by the end of the twentieth century there were over 1600 Starbucks scattered across the world with a new one opening its doors each day.

Starbucks' first store was opened by Jerry Baldwin, Gordon Bowker and Zev Siegl in 1971. It was not the best time to start up a business in Seattle, as Boeing the major employer in the area was in financial difficulties and laying off staff prompting the famous billboard – 'Will the last person to leave Seattle please turn off the lights'. The three founders of Starbucks were coffee lovers – proper coffee – rather than the instant products that were at the time filling supermarket shelves. That they had struck a chord at the right time is evidenced not only by the success of Starbucks but also by the success of other similar operations. From nowhere Costa Coffee shops began to appear on high streets and railway/airport terminals in the UK in the 1990s showing how consumers were seeking authentic tastes. Initially Starbucks was a supplier of high quality coffee products to other coffee shops rather than the now familiar coffee shop operation it has become.

Zev Siegl sold out his holding in 1980 and in 1982 Howard Schultz (now chairman and chief global strategist) joined the company as the director of retail operations and marketing. Visiting Italy, Schultz decided that the espresso bar type culture might go down well in Seattle and started Il Giornale – a coffee bar operation using beans from Starbucks. The European bistro/coffee bar idea was alien to the US where milk bars and diners had filled that role. So successful did this prove that in 1987, Il Giornale acquired Starbucks' assets and the name of the company was changed to the Starbucks Corporation and outlets opened in Chicago and Vancouver, British Columbia, just across the US–Canadian border from Washington State. By then Starbucks had grown to 17 outlets.

Growth in another direction occurred in 1988 when the company began a mail order operation encompassing the whole of the US as well as increasing its number of outlets to 33. Mail order brought the Starbucks name to a much wider audience.

In considering staff needs, in 1991 Starbucks became the first privately owned US company to offer stock options to part-time employees. The nature of the coffee shop business is such as to attract a considerable number of part-time employees and this type of recognition is an important motivator showing that they are considered as much a part of the organization as those working full time. The care for staff is undoubtedly one reason why the number of outlets grew by a factor of nearly four between 1988 and 1991 (from 33 to 116).

In 1993 Starbucks began its relationship with the book-selling giant, Barnes and Noble. While this might seem a strange synergy, books and coffee, it is not as unusual as all that as many bookstores offer coffee to browsers. Coffee and reading go together exceptionally well. Since then Starbucks has also formed relationships with the Canadian bookseller, Chapters and also with Borders. The author often enjoys a cup of coffee in the Starbucks' outlet in the Borders Bookshop main Glasgow branch.

While the move into an adjacent part of Canada was predictable, Starbucks' next international growth was to a market that might not be immediately associated with a US or European style coffee shop operation. A 1995 joint venture with Sazaby Inc. was completed to develop a chain of Starbucks in

Japan. With additional US outlets opening in a number of major cities in 1995, the total number of Starbucks reached 676. The Japanese coffee shops opened in 1996 together with outlets in Hawaii (although a US state, Hawaii has a large Japanese population) and Singapore. Starbucks also introduced ice cream sales and negotiated a partnership with Pepsi Cola to sell a bottled version of Starbucks Frappuccino® blended beverage. The number of outlets reached 1015. The next year the company expanded into the Philippines with further growth into Thailand, New Zealand and Malaysia in 1998.

The way Starbucks had globalized had been west and south of Washington State moving across the Pacific into regions where either there was a considerable US influence or English was a common language: Japan, the Philippines, New Zealand etc. The Pacific Northwest of the US looks towards Asia and Australasia in the way that the Eastern seaboard is more oriented towards Europe.

It had been developing a similar concept with 60 outlets in the UK. It does not follow that UK tastes will exactly mirror those of the US but there are cultural and, of course, linguistic similarities. By acquiring the Seattle Coffee Company UK operation in 1998, Starbucks made an important move into the wider European market complete with premises and customers. 1999 and 2000 saw the Starbucks concept extended geographically into China, Dubai (in the Persian Gulf), Hong Kong (by then handed back by the UK to China but still with a considerable Western influence), Kuwait, South Korea and even Lebanon.

Another important move in 2000 was Starbucks alliance with Trans Fair USA to market and sell 'Fair Trade' certified coffee in over 2000 outlets. The concerns about fairness to coffee growers have been part of the wider concerns about globalization and the domination of supplies by large corporations. By signing such an agreement, Starbucks has sent a very powerful message to others in the business world. Plans for 2001 included further European growth into Switzerland and Austria in partnership with Swiss Bon Appétit Group AG. It is expected that there will be 15 Swiss stores by 2003 plus a number in Austria.

Starbucks growth has been logical and its global moves carefully chosen to ensure success. They can be summarized as shown in Table 10.2.

Table 10.2 Growth of Starbucks.

Year	Expansion into	Total outlets
1971	Seattle	1
1987	US, Canada	17
1988–95	US	676 (1995)
1996	US, Japan, Hawaii, Singapore	1015
1997	US, Philippines	1412
1998	US, UK	1886
1999	US, Canada, China, Kuwait, South Korea, Lebanon	2135
2000	US, Dubai, China	3300

One of the difficulties of growth a company such as Starbucks is the reliance on a single product – coffee. A bad harvest can have a devastating effect even if it is not in an area that the company sources from. Such a supply problem is likely to drive up global prices. This occurred in 1994 when the Brazilian coffee crop was blighted by severe frost. Starbucks did not use Brazilian coffee but as Brazil traditionally supplies over 25 per cent of the world's coffee, a shortage in Brazil would drive up the price on the world market. With over 300 outlets, Starbucks would be hit heavily by such a price hike. The last similar situation had been 20 years earlier at a time when Starbucks had only three stores – 1994 was going to be difficult. The problem for Starbucks was a medium term one. The company already had advance purchases that would last for nearly a year but should it continue to buy as the price rose? If it did not it was possible that others would and that there would be problems supplying the operation after the year had passed. There was also the issue of what to do about the price charged in the outlets – when should it rise and by how much?

The decision was made not to raise prices immediately. However, a second frost hit the Brazilian crop, the cumulative effects destroying about 40 per cent of the coffee. The price of green coffee rose by 330 per cent in three months. Eventually Starbucks had to raise its prices but only by 10 per cent reflecting the actual cost increases for that fiscal year. While there was concern about whether customer demand would drop these proved unfounded – coffee proved to be fairly price elastic – the customer would still buy despite the rise. Starbucks customers were prepared to pay a little extra for a quality product. The company made the decision to continue buying stocks reasoning that it was better to have product than to run out. This caused a few financial problems as some of the buying was at the very peak of the coffee price rise and retail prices had to be increased again. However, the strategy was the right one. Customers could still be supplied.

It has made sense for Starbucks to branch out to a degree given this dependence on one product. The Tazo® operation started in 1996 aims to do for tea what Starbucks has done for coffee. Tea is supplied to restaurants, specialist outlets and of course the Starbucks chain.

In July 2001, Starbucks announced its third-quarter results with an anticipated 25 per cent growth in total revenues in fiscal 2002. In that same period it is the intention to open 1200 new stores and a loyalty card scheme.

By the end of fiscal 2005 Starbucks intends to have more than 10,000 stores and a revenue of $6.6 billion.

Coffee may be a mundane product but for generations it has been associated with social intercourse and business. The insurance operation of Lloyds started in a London coffee shop. What Starbucks and other similar companies such as Costa Coffee have done is to bring this experience to a wider audience in a modern setting.

CASE STUDY QUESTIONS

1   Why was tea such a natural diversification for Starbucks?

2 Coffee has proved to be fairly price elastic – why do you think this is?
3 Coffee outlets such as Starbucks provide coffee but what else do they provide that adds customer value?

Summary and key learning points

- That things are done differently in other countries must be kept in mind when planning to grow by global expansion.
- Local culture must be taken into account when growing on a global basis.
- Those planning to grow by expanding into a more global market should do so carefully and in incremental steps.
- Business may be conducted very differently in other countries and this may cause a conflict with rules and legislation in the company's home country.
- Organizations can grow either organically or by mergers and acquisitions.
- Organic growth may be by expanding the portfolio, horizontal diversification, vertical diversification or a mixture of all three.
- Growth should be in line with the organization's mission and vision.
- Alliances and franchising are less risky means of achieving organizational growth.
- Growing organizations need to prepare a business plan.
- Organizational and external analysis allow the organization to identify opportunities and threats that will affect growth.
- Organizational structures and systems may have to change as the organization becomes global.

QUESTIONS

1 What are the advantages of (a) using an agent and (b) being an agent in the globalization process?
2 What is franchising and why is it so popular?
3 What is meant by the span of control and how might organizational structures need to be amended to take into account a wider global network?
4 Why are so many manufacturers subcontracting the whole process rather than just component manufacture?

Recommended further reading

For information about mergers and alliances consult:

Anslinger P L and Copeland T E (1994) *Growth through acquisitions*. In *Strategies for Growth*. Cambridge, MA: Harvard Business School.

Lorange P and Roos J (1992) *Strategic Alliances*. Cambridge, MA: Blackwell.

For information about Starbucks see:

Schultz H and Yang D J (1997) *Pour Your Heart into it – How STARBUCKS Built a Company One Cup at a Time*. New York: Hyperion.

Ⅲ 11 Key thinkers on globalization

Listed below are some of the key thinkers on globalization. The key texts referred to are those relating to globalization. A number of the thinkers listed have also written on other business, management, political and social issues. Full details of the books referred to will be found in the Bibliography.

James C W Ahiakpor

In *Multinationals and Economic Development* (1990, with a foreword by Alan M Rugman – see later), James Ahiakpor of California State University makes the valid point that multinationals dominate world trade and direct investment and that less developed countries have often regarded this power as detrimental to their fragile, growing economies and have pursued a policy of regulation. Modern economic theories of multinationals need to evaluate the effects of such policies. He offers an alternative to restrictive policies, arguing that multinationals are best treated in the same way as local private firms. By integrating new theories of multinational enterprise and of development economics he presents a critical analysis of the various competing policy options and their consequences. Using empirical evidence from Asia, Africa and Latin America and covering such areas as imports, exports, resource utilization and new technology, Ahiakpor asserts that a classical, neutralist policy towards multinational companies would be the most effective way of stimulating growing economies. Ahiakpor is well known as an author of economic texts.

Key text

Multinationals and Economic Development

Patricia L Anslinger

Globalization and organizational growth go together. Global expansion has become one of the vehicles of organizational growth. Patricia Anslinger is a principle of the McKinsey & Company New York Office. As one of the world's premier consulting firms, McKinsey was responsible for commissioning the research that led to Tom Peters and Bob Waterman writing *In Search of Excellence* – still one of the best-selling business books of all time. In a contribution to the *Harvard Business Review*, 'Strategies for growth', Anslinger together with her colleague Thomas Copeland (see below) have challenged the perceived wisdom that acquisitions should be based on synergy. They have provided evidence that with care, even non-synergical acquisitions can make a large and swift contribution to a company's bottom line. This work is important in a study of globalization given the concerns expressed about the emphasis placed on short-term returns covered earlier in this text.

Anslinger is a notable contributor to the *Harvard Business Review*.

Key text

'Growth through acquisitions' (with T Copeland) in *Harvard Business Review – Strategies for Growth*

Philip Bobbitt

Bobbitt has served as a senior White House advisor and a member of the National Security team for both Republican and Democrat administrations. In addition to holding the Walker Chair in constitutional law at the University of Texas he has also been Anderson Senior Research Fellow at Nuffield College, Oxford, UK and Marsh Christian Senior Fellow in War Studies at King's College, London.

Most of Bobbitt's writing has concerned nuclear strategy, social choice and constitutional law. However, in *The Shield of Achilles – War, Peace and the Course of History* he examines the twentieth century from the viewpoint of what he describes as the 'long war'. He contends that this conflict lasted from 1914 until the fall of the soviet system in the 1990s. His 'long war' includes both World Wars and the Korean War, Suez, Vietnam etc. Had it been written after the events of 11 September 2002 he might have extended this to include the campaign in Afghanistan and the US/UK invasion of Iraq in 2003. He sees the war in terms of a conflict between three competing ideologies – democracy/capitalism, fascism and communism. Democracy and capitalism proved the stronger.

In the book Bobbitt looks at how the future of the state will change following the end of the 'long war'. Bobbitt does not see companies ruling the world – the fear of Korten – but he does envisage a move from the nation state to the market state. While the nation state as it is known today maximizes free health care for at least a part of the population (especially in the US), welfare, public education, universal franchise etc. in order to guarantee the welfare of the nations, the market state, the first of which he sees as the US, offers to maximize the opportunities for people. He believes that this will lead to more and more privatization and may lead to voting and representative government being less important. The policies of both Reagan in the US and Thatcher in the UK during the 1980s seemed to begin this trend towards a form of government by market forces.

Key text

The Shield of Achilles – War, Peace and the Course of History

Thomas Copeland

A co-worker of Anslinger (see above), Copeland was a professor of finance at UCLA before becoming Director of Financial Services at the consulting firm of McKinsey and Company in New York. Of particular interest in the context of this material is his work with Anslinger on the benefits of non-synergical growth and the links between finance and policy as described in his 1988 text *Financial Theory and Corporate Policy*. All growth depends on finance and thus any study of globalization cannot neglect the vital role of finance.

Key text

Financial Theory and Corporate Policy
'Growth through acquisitions' (with T Copeland) in *Harvard Business Review – Strategies for Growth*

Arnold C Drainville

In *Contesting Globalization* Drainville examines the tensions between global civil society and global market capitalism. He traces the history and development of global governance through the IMF, World Bank, WTO and also the opposition to these developments. Through the use of case studies Drainville links industrial unrest in the nineteenth century to the protests against globalization at the beginning of the twenty-first century.

Key text

Contesting Globalization

Anthony Giddens

Anthony Giddens is the director of the London School of Economics and the pioneer of the 'Third Way' concept between left and right wing that has been adopted by the UK Prime Minister, Tony Blair. In 1999 he presented the BBC Reith Lecture and did so on the implications of globalization and the world becoming more homogeneous. A highly challenging lecture, it has now been produced in book form and makes fascinating reading as Giddens looks not only at business but also at traditions and the family etc. The book (*Runaway World*) also contains a superb reading list on globalization. Frequently consulted by heads of state, Giddens has written a large number of books on political and social themes that are outside the scope of this material.

Key texts

Runaway World
On the Edge: Living with Global Capitalism (Giddens A and Hutton W, editors).

Philip R Harris and Robert T Moran

Harris and Moran are US academics who have studied management and business across cultural differences. Their materials take a US perspective and provide examples of the differences between other cultures and that of the US. Their comments on the UK are particularly interesting and highlight some of the more subtle differences between two apparently closely related cultures. They have also stressed the importance of business leaders developing a global approach to modern business leadership.

Key texts

Developing the Global Organization (with W G Stripp)
Managing Cultural Differences

Noreena Hertz

Noreena Hertz, associate director of the Centre for International Management at the Judge Institute of the University of Cambridge in the UK wrote *The Silent Takeover* in which she argues that global capitalism could cause the death of the very democracy that has allowed it to flourish in 1999. The title reflects the fact that while there are few major corporate takeovers and mergers that are not reported widely in the media, the takeover that she is referring to is of an altogether different, and often non-reported order. She is referring to the takeover of the planet itself rather than the takeover of a business rival. This is a silent takeover because few have realized that it may be happening. She points out that of the world's largest economies, 51 are now corporations and only 49 are nation states. Hertz has produced a highly readable account of economic change over the past two decades.

Her view of globalization is that not everyone benefits from the capitalist dream and that chief executives of major corporations often have more power than elected leaders. Hertz sees a time in the not too distant future when it is consumers' wallets that will decide policy and not the ballot box.

Her first book, *Russian Business Relationships in the Wake of Reform* was based upon a series of case studies of Russian enterprises that were tracked during the 1990s. It provides insight into the initial conditions that have been established in Russia, and which determine the kind of market system that is now emerging – a system that has had to take account of globalization as much of the finance has been from outside Russia.

Key texts

Russian Business Relationships in the Wake of Reform
The Silent Takeover

Will Hutton

Ex-editor in chief of the *Observer* newspaper and now chief executive of the Work Foundation Hutton has written a number of books for the popular market looking at the UK and in particular the UK and the EU. While professing himself as not 'anti-American' he is nevertheless a critic of the US administration of G W Bush. Hutton is a supporter of UK adoption of the euro and of Europe acting as a counter-balance to US financial power. He is a trenchant critic of short termism and the placing of shareholder value above all other aspects of a business. Hutton sees the UK at the heart of a strong EU.

Key texts

On the Edge: Living with Global Capitalism (A Giddens and W Hutton, editors – bibliography entry under Giddens A)
The Revolution that never was: An Assessment of Keynesian Economics
Why Britain Should Join the Euro (with R Layard, W Buiter, C Huhne, P Kenen and A Turner)
The State We're In: Why Britain is in Crisis and How to Overcome it
The World We're In

Nordström Kjell and Jonas Ridderstrale

Kjell is based at the Institute of International Business at Stockholm University while his colleague works at the University's Centre of Advanced Studies in Leadership. Their 'popular' market book – *Funky Business* – has a serious message. In the twenty-first century no organization or individual can afford to ignore the global aspects of commerce. They do see a danger in nations handing over power to supra national institutions such as the EU. Their key message is that to compete in a global market, organizations need to rethink the way they do things – they need a culture shift. The authors see 'funky' business as being innovative, responsive to rapid change, nurturing talent and welcoming unpredictability. A fun read but a serious message. Jonas Ridderstrale is the author of a study of global innovation by ABB and Electrolux – companies that have succeeded in the global marketplace.

Key texts

Funky Business (Nordström Kjell and Jonas Ridderstrale)
Global Innovation – Managing Projects at ABB & Electrolux (Jonas Ridderstrale)

Naomi Klein

A Canadian, Naomi Klein is a journalist and commentator who has been especially concerned with the effects of branding and globalization on society. In her book, *No Logo* (short-listed for the Guardian First Book Award in 2000) she explores the effects of export processing zones on the economies of countries such as the Philippines and argues that there appears to be little benefit to workers in such areas. Indeed, according to Klein the workers may well see their living standards decline. She also examines the power of the consumer to make large organizations accountable by the use of boycotts etc. While her work concentrates on the activities of US based multinationals she also examines the behaviour of Shell and other European operations. *No Logo* contains a useful reading list for those interested in studying globalization. Klein writes a weekly column in the *Canadian Globe* and *Mail* newspapers.

Key text

No Logo

David C Korten

The author of the best-selling *When Corporations Rule the World*, Korten addresses the issue of modern corporate power, exposing the harmful effects he believes globalization is having not only on economics, but also on politics, society and the environment. His work documents the devastating consequences that can occur when corporations recreate values and institutions to serve their own and their stockholders' narrow financial interests. Korten outlines a strategy for creating localized economies that empower people and communities within a system of global cooperation. While his work is controversial, Korten does attempt to put a model in place to remedy what he sees as the disastrous effects of globalization.

In *The Post Corporate World* Korten examines what he perceives as the deep and growing gap between the promises of the new global capitalism and the reality of insecurity, inequality, social breakdown, spiritual emptiness and environmental destruction that he believes it leaves in its wake. The book looks at what went wrong and why, drawing on insights from the new biology and a growing human understanding of living systems to propose a solution – an economy that takes market principles seriously but also reflects the creativity and uniqueness of the individual. Korten also suggests specific actions to free the creative powers of individuals and societies through the realization of real democracy, the local rooting of capital through stakeholder ownership and a restructuring of the rules of commerce to create market economies that combine market principles with a culture that nurtures social bonding and responsibility. This book is a useful complement to one of his earlier works – *Globalizing Civil Society*.

Richard D Lewis

Richard D Lewis is an authority on the management of cultural difference. He is the founder of the magazine *Cross Culture*, of considerable interest to those involved in global expansion. Speaking over 12 languages, Lewis worked with a large number of major multinational organizations in order to improve the way that they communicate with their global workforce, customers and suppliers. Lewis makes the vital point that mutual understanding and sensitivity lie at the heart of managing across cultures and are thus key factors in successful global expansion. In both *When Cultures Collide* and *Cross-Cultural Communications – A Visual Approach* he stresses the importance of ensuring that the communications process is as robust as possible. The same words and phrases can mean different things in different cultures and this is an important point to consider when the global organization is issuing policy documents etc.

Having developed a model for cultural analysis, Lewis has produced two PC-based packages, the first being the Cross Cultural Assessor, which is a tool for cross-cultural analysis applicable to both individuals and across an organization and in the second, Gulliver provides both cross-cultural training and a database to set up 'what if scenarios'. Details of Lewis' books and these products are given below.

Richard D Lewis Communications and the associated Institute of Cross Cultural Communication (both based in the UK but operating globally) also produce a *Cross Cultural Letter to International Managers* 10 times per year and available on subscription.

Peter Lorange (and Johan Roos)

Peter Lorange, president of IMD in Switzerland and formerly president of the Norwegian School of Management and a teacher at Wharton and MIT, has contributed to the issue of growth through his work with Johan Roos on strategic alliances. Such alliances are often the first steps towards global expansion for an organization.

Together they produced the classic text on alliance and joint ventures – *Strategic Alliances*.

The number of such alliances grew rapidly throughout the last decade of the twentieth century, growth that seems set to continue into the twenty-first.

By studying a large number of such operations, Lorange (and Roos) have been able to generate a blueprint for managing growth through this means. The point is made that the process is one that occurs over time and comprises steps that are commercial, analytical and political, the latter of critical importance in global expansion. Lorange and Roos stress the importance of trust in the relationships – not always the easiest task in a competitive environment.

Key texts

Strategic Alliances – Formation, Implementation and Evolution (with J Roos)
The Strategic Planning Process

Grady E Means

Grady E Means is global leader of the Strategy Consulting group of the Management Consulting Services (MCS) practice of the international PricewaterhouseCoopers consultancy. In this role he oversees a global organization that integrates a full range of consulting services – from business strategy development and operations to resource productivity and cost reduction and organizational restructuring to technology design – into a coherent package of solutions to help large companies succeed in today's global new economy.

Means has been a business strategy consultant and adviser to top management and government leaders for nearly 30 years. During that time, he has managed projects for many companies in nearly all sectors of the economy. He has also served in the White House as assistant to Vice President Nelson Rockefeller for domestic policy development and at the US Department of Health, Education and Welfare, where he was staff economist in the Office of the Secretary. He is a former staff member of the Graduate School of Business at Stanford University.

Means is frequently interviewed and quoted in national and international business media. He is co-author of the books, *The Wisdom of the CEO, MetaCapitalism: The E-Business Revolution and the Design of 21st Century Companies and Markets*.

In *MetaCapitalism*, written with David M Schneider, Means provides a comprehensive analysis of how the Internet, combined with major improvements in business management, efficiency and productivity in the 1990s is leading to a fundamental transformation of global business by creating unprecedented economic value and wealth and accelerating the growth of worldwide capital markets from $20 trillion to levels potentially approaching $200 trillion in less than 10 years.

Means and Schneider show how through the formation of e-markets, online exchanges and networked business communities, traditionally successful business models are turned on their heads with the transition towards decapitalization and external networks, rather than owning every aspect of production.

MetaCapitalism describes how global capital markets are increasingly rewarding companies that are using new technology to constantly reorganize themselves by integrating new players and forging new partnerships and alliances (see the work of

Lorange, above), rather than companies who continue to maintain a large internal capital base of manufacturing sites, distribution centres and retail outlets.

They also show how modern growth leads to an increase in outsourcing thus providing a useful link to many of the writers on globalization.

In *The Wisdom of the CEO*, Means and his associates have gathered together contributions from those running some of the best-known high growth organizations and provide an analysis of recent changes to the way business is conducted and predictions for the future.

Key texts

The Wisdom of the CEO
MetaCapitalism: The E-Business Revolution and the Design of 21st Century Companies and Markets

Mike Moore

Mike Moore is an ex prime minister of New Zealand and was the director general of the World Trade Organization between 1999 and 2002. His book *A World Without Walls* is a reflection on his time as director general of the WTO. As such it provides a useful addition to the debate about globalization. Arriving at the WTO shortly before the ill-fated Seattle meeting, Moore sought to reform the WTO, addressing the concerns of poorer countries and engaging in open debate with the often-hostile NGOs. He is clearly proud of the outcome of the Doha meeting in November 2001 that secured commitment to a new round of trade talks with a focus on development. Moore uses the book to rebut the attacks against the WTO arguing that the WTO's promise of rules-based free trade offers the best hope for lifting millions of the world's poorest citizens out of poverty. While there are a number of books that attack the WTO it is useful to read an insider account of the philosophy and the workings of the organization.

Key text

A World Without Walls

Michael Porter

A renowned professor at Harvard Business School, Porter has been the world authority on competition and competitive strategies since the 1980s. His writing has informed both those in industry and academia on the nature of competition and the forces that drive the process. It was Porter who introduced the famous 'Five Forces' model: the bargaining power of the supplier, the bargaining power of the customer, competition between existing players, the threat of new entrants and the treat of substitution, that has been used by many to explain how the competitive process has worked in particular industries. In *The Competitive Advantage of Nations* he turned his ideas and attention to the global stage identifying the fundamental determinants of national competitive advantage in an industry and how they work together to give international advantage. The findings had implications for firms and governments and help set the agenda for discussions of global competition. A prolific author, the most relevant of his books for a study of globalization are listed below.

Key texts

Competitive Advantage
Cases in Competitive Strategy
Competitive Strategy
On Competition
The Competitive Advantage of Nations

Alan M Rugman

The Thames Water Fellow in Strategic Management at Templeton College, University of Oxford Rugman is a major authority on international business, multinationals and globalization.

In *The End of Globalization* Rugman shows how he believes that his view of regionalization is more akin to reality than globalization. He links this work to his earlier works on the 'triad' of North America, Japan and the European Union. It is these regional triad markets that Rugman believes are often confused with global markets. As an example he quotes the fact that 95 per cent of European motorcar output is sold in Europe with only a small percentage leaving the regional market. It should be noted, however, that the Japanese have invested heavily in European (and North American) plants so that their output can be deemed indigenous.

Rugman and Joseph D'Cruz have introduced the concept of the flagship firm in *Multinationals as Flagship Firms*. In each business network strategic leadership is provided by the flagship firm, which is (by their definition) a multinational enterprise. It has other partners: key suppliers, key customers, key competitors and key partners in the non-business infrastructure. These business networks are usually located in the 'triad' regions of the EU, North America and Japan. There are strong cross-border network linkages within these regions, but less globalization than regional economic integration. The theory of the flagship firm/five partners model is applied to the telecommunications, chemicals, automotive and electronics sectors, among others. Within this framework they have considered both empirical studies and field research of the international competitiveness of these sectors.

Rugman has stated that globalization is a myth – it cannot end, as it never really started. He further contends that multinational enterprises are the engines of international business especially when they think regionally and act locally.

Much of Rugman's writing has been on multinational enterprises as can be seen in the list below. He has also edited many texts that relate to globalization (or regionalization as he contends).

He disagrees with Giddens (see earlier) that globalization causes cultural complexes and that it is new. Rugman argues that globalization is at least 2000 years old if not older. He also argues that examples of multinational enterprises can be found in civilizations as ancient of those of the Assyrians and Phoenicians.

Key texts

The End of Globalization
International Business: A Strategic Management Approach (with R M Hodgetts)
Multinationals and Canada – United States Free Trade (Critical Issues Facing the Multinational Enterprise)
The Theory of Multinational Enterprises
Foreign Investment and NAFTA
Multinationals in Canada: Theory, Performance and Economic Impact
International Diversification and the Multinational Enterprise
Inside the Multinationals
Multinationals as Flagship Firms: Regional Business Networks (with J R D'Cruz)
International Business (with D J Lescraw)
Research in Global Strategic Management: Global Competition and the European Community (editor)
Multinationals and Technology Transfer (editor)
Oxford Handbook of International Business (editors A M Rugman and T L Brewer)
The World Trade Organization in the New Global Economy (editors A M Rugman and G Boyd)

Saskia Sassen

Working at both the University of Chicago and the London School of Economics, Sassen has produced a number of texts that look at how the new, more global economy works. She believes that globalization has led to a change in the way national sovereignty is perceived rather than its destruction.

In *The Global City* Sassen argues that certain cities in today's post-industrial world have become central nodes in the new service economy, strategic sites for the acceleration of capital and information flows as well a spaces of increasing socio-economic polarization. One effect has been that such cities have gained in importance and power relative to nation states. In a further work, *Global Networks, Linked Cities*, Sassen and a group of contributors expand on her earlier work focusing on two key issues. The first concerns how information flows have bound global cities together in networks, creating a global city web whose constituent cities become global through the networks they participate in. Second is an investigation into emerging global cities in the developing world – Sao Paulo, Shanghai, Hong Kong, Mexico City, Beirut, Dubai and Buenos Aires. They show how these globalizing zones not only replicate many features of the top tier of global cities, but also generate new socio-economic patterns. These new patterns of development promise significant changes in the structure of the global economy, as more and more cities worldwide are integrated into globalization's circuitry.

Sassen has also studied labour mobility and international investment. In *Guests and Aliens* she provides a useful commentary on how immigration can have positive and negative results on economies and societies. Her work should be considered by all those interested in globalization.

Key texts

The Global City
Losing Control: The Decline of Sovereignty in an Age of Globalization
Global Networks, Linked Cities
The Mobility of Labor and Capital – A Study in International Labor and Investment Flow
Globalization and its Discontents
Guests and Aliens

Joseph E Stiglitz

In 1993 Joseph E Stiglitz left the academic world to become the chairperson of President Clinton's Council of Academic Advisors. In 1997 he was appointed to the position of chief economist and senior vice president of the World Bank. In 2000 he returned to academia. He was awarded the Nobel Prize for Economics in 2001.

Stiglitz is the author/editor/contributor to a large number of volumes on global finance and economics, the most relevant of which are listed below.

Stiglitz makes the point in his considerations of global finance and the role of the IMF and WTO that the widespread financial crises of recent years have all too dramatically illustrated the shortcomings of financial policy under liberalization. The complexity of the issues mocks any idea that a standard liberalization template will be universally effective.

In *Globalization and its Discontents* he explains the functions and powers of the main institutions that govern globalization – the IMF, the World Bank and the WTO together with the ramifications, both good and bad, of their policies. Stiglitz strongly believes that globalization can be a positive force around the world, particularly for the poor, but only if the IMF, World Bank and WTO dramatically alter the way they operate, beginning with increased transparency and a greater willingness to examine their own actions closely.

Key texts

Whither Socialism?
The Economic Role of the State (editors J E Stiglitz and A Heertje)
Rethinking the East Asian Miracle (editors J E Stiglitz and Y Shaid)
Financial Liberalization: How Far, How Fast? (editors J E Stiglitz G Caprio and P Honohan)

Noel M Tichy

Noel M. Tichy is a professor of organizational behavior and human resource management at the University of Michigan Business School, where he is the director of the Global Leadership Program and an authority on business growth and globalization.

Between 1985–87, Tichy was responsible for management education at General Electric where he directed its worldwide management development programmes. Prior to joining the Michigan Faculty he had served for nine years on the Columbia University Business School Faculty.

Tichy is the author of a large number of books and articles. His most relevant texts to a study on globalization are listed at the end of this entry. His texts have covered strategic growth, global citizenship and change management.

Tichy has served on the editorial boards of the *Academy of Management Review*, *Organizational Dynamics*, *Journal of Business Research* and *Journal of Business Strategy*. He is past chairman of the Academy of Management's Organization and Management Theory Division and is a member of the Board of Governors of the American Society for Training and Development. He was the 1987 recipient of the New Perspectives on Executive Leadership Award by Johnson Smith and Knisely for the most outstanding contribution to the field as captured in *The Transformational Leader* written with Mary Anne Devanna. He received the 1993 Best Practice Award from the American Society for Training and Development and the 1994 Sales and Marketing Executives International Educator of the Year Award. Tichy is the founder and editor in chief of the *Human Resource Management Journal*.

Noel Tichy has been widely consulted by a variety of organizations. He is a senior partner in Action Learning Associates. His clients have included Ameritech, AT&T, Mercedes-Benz, BellSouth, CIBA-GEIGY, Chase Manhattan Bank, Citibank, Exxon, General Electric, General Motors, Honeywell, Hitachi, ICI, IBM, NEC, Northern Telecom, Nomura Securities and 3M – the vast majority of which are global players.

Key texts

Managing Strategic Change
Control Your Destiny or Someone Else Will: How Jack Welch is Making General Electric the World's Most Competitive Company (with S Sherman)
Every Business Is A Growth Business (with R Charan)
The Leadership Engine: How Winning Companies Build Leaders at Every Level
Corporate Global Citizenship

Fons Trompenaars

Fons Trompenaars has been one of the most influential writers on the management of cultural differences for global organizations. His initial studies were undertaken while working for Royal Dutch Shell in the Netherlands. As a global organization Shell has considerable experience in managing different cultural groups and Trompenaars set out to put these experiences into a conceptual framework that could be transferred to other organizations. It is hard to find work on cultural diversity within the work situation and global operations that does not cite Trompenaars.

His initial work – *Riding the Waves of Culture* – published in 1993 was bought in large quantities by organizations operating on a global basis. The book not only provided a contextual framework but also provided concrete examples of the differing cultural norms that managers were likely to encounter and strategies for dealing with them in a sensitive and effective manner.

In association with Charles Hampden-Turner, Trompenaars looked in more detail at the competencies required for cross-cultural management (*Building Cross-Cultural Competence*) and the requirements for twenty-first century business leaders in a more globalized environment (*21 Leaders for the 21st Century*) as well as a detailed examination of social, cultural and economic differences between Asia and the West in *Mastering the Infinite Game*.

Key texts

Riding the Waves of Culture
Mastering the Infinite Game (with C Hampden-Turner)
Building Cross-Cultural Competence (with C Hampden-Turner)
21 Leaders for the 21st Century (with C Hampden-Turner)

George S Yip

A teacher of business strategy and international marketing at UCLA and a former faculty member at Harvard Business School, Yip has written a useful guide on the processes involved in global expansion for organizations in his book, *Total Global Strategy*. Very much concerned with the gaining of competitive advantage (cf. Michael Porter), Yip provides clear practical advice on global marketing, product design, competition and the structure of a global organization.

Well qualified to comment on global organizations as he is Asian by birth, lives in the US, and has EU citizenship, Yip has also written on developing strategies for Central and Eastern European expansion and on expanding into Asian markets.

Key texts

Total Global Strategy
Strategies for Central and Eastern Europe (editors G S Yip and A Kozminski)
The Asian Advantage: Key Strategies for Winning in the Asia-Pacific Region

▪ ☒ Bibliography

Ahiakpor J C W (1990) *Multinationals and Economic Development*. London: Routledge.

Aldrich D F (1999) *Mastering the Digital Marketplace*. Chichester: Wiley.

Alsop R (1999) Brand loyalty is rarely blind loyalty. *Wall Street Journal*, 19 October.

Anslinger P L and Copeland T E (1994) Growth through acquisitions. In *Strategies for Growth*. Cambridge, MA: Harvard Business School.

Ardrey R (1966) *The Territorial Imperative*. London: Atheneum.

Black J S, Morrison A J and Gregersen H B (1999) *Global Explorers*. New York: Routledge.

Bobbitt P (2002) *The Shield of Achilles – War, Peace and the Course of History*. New York: Alfred A Knopf.

Cartwright R (2000) *Mastering Customer Relations*. Basingstoke: Palgrave Macmillan.

Cartwright R (2001) *Mastering the Business Environment*. Basingstoke: Palgrave Macmillan.

Cartwright R (2002) *Mastering Marketing Management*. Basingstoke: Palgrave Macmillan.

Cartwright R (2003) *Managing Talent*. Oxford: Capstone.

Cartwright R and Baird C (1999) *The Development and Growth of the Cruise Industry*. Oxford: Butterworth Heinemann.

Cartwright R and Green G (1997) *In Charge of Customer Satisfaction*. Oxford: Blackwell.

Clutterbuck D, Clark G and Armistead C (1993) *Inspired Customer Service*. London: Kogan Page.

Clutterbuck D and Goldsmith W (1983) *The Winning Steak*. London: Orion.

Clutterbuck D and Goldsmith W (1997) *The Winning Steak Mark 2*. London: Orion.

Clutterbuck D and Kernaghan S (1992) *Making Customers Count*. London: Mercury.

Collier P and Horowitz D (1976) *The Rockefellers – An American dynasty*. New York: Simon & Schuster.

Copeland T (1988) *Financial Theory and Corporate Policy*. New York: Addison Wesley.

Davies C (1997) *Divided by a Common Language*. Sarasota, FL: Mayflower Press.

Dearlove D (2001) *Doing Business the Bill Gates' Way*. Oxford: Capstone.

Dickinson R and Vladimir A (1997) *Selling the Sea*. New York: Wiley.

Drainville A C (2003) *Contesting Globalization*. London: Routledge.

Eddy P, Potter E and Page B (1976) *Destination Disaster*. London: Hart Davis.

Ellwood W (2001) *The No-nonsense Guide to Globalization*. Oxford: New Internationalist.

Fowler A (2000) *The Virtuous Spiral: A Guide to Sustainability for NGOs in International Development*. London: Earthspan.

Gale G T and Wood R C (1994) *Managing Customer Value: Creating Quality and Service that Customers Can See*. New York: Free Press.

Giddens A (1999) *Runaway World*. London: Profile Books.

Harris P R and Moran R T (2000) *Managing Cultural Differences*. Houston: Gulf.

Harris P R, Moran R T and Stripp W G (1998) *Developing the Global Organization – Strategies for Human Resource Professionals*. Houston: Gulf.

Harvey D (2002) *Customers – The Hidden Threat to Your Business*. Oxford: Capstone.

Hastings C, Bixby P and Chaudhry-Lawton R (1994) *Superteams*. London: Harper Collins.

Hertz N (1997) *Russian Business Relationships in the Wake of Reform*. Basingstoke: Palgrave Macmillan.

Hertz N (2001) *The Silent Takeover*. London: Heinemann.

Hutton W (1996) *The State We're In: Why Britain is in Crisis and How to Overcome it*. London: Vintage.

Hutton W (2001) *The Revolution that Never was: An Assessment of Keynesian Economics*. London: Vintage.

Hutton W (2002) *The World We're In*. London: Little Brown.

Hutton W, Layard R, Buiter W, Huhne C, Kenen P and Turner A (2002) *Why Britain Should Join the Euro*. London: Britain in Europe.

Iriye A (2002) *Global Community: the Role of International Organizations in the Making of the Contemporary World*. Berkeley: University of California Press.

Jay R (2000) *Smart Things to Know about Customers*. Oxford: Capstone.

Jones T O and Strasser W E Jnr (1995) Why satisfied customers defect. *Harvard Business Review*, Nov–Dec, 88–99.

Joynt P and Morton R (eds) (1999) *The Global HR Manager*. London: Chartered Institute of Personnel and Development.

Kapur D, Lewis J P and Webb R (1997) *The World Bank. Its First Half Century*. Washington, DC: Brookings Institution Press.

King D (1987) *The New Right – Politics, Markets and Citizenship*. Basingstoke: Palgrave Macmillan.

Kjell N and Ridderstrale J (2002) *Funky Business*. Stockholm: Bookhouse.

Klein N (2000) *No Logo*. London: Flamingo.

Korten D C (1990) *Getting to the 21st Century – Voluntary Action and the Global Agenda*. New York: Kumarian Press.

Korten D C (1996) *When Corporations Rule the World*. San Francisco: Berrett-Koehler.

Korten D C (1997) *Globalizing Civil Society*. New York: Seven Stories Press.

Korten D C (1999) *The Post Corporate World*. San Francisco: Berrett-Koehler.

Kroc R (1990) *Grinding it Out*. New York: Saint Martin's Press.

Langworth R (1987) *A Complete History of the Ford Motor Company*. New York: Random House.

Lewis R D (1999) *Cross-Cultural Communications – A Visual Approach*. London: Transcreen.

Lewis R D (2000) *When Cultures Collide*. London: Nicholas Brealey.

Lorange P (1994) *The Strategic Planning Process*. London: Dartmouth.

Lorange P and Roos J (1992) *Strategic Alliances.* Cambridge, MA: Blackwell.

Love J (1995) *Behind the Arches.* New York: SOS Free Stock.

Macmillan M (2001) *Peacemakers – Six Months that Changed the World.* London: John Murray.

Manes S and Andrews P (1994) *Gates.* New York: Simon & Schuster.

Mason E and Asher R E (1973) *The World Bank Since Bretton Woods.* Washington, DC: Brookings Institution.

Means G E, Dauphinais G W and Price C (2000) *The Wisdom of the CEO.* New York: Wiley.

Means G E and Schneider D (2000) *MetaCapitalism: The E-Business Revolution and the Design of 21st Century Companies and Markets.* New York: Wiley.

Menzies G (2002) *1421 – The Year China Discovered the World.* London: Transworld.

Moore M (2003) *A World Without Walls.* Cambridge: Cambridge University Press.

Morris D (1969) *The Human Zoo.* London: Jonathon Cape.

Nicholson N (2000) *Managing the Human Animal.* New York: Crown.

Pendergrast M (2000) *For God, Country, and Coca-Cola.* London: Orion.

Peters T (1987) *Thriving on Chaos.* New York: Alfred A Knopf.

Peters T and Waterman R (1982) *In Search of Excellence.* New York: Harper & Row.

Pettinger R (1998) *The European Social Charter – A Manager's Guide.* London: Kogan Page.

Pitt B (1962) *1918 – The Last Act.* London: Cassell.

Porter M (1980) *Competitive Advantage.* New York: Free Press.

Porter M (1985) *Competitive Strategy.* New York: Free Press.

Porter M (1992) *Cases in Competitive Strategy.* New York: Free Press.

Porter M (1996) *On Competition.* Cambridge, MA: Harvard University Press.

Porter M (1998) *The Competitive Advantage of Nations.* Basingstoke: Palgrave Macmillan.

Price C (2000) *The Internet Entrepreneurs.* Harlow: Pearson.

Quinn W (2000) *How Wal-Mart is Destroying America (and the World).* Berkeley: 10 Speed.

Ransom D (2001) *The No-nonsense Guide to Fair Trade.* Oxford: New Internationalist.

Ridderstrale J (1996) *Global Innovation – Managing Projects at ABB and Electrolux.* Stockholm: Coronet.

Rugman A M (1979) *International Diversification and the Multinational Enterprise.* Lexington: Lexington Books.

Rugman A M (1980) *Multinationals in Canada: Theory, Performance and Economic Impact.* New York: Kluwer.

Rugman A M (1981) *Inside the Multinationals.* London: Croom Helm.

Rugman A M (ed.) (1983) *Multinationals and Technology Transfer.* Westport: Praeger.

Rugman A M (1990) *Multinationals and Canada – United States Free Trade (Critical Issues Facing the Multinational Enterprise).* Columbia: University of South Carolina Press.

Rugman A M (ed.) (1991) *Research in Global Strategic Management: Global Competition and the European Community.* Greenwich: JAI Press.

Rugman A M (1994) *Foreign Investment and NAFTA.* Columbia: University of South Carolina Press.

Rugman A M (1996) *The Theory of Multinational Enterprises*. Cheltenham: Edward Elgar.

Rugman A M (2000) *The End of Globalization*. London: Random House.

Rugman A M and Boyd G (eds) (2001) *The World Trade Organization in the New Global Economy*. Cheltenham: Edward Elgar.

Rugman A M and Brewer T L (eds) (2001) *Oxford Handbook of International Business*. Oxford: Oxford University Press.

Rugman A M and Hodgetts R M (2002) *International Business – A Strategic Management Approach*. London: FT/Prentice Hall.

Rugman A M and D'Cruz J R (2003) *Multinationals as Flagship Firms: Regional Business Networks*. Oxford: Oxford University Press.

Rugman A M and Lescraw D J (1985) *International Business*. New York: McGraw-Hill.

Sabbach K (1995) *21st Century Jet – The Making of the Boeing 777*. Basingstoke: Palgrave Macmillan.

Salda A C M (1997) *Historical Dictionary of the World Bank*. Lanham, Maryland: The Scarecrow Press.

Sassen S (1990) *The Mobility of Labor and Capital – A Study in International Labor and Investment Flow*. Cambridge: Cambridge University Press.

Sassen S (1996) *Losing Control: The Decline of Sovereignty in an Age of Globalization*. New York: Columbia University Press.

Sassen S (1999) *Globalization and its Discontents*. New York: New Press.

Sassen S (2000) *Guests and Aliens*. New York: New Press.

Sassen S (2001) *The Global City*. Princeton, NJ: Princeton University Press.

Sassen S (2002) *Global Networks, Linked Cities*. New York: Routledge.

Saunders R (2000) *Amazon.com*. Oxford: Capstone.

Schultz H and Yang D J (1997) *Pour Your Heart into it – How STARBUCKS Built a Company One Cup at a Time*. New York: Hyperion.

Seybold P B (1998) *Customers.com*. New York: Random House.

Spector R (2000) *Amazon.com – Get Big Fast*. London: Random House.

Stiglitz J E (1996) *Whither Socialism?* Cambridge, MA: MIT Press.

Stiglitz J E (2000) *Economics of the Public Sector*. New York: W W Norton.

Stiglitz J E (2002) *Globalization and its Discontents*. New York: W W Norton.

Stiglitz J E and Heertje A (eds) (1989) *The Economic Role of the State*. Oxford: Blackwell.

Stiglitz J E and Shaid Y (eds) (2000) *Rethinking the East Asian Miracle*. Oxford: Oxford University Press.

Stiglitz J E, Caprio G and Honohan P (eds) (2001) *Financial Liberalization: How Far, How Fast?* Cambridge: Cambridge University Press.

Stiglitz J E and Sah R K (2002) *Peasants Versus City Dwellers: Taxation and the Burden of Economic Development*. Oxford: Oxford University Press.

Strouse J (2000) *Morgan: an American Financier*. New York: Harper Perennial.

Studder M (2001) *The Global Strategies of MME and Government Policies: Ford Motor Company and the Automobile Industry in Canada and Mexico*. New York: Routledge.

Tichy N (1983) *Managing Strategic Change*. New York: Wiley.

Tichy N (1997) *Corporate Global Citizenship*. San Francisco: Jossey Bass.

Tichy N (1997) *The Leadership Engine: How Winning Companies Build Leaders at Every Level*. New York: HarperCollins.

Tichy N and Charan R (1998) *Every Business is a Growth Business.* New York: Random House.

Tichy N and Sherman S (1994) *Control Your Destiny or Somebody Else Will – How Jack Welch is Making General Electric the World's Most Competitive Company.* New York: Harper Business.

Trompenaars F (1993) *Riding the Waves of Culture.* London: Economist Book.

Trompenaars F and Hampden-Turner C (1997) *Mastering the Infinite Game.* Oxford: Capstone.

Trompenaars F and Hampden-Turner C (2000) *Building Cross-Cultural Competence.* London: Nicholas Brealey.

Trompenaars F and Hampden-Turner C (2001) *21 Leaders for the 21st Century.* Oxford: Capstone.

Tulgan B (1996) *Managing Generation X.* Oxford: Capstone.

Tulgan B (2001) *Winning the Talent Wars.* Naperville, IL: Nicholas Brealey.

United Nations (1999) *Human Development Report.* Oxford: UN Development Program/Oxford University Press.

Vance S S and Scott R V (1994) *Wal-Mart – A History of Sam Walton's Retail Phenomenon.* New York: Twayne.

Walcoff P (1999) *The Fast Forward MBA in Business Planning for Growth.* New York: Wiley.

Waller D (2001) *Wheels of Fire.* London: Hodder & Stoughton.

Watson J L (ed.) (1998) *Golden Arches East: McDonalds in East Asia.* Stanford, CN: Stanford University Press.

Wickens P (1987) *The Road to Nissan.* Basingstoke: Palgrave Macmillan.

Wild A (2000) *The East India Company.* London: Collins.

Wind J (1982) *Product, Policy and Concepts, Methods and Strategy.* New York: Addison-Wesley.

Yip G S (1992) *Total Global Strategy.* Englewood Cliffs, NJ: Prentice Hall.

Yip G S (2000) *The Asian Advantage: Key Strategies for Winning in the Asia-Pacific Region, updated edition, After the Crisis.* New York: Perseus.

Yip G S and Kozminski A K (eds) (2000) *Strategies for Central and Eastern Europe.* Basingstoke: Palgrave Macmillan.

Web sites

www.amazon.com	Amazon.com main web site
www.amazon.co.uk	Amazon UK web site
www.asda.co.uk	Asda
www.aseansec.com	ASEAN
www.boeing.com	Boeing
www.canon.com	Canon
www.carnival.com	Carnival Corporation
www.cocacola.com	Coca-Cola
www.corpwatch.org	Globalization 'watchdog' network
www.ecb.int	European Central Bank
www.efta.int	European Free Trade Association

www.europa.eu.int	European Union
www.ford.com	Ford main web site
www.ford.co.uk/ie/	Ford UK
www.ilo.org	International Labor Organization
www.imf.com	International Monetary Fund
www.kodak.com	Kodak
www.mcdonalds.com	McDonald's
www.microsoft.com	Microsoft
www.nafta.customs.org	NAFTA web site
www.ngo.com	NGO Global Network
www.nike.com	Nike
www.open.gov.uk	UK public sector information
www.oxfam.org.uk	Oxfam
www.politicalresources.net	NGO information
www.poprincesscruises.com	P&O Princess Cruises
www.starbucks.com	Starbucks
www.statistics.gov.uk	UK Government Office of National Statistics
www.un.org	United Nations
www.walmart.com	Wal-Mart
www.worldbank.org	World Bank
www.wto.com	World Trade Organization

⊻ Index